40 YEARS OF MATCH OF THE DAY

Martyn Smith

4O YEARS OF MATCH OF THE DAY

BBC
BOOKS

Credits

All pictures © *Empics* except the following:
© *Action Images* 157; © BBC 8, 10, 13b, 15b (courtesy Alec Weeks), 18, 19, 25, 30, 34, 37, 40, 41b, 45, 47r, 54, 55t, 56, 60, 65, 67t, 68, 71, 75b, 77, 84 (both), 88, 91, 97t, 113, 123 (courtesy Gerald Sinstadt), 130, 133, 143, 156, 158, 165, 177, 181, 191, 192, 198, 201, 218, 220l; © *Colorsport* 74, 106, 145b, 150, 152, 171, 208; © *Steve Hale* 118; © *Hulton Getty* 9t, 51; Chris Lewis 62b; © *Liverpool Daily Post & Echo* 42; © *Mike Pierce* 109; © *Radio Times/BBC Worldwide* 12, 66, 78t, 86; © *Martyn Smith* 57, 219 (both), 220r, 221 (all).
Matchday notes on page 47 courtesy Barry Davies, page 90 courtesy John Motson.
Memorabilia supplied by the author, BBC Written Archives, Alan Griffiths (matchday programme on page 13) and the *Match of the Day* office.

First published in 2004
Copyright © Martyn Smith 2004
The moral right of the author has been asserted.

ISBN 0 563 52181 3

Published by BBC Books, BBC Worldwide Ltd, Woodlands, 80 Wood Lane, London W12 0TT

BBC Worldwide would like to thank those who supplied photographs and for permission to reproduce copyright material. While every effort has been made to trace and acknowledge all copyright holders, we would like to apologize should there have been any errors or omissions.

Commissioning editors Ben Dunn, Vivien Bowler, Tracey Smith

Produced for BBC Books by Butler and Tanner

Design, layout, colour reproduction, printing and binding by Butler & Tanner, Frome, Great Britain
Editors Julian Flanders, Helen Burge
Picture Research Julian Flanders, David Cottingham
Designers Lyn Davies, Jennie Hoare, Craig Stevens and Kathie Wilson
Index by Indexing Specialists (UK) Ltd

Author's Acknowledgements

Like *Match of the Day*, I also turn 40 this year and my earliest memories are of going with my Dad and his brothers, Stan and Alan, to watch Chelmsford City play in the Southern League in the late 1960s and early 1970s. The post match ritual was always the same. They would walk to the edge of the terrace next to the gate just ahead of the final whistle, moan about the terrible performance and then cross New Writtle Street to their mother's house to hear Len Martin read out the results on *Grandstand* as they checked the Pools.

After tea came the weekly battle with my parents, Mike and Nettie, to be allowed to stay up and watch *Match of the Day*. Little did I imagine that one day I would be working on the show, firstly as a Floor Manager and then as an Assistant Producer, albeit not a very good one. Editing football matches requires a skill and concentration level that I have never possessed but I saw enough to admire the abilities of those who bring the matches to our screens.

The other great memories are of FA Cup Final days and the excitement of actually being able to watch a match live on television. Every year we would go to my Granny and Grandad's as they had that rare thing – a colour TV. All their friends would be there and they would gather from mid-morning so that every part of the build up, from 'It's a Cup Final Knockout' to 'Meet the Teams', was seen. It was a ritual that helped establish my great love of sport, much to the chagrin of my brother and sister, Simon and Jane, who must have been very bored with years of sports talk.

A lot of people have helped me with the writing of this book and I would like to thank a few of them. I'm grateful to all the presenters, commentators, pundits, fans and members of the production teams from across the decades who so kindly gave up their time and memories; to the BBC Sports Library, BBC Written Archives, Paul Wright and Zak Oomer in BBC Sport for all their generous help; to Kay Satterley and Claire Donohoe-Lane in the *Match of the Day* office for the massive amount of assistance that they have given me across many years; to Phil Bigwood for putting up with my many questions, and, of course, the legend who is Albert Sewell for, as ever, getting me out of a few holes and offering invaluable guidance and advice.

I'd like to also thank Edward Lidster for his support and patience during the past few months, Steve Whitehead and Steve Moreschi for humouring my absences and not lobbying too hard on behalf of Chelsea and Plymouth and Jay Ramirez for keeping me grounded.

This book is dedicated to the memory of Peter Talbot, a Middlesbrough fan who loved the club but didn't get the chance to see them achieve success.

MARTYN SMITH

contents

Foreword

As someone who has had the enormous privilege of being the Editor of *Match of the Day* I am incredibly proud that it has reached its 40th anniversary. For me, growing up in Northern Ireland in the 1960s, it gave entrance to a world of football to which Co Armagh offered no ready accessibility. The images we saw and the voices we heard in those early years were everything to a generation which previously got one televised game per year – the FA Cup Final. Suddenly we were transported every Saturday night around the grounds of England and the newsprint of heroic deeds was now writ large upon the screen.

Colour arrived and with it the skill, beauty, rawness and sheer exhilaration of the game leapt into our living rooms. The players and managers became known to millions who had previously been indifferent. Presenters, pundits, reporters all became national names from working on a programme with no other brief than to deliver a compendium of the day's events.

Sky's arrival on the football landscape changed the game irrevocably but the essential ethos of the *Match of the Day* brand did not waver and we at the BBC are delighted to have it back after its temporary Saturday night transfer. We hope it is a programme that you can trust. We hope it is a programme that the audience values. We hope it is a programme that still makes sense in a rapidly changing broadcast world. And we hope the football continues to thrill.

And then there's the music...

NIALL SLOANE
Head of Football, BBC Sport

1937

Although *Match of the Day* started in 1964 the story of football on BBC Television actually began on 15 February 1937 when the Corporation first wrote to Arsenal's manager, George Allison, to say that they were 'anxious to experiment with the broadcasting of Association Football'. They wondered if Arsenal's players could demonstrate the sport in front of cameras at Alexandra Palace near to the BBC transmitter. Television had only been launched in the previous November but already it was thought that sport could have an important role to play in encouraging people to buy the new sets. Arsenal were interested in the idea but apologized and declined to take part as they didn't have enough spare time.

In August the Assistant Director of Television, Mr R.A. Rendall, suggested taking the BBC's new mobile television unit to Highbury so that they could televise live from Arsenal's ground. This was agreed and three short transmissions were shown in the following month. The van costs, including the scanner and power, were put at £35 and the BBC felt that there had to be several broadcasts from the ground to justify the cost of moving all the new kit there.

After many weeks of planning the first ever live televising of footballers took place on Wednesday 15 September 1937. It only consisted of two minutes of mute pictures from Highbury at 3.45 p.m., and went out as part of a magazine show called *Picture Page*.

On that same evening a handful of BBC bigwigs gathered in a special viewing room at Alexandra Palace to watch a test transmission of that night's reserve match between Arsenal and Millwall. It was also at Highbury as the

Radio Times listing for 16 September 1937.

DANCE, a little ar and a Ballet, Music by Spike phy by Antony y Dallas Bower. ion Orchestra, , conducted by d Spike Hughes

: British Movie-

D THE BE- play by Stephen -Don Gemmell. nk Birch. Lady a Churchill. A Davies. Jack ggs. Ernestine Mrs. Harding— t 1: Sir John ondon. Act 2: s. Act 3: Mrs. ondon. Produc-

ERSONALLY' ole

dike Kid '

ERS. Mildred

and Pepys will be discussed, with illustrations by televised reproductions of paintings in the National

WEDNESDAY, Sept. 15

11.0-12.0 FILM for Demonstration Purposes

3.0 JUST FOR FUN! with Edward Cooper and Richard Murdoch. Presentation by Reginald Smith

3.20 NEWS FILM: Gaumont British News

3.30-4.0 'PICTURE PAGE' (Seventy-Seventh Edition). A Magazine Programme of general and topical interest, edited by Cecil Madden, produced by Jan Bussell. The Switchboard Girl: Joan Miller

9.0 JUST FOR FUN! with Edward Cooper and Richard Murdoch. Presentation by Reginald Smith.

bridge demonstrations.

'THE SCANNER'

THURSDAY, September 16

11.0-12.0 FILM for Demonstration Purposes

3.0 Douglas Byng in 'FANCY THAT!' with Elaine Mara, Muriel Robbins, Betty Shepard, Peggy Stacey, and Dennis van Thal and Bob Probst. Presentation by Reginald Smith

3.30 NEWS FILM: British Movietonews

3.40 FOOTBALL AT THE ARSENAL. A demonstration by members of the Arsenal team at the Arsenal Stadium, Highbury (by courtesy of the Directors of the Arsenal Football Club). Introduced by George F. Allison. (Conditions permitting)

3.55-4.0 FILM

9.30-10.0 THE THE WINDOW as 3.30)

SATURDAY

11.0-12.0 FILM Purposes

3.0 IN OUR G. Findlay, Keeper o cultural Society's will pay an infor garden in Alexand

3.20 NEWS FIL tonews

3.30-4.0 'OLD (Details as Thursc

9.0 'THE PROP one act by Chek landowner—Willia sha, his daughte Lomov, their nei Brandt. Production

SNAGGE.   Now the viewers've had a look round

your very fine stadium

expect they'd like to

would, how many peopl

ALLISON.   Well, Mr. Snagge, it

(and he gives the fi

other interesting d

stadium, with any

interjections from

SNAGGE.   I see you're very

your turf.

ALLISON.   Yes, it gets cut just as often as

your lawn at home.

SNAGGE.   More, I hope!

ALLISON.   Would you like to have a word with

our Clerk of Works, Mr. Campbell?

SNAGGE.   Certainly, if he can spare the time.

ALLISON.   (Calling away from mic.) Campbell!

Come here a minute, will you?

On 16 September 1937 history was made at Highbury in London as broadcaster John Snagge (left) chatted with Arsenal manager George Allison (below) and viewers watched the Arsenal team being put through their paces during training (above).

transmitters could only cover a very limited distance. The intention was to determine whether or not live football match broadcasts would be possible and what they saw that night was encouraging.

The following day, Thursday 16 September, football appeared in the *Radio Times* as a separate show for the very first time. At 3.40 in the afternoon, *Football at the Arsenal* began and the great broadcaster, John Snagge, welcomed viewers as he stood on the pitch accompanied by George Allison. The show lasted just under 15 minutes but that was enough time to meet the Clerk of Works who discussed the pitch; Mr Whittaker, the trainer, who put the team through exercises in front of the cameras; and one of the players, Cliff Bastin, who gave a demonstration of good and bad trapping.

When the programme returned on the next afternoon George Male became the first footballer to be interviewed live on television. As the other players were introduced to the camera John Snagge remarked that it seemed that you didn't have to be a Londoner to get into the team. 'Not at all', replied Allison, 'they are from Scotland, Yorkshire, Wales, all over the place ... just provided they are British subjects. We couldn't put a foreigner in the team.' Times have certainly changed at Highbury.

1946–1963

When the television service reopened after the war in 1946 the BBC was keen to begin showing football as soon as possible. The Football League once again refused to allow matches to be covered but the FA was still very open to the idea.

Ian Orr-Ewing was the Television Outside Broadcast Manager but he was still only able to televise matches that took place within 20 miles of Alexandra Palace which, once again, limited them to broadcasting games from London. There were now believed to be about 15,000 television sets in the area but Orr-Ewing was convinced that televising a match wouldn't stop fans from going to it.

The Athenian Football League also took this view, were keen to help the BBC and offered their matches for coverage. As a result, live televised football resumed from Barnet on the afternoon of Saturday 19 October 1946, when the home team, who were the Amateur Cup holders, took on Wealdstone.

There were still a number of technical problems to overcome and the broadcast was only able to go ahead after a nearby resident allowed the engineers to borrow their telephone line and when the owner of a local allotment, Mr Overall, had given permission for scaffolding to be erected on his plot. This was obtained after Peter Dimmock, then the Assistant Television Outside Broadcast Manager, promised to compensate him for any crop damage incurred! Edgar Kail provided the commentary and the broadcast went fairly well although bad light curtailed the coverage 15 minutes from the end of the game.

Following the success of that first programme the FA agreed to the BBC's request to televise selected FA representative and Cup matches in the London area and on 8 February 1947, Peter Dimmock introduced live coverage of Blackburn's fifth-round FA Cup tie against Charlton at The Valley. Alongside him was Jimmy Jewell, a former referee who had given the penalty that decided the 1938 Cup Final.

The BBC were later also allowed to cover the FA Cup Final and England against Scotland as sports broadcasting began to develop.

The Coronation in 1953 saw a big rise in the number of television sets purchased and the man who was in charge of that broadcast, Peter Dimmock, was also now Head of Sport.

Peter Dimmock played a major part in championing the BBC's coverage of football in the early years as a commentator, presenter and, eventually, Head of Sport.

In 1954, he and Paul Fox began to build on the increasing popularity of televised sport by launching a new midweek magazine programme, *Sportsview*. It was the first regular show to feature football match highlights, profiles and news stories as well as reports from many other sports.

Such was its popularity that in the following year they introduced a Saturday evening programme aimed mainly at football fans that became the forerunner to *Match of the Day*. Presented by the BBC's football commentator, Kenneth Wolstenholme, edited by Paul Fox and beginning on BBC1 at 10.15 p.m. on Saturday 10 September, *Saturday Sports Special* was a revolutionary new show that contained film reports and match action from around the UK.

At the start of the first edition, Peter Dimmock, who was also the face of *Sportsview*, appeared in vision. He welcomed the viewers and stressed that it was a show especially for sports enthusiasts that would be based in London but have live outside broadcast cameras all over the country to bring news, interviews and features in addition to the film reports. 'The accent is on soccer and that's why we have asked Kenneth Wolstenholme to occupy the *Sportsview* chair to introduce *Saturday Sports Special* to you each week at around 10 o'clock. So Kenneth, please take over and good luck for the new *Sportsview* unit Saturday programmes.' Kenneth then walked on to the set and took the chair from Dimmock.

The programme featured action from Luton Town against Newcastle United, Cliff Michelmore commentating on Charlton Athletic's 2-0 loss to Everton, highlights of Rangers' encounter with Stirling Albion and a spotlight on Wolverhampton Wanderers who had scored 25 goals in their first six matches of the season. In addition, Walley Barnes was in the studio to talk about Tottenham Hotspur's defeat of Arsenal, David Coleman was in the Midlands' studio to round up the local news, and cycling, rugby, tennis, racing and motor cycling were all featured.

The programme got a very favourable press but overran by several minutes and incurred the wrath of the Controller of Programmes, Cecil McGivern, who also felt that there was far too much talking and not enough action. It had been a technical nightmare with the teleprompter not working properly, a number of faults and the Scottish report being accidentally faded out in mid-sentence. Paul Fox, the editor, held out, however, and the programme was quickly established with football as the essential ingredient.

Fox had to rely on the regional contributors who were out of his direct control and sent a memo to remind them that 'the number one essentials' were the slickness and punch in the round-ups, plus, of course, strict timekeeping. He wanted follow-ups, manager and player interviews, comment, news and a spotlight on the incidents. It was a show that should have the feel of a Monday morning paper, not a Sunday one.

The series ran for eight years and was supplemented in October 1958 by the launch of *Grandstand*. However, it eventually ended in 1963. Broadcasting was led, as ever, by new technology and *Saturday Sport Special* comprised short match reports that had been shot on 16 mm film that then had to be processed in time for transmission. This meant that it had to be rushed to the laboratories, returned as a wet negative and edited at Lime Grove by editors who had to work miracles every week to get the show on air.

As there was usually only one camera in operation at matches it meant that occasionally, and embarrassingly, the winning goal might be scored while the film was being changed. When videotape and the reality of multi-camera coverage developed, the programme died a natural death. Viewers could still see midweek highlights on *Sportsview* as well as the occasional live European match, but 1963 to 1964 was a barren year for football fans until the new BBC2 channel was launched and the Head of Sport, Bryan Cowgill, spotted a wonderful opportunity to get regular football back on the BBC.

Charlton keeper Sam Bartram (centre) challenges a Blackburn forward in the first live post-war FA Cup tie on 8 February 1947. The Londoners won the match 1-0.

1964–1965

Presenter
Kenneth Wolstenholme

League Champions   Manchester United

FA Cup winners   Liverpool

League Cup winners   Chelsea

European Cup-Winners' Cup winners
West Ham United

The show

On 22 August 1964 the BBC1 evening line-up was standard for its time and included *The Telegoons*, *Dr Who* with William Hartnell, *Juke Box Jury* hosted by David Jacobs, *Dr Finlay's Casebook* and *Perry Mason*.

Over on the new BBC2, following on from *Compact*, *Open House* and *Line Up*, the *Match of the Day* titles were ready to play for the very first time. As the Beatles had just begun a five-month run at number one in the album chart with *A Hard Day's Night* it was appropriate that Kenneth Wolstenholme's opening link should come pitchside from Anfield as the crowd sang 'She Loves You' behind him.

'Welcome to *Match of the Day*, the first of a weekly series coming to you every Saturday on BBC2. As you can hear we're in Beatleville for this Liverpool versus Arsenal match.'

After looking at graphic captions of both teams, Ken was joined by his summariser, Walley Barnes, who previewed the game. Liverpool were the defending champions, the ground was full and the first ever *Match of the Day* goal came when Ian Callaghan crossed to Roger Hunt who hooked the ball into the top left corner with a right-foot volley. Liverpool won 3-2, Barnes gave his views at half-time and at the end of the game, Wolstenholme provided a brief news round-up and the legend was born – although only an estimated 20,000 viewers actually saw the show.

Not everyone liked it, however, and in the *Sunday Citizen* the following day, F.W. Deedes wrote , 'Why are the BBC lashing out on, by all commercial standards, a flop? Because they see it as pulling another minority interest towards their second channel which seems to be almost a bigger flop than the soccer flop they are buying... It looks like a real clanger to me.'

Kenneth Wolstenholme presented 27 of the shows during that season with Walley Barnes hosting six and Frank Bough

transplantation by deep-freezing, and basic questions such as the chemistry of the brain. It is the largest medical research institute in Britain and it costs some £6,700 a year to maintain each scientist (inclusive of his salary).

But it is not the purpose of the programme to report on their research—it seeks instead to show to tell in advance which facts will prove to be of decisive importance.

The work at the N.I.M.R. is in essence typical of scientific research in general; and the way in which its scientists largely spend their time conveys, I believe, something of what it means to be a scientist.
G. RATTRAY TAYLOR

Dora Bryan
2
8.50
WHETHER it is as a dizzy Information Desk girl, as a patient on a psychiatrist's couch, or as a harassed shop assistant, there is no doubt that Dora Bryan is one of Britain's most effective comediennes. Tonight you can see her in these and many other roles when she sings and performs sketches from the London revues and musicals which made her famous.

Match of the Day
2
6.30
TODAY for the first time soccer fans can watch a feature-length version—as opposed to a potted 'highlights' version—of a regular League fixture. Which one? That, by agreement with the Football League, remains a secret until 4.0 this afternoon. But Bryan Cowgill, BBC-tv's sports chief, promises that it will be a top match.

The agreement by which BBC-tv won permission for this came after careful negotiations between Bryan Cowgill and League Secretary Alan Hardaker. It allows for fifty-five minutes of coverage, enough to show the whole development of the game, and for its screening at a more popular hour.

'Up to now we have only been able to show ten-minute edited films of any given match, which effectively meant a machine-gun succession of goal-goal-goal,' says Cowgill. 'Now we can fall in line with BBC-2's policy by offering "depth" treatment of our most popular sport.' To those who think this breakthrough is a further blow to turnstile takings, he offers his experienced opinion that 'television never kept anyone away from the best in sport.'

In charge of the new venture as producer is **Alan Chivers**, BBC-tv's most experienced soccer specialist. He intends to make full use of the technical advantages of 625 lines, and says: 'We're no longer restricted mainly to the close-up. With 625's greater definition we can use wider shots without losing clarity, and so show much more of the overall pattern of a game.'

three; 28 different teams were seen with four of the most featured sides coming from London where the bulk of the audience lived. Spurs appeared nine times, Manchester United eight, Arsenal and West Ham seven and Chelsea six.

As BBC2 was a new channel it was only available in the London area at first. However, on 3 December new transmitters were opened in the Birmingham area and another two million people had potential access to the service. The highlights were not just confined to Division One because, under the agreement with the Football League, three programmes were devoted to Division Two. From as early as September, the League were complaining about the matches chosen, and that too many London clubs were being shown.

But, despite the doubters the new programme was seen as a success, not least because it seemed to be a big hit overseas. By mid-October it had already been sold to Hong Kong, Australia, New Zealand, Rhodesia, Mexico, Saudi Arabia, Liberia, Egypt, the Philippines, Kenya, Aden, Gibraltar, Trinidad and Malta.

The season

The 1964–65 season began with Liverpool as Champions and West Ham United as FA Cup holders. Manchester United's Denis Law was the reigning European Footballer of the Year. One famous name was missing, however, when the new campaign kicked off; 26-year-old John White, a member of Tottenham Hotspur's double-winning side, was tragically killed by lightning in July while sheltering under a tree on a golf course at Enfield.

Despite the inevitable difficulties involved in selecting matches to cover several weeks in advance, the cameras got lucky on many occasions and were there to see nine of Denis Law's 28 League goals as he, George Best and Bobby Charlton propelled Manchester United towards the title again. They were seen beating Tottenham Hotspur 4-1 in

Right Liverpool's Roger Hunt (left) celebrates the first ever *Match of the Day* goal with team-mates Ron Yates and Ian Callaghan. The match featured five goals as Liverpool beat Arsenal 3-2. Roger Hunt's opening goal was followed by two from Gordon Wallace. *Above* Wallace rises above Arsenal's Don Howe to head past Jim Furnell.

Walley Barnes

Walley Barnes was the original *Match of the Day* pundit who would give his comments from the side of the pitch before the match, at half-time and at the end of the game. He appeared alongside Kenneth Wolstenholme in the first programme from Anfield and presented several shows later in the same season.

Barnes was a talented left-back who captained both Arsenal and Wales. He made more than 300 appearances for his club, winning the League Championship in 1948 and the FA Cup in 1950. He was also capped 22 times by Wales before retiring in 1955 to become a BBC football 'adviser' and commentator. His name is one of the most misspelled in football. Walley Barnes died in September 1975 aged 55.

Another pundit who was occasionally used was the former Tottenham Hotspur and Northern Ireland captain, Danny Blanchflower. He had led Spurs to the League and Cup double in 1961, the FA Cup in 1962 and the European Cup-Winners' Cup in 1963.

September, travelling to Highbury in November to beat Arsenal 3-2 and defeating Chelsea 4-0 in March.

It was a time when goalscorers were king and teams regularly put five or six past their opponents. The highlights were Spurs' 7-4 win against Wolverhampton Wanderers, Manchester United beating Aston Villa 7-0 and an astonishing encounter between Blackburn Rovers and Birmingham City that ended 5-5.

As well as George Best, several other young players were making their mark including 19-year-old Alan Ball who scored a hat-trick in front of the cameras for Blackpool as they drew 3-3 with Fulham at Craven Cottage.

Newly promoted Leeds United had an incredible first year in the top flight under manager Don Revie and almost beat Manchester United in the title race. They gained a reputation for being an aggressive side and in November, when they travelled to Goodison Park, both

Bobby Moore triumphantly raises the European Cup-Winners' Cup after West Ham's 2-0 win over Munich 1860 at Wembley.

they and Everton were ordered off the pitch after 38 minutes as the referee tried to calm a heated atmosphere. It was ten minutes before the match was able to resume.

The crucial encounter between Leeds and Manchester United in April was the featured game on the penultimate show. John Connelly's goal was the difference as Leeds lost at home for only the second time that season. They both finished on 61 points, but the Championship went to Manchester United on goal average. Tommy Docherty's young Chelsea side were third, and were winners of the League Cup, beating Leicester City 3-2 on aggregate in the two-legged Final.

In August the axe had fallen on one of football's legendary managers, Stan Cullis, who was sacked by Wolverhampton Wanderers after 16 years at the helm and having led them to three Championships and two FA Cups. His

Leeds United's combative midfielder Bobby Collins was voted Footballer of the Year in 1965.

Alec Weeks (below right) directed some 1600 matches for the BBC between 1959 and 1987 including the 1966 World Cup Final.

successor, Andy Beattie, was unable to prevent them being relegated at the end of the season along with neighbouring Birmingham City. At the time only two clubs were relegated and promoted. They were replaced in Division One by Newcastle United and Northampton Town.

West Ham United beat Munich 1860 2-0 at Wembley to win the European Cup-Winners' Cup. They were only the second British team to lift a European trophy and as Bobby Moore climbed the famous steps to receive the cup it proved to be the perfect rehearsal for the World Cup in the following year.

The FA Cup

The first *Match of the Day* double header was broadcast on 9 January 1965 when Frank Bough presented highlights of Everton's 2-2 draw against Sheffield Wednesday in the third round of the FA Cup. It was the only cup match to be shown that season. The second featured game was Oxford United's Division Four encounter with Tranmere Rovers. Oxford won but the loudest voice heard that day was that of the Oxford captain, Ron Atkinson, whose instructions to his team-mates could clearly be heard above Bough's commentary.

The Final itself was a tough encounter between Leeds United and Liverpool. Goalless after 90 minutes, Roger Hunt headed Liverpool into the lead after three minutes of extra time. Eight minutes later Billy Bremner equalized before Ian St. John scored the winner for the Merseysiders with less than 10 minutes remaining to enable them to lift the FA Cup for the first time in their history.

1964 European Nations Cup

Spain beat the defending champions USSR 2-1 in the Final, held in front of 100,000 spectators in Madrid in June 1964. Hungary were third with Denmark in fourth place. England had failed to qualify for the finals having been knocked out of the first qualifying round in 1963 by France who beat them 6-3 on aggregate.

Liverpool's Ian St. John (number 9 on ground) forces the ball over the Leeds line for the winning goal in the FA Cup Final much to the despair of Giles, Reaney and Gary Sprake.

Stanley Matthews is chaired off the pitch, at the end of his testimonial match in 1965 between Stoke City and a World Stars XI, by Lev Yashin (left) and Ferenc Puskas.

Sir Stanley Matthews retired aged 50 after a 33-year career without a single booking or dismissal. Although he began and ended his playing days with Stoke City, Matthews was best known for his 14 seasons with Blackpool that included their famous FA Cup Final win in 1953 when he helped inspire the club to a memorable 4-3 victory over Bolton Wanderers. On 6 February 1965 Matthews became the oldest active player in the history of first-class football when he helped Stoke City beat Fulham. In the New Year's Honours List Stanley had become the first footballer to be knighted.

Footballer of the Year
Bobby Collins, Leeds United

European Footballer of the Year
Eusebio, Benfica

Match of the Day Results 1964–1965

22 August 1964 – Division One
Liverpool 3-2 Arsenal
Hunt, Wallace (2)   Strong, Baker

29 August 1964 – Division One
Chelsea 3-1 Sunderland
Murray, Graham, Shellito   Herd

5 September 1964 – Division One
Fulham 2-1 Manchester United
Stiles (o.g.), Haynes   Connelly

12 September 1964 – Division One
West Ham United 3-2 Tottenham Hotspur
Byrne (3)   Greaves (2, 1 pen)

19 September 1964 – Division One
Chelsea 2-0 Leeds United
Venables, Hollins

26 September 1964 – Division One
Manchester United 4-1 Tottenham Hotspur
Crerand (2), Law (2)   Robertson

3 October 1964 – Division One
Chelsea 5-1 Blackburn Rovers
Bridges (3), Tambling,   McEvoy
R. Harris

10 October 1964 – Division One
Tottenham Hotspur 3-1 Arsenal
Robertson, Greaves, Saul   Baker

17 October 1964 – Division One
Leicester City 3-2 Nottingham Forest
Hodgson, Armstrong (pen),   Crowe, Wignall
Stringfellow

24 October 1964 – Division One
Tottenham Hotspur 1-1 Chelsea
Jones   Graham

31 October 1964 – Division One
Arsenal 3-1 Everton
Baker (2), Anderson   Pickering

7 November 1964 – Division One
West Ham United 1-1 Blackburn Rovers
Sissons   Byrom

14 November 1964 – Division One
Wolverhampton 3-1 Tottenham Hotspur
Wanderers   Brown
Wharton, Crawford, Le Flem

21 November 1964 – Division One
Fulham 3-3 Blackpool
Earle, Chamberlain, Howfield   Ball (3)

28 November 1964 – Division One
Arsenal 2-3 Manchester United
Anderson, Eastham   Law (2), Connelly

5 December 1964 – Division One
West Ham United 0-0 Leicester City

12 December 1964 – Division One
Chelsea 2-1 Wolverhampton
Bridges (2)   **Wanderers**
   Crawford

19 December 1964 – Division One
Aston Villa 3-1 Arsenal
A. Baker (2), MacLeod   J. Baker

26 December 1964 – Division One
Nottingham Forest 1-2 Tottenham Hotspur
Chapman   Gilzean, Jones

28 December 1964 – Division One
West Ham United 2-1 Birmingham City
Byrne, Kirkup   Sharples

2 January 1965 – Division One
Stoke City 1-0 West Ham United
Viollet

9 January 1965 – FA Cup 3rd Round
Everton 2-2 Sheffield Wednesday
Pickering, Burgin (o.g.)   Fantham, Quinn

9 January 1965 – Division Four
Oxford United 1-0 Tranmere Rovers
Beavon (pen)

16 January 1965 – Division One
Nottingham Forest 2-2 Manchester United
Hinton (2)   Law (2)

23 January 1965 – Division One
West Bromwich Albion 2-0 Tottenham Hotspur
Cram, Clark

30 January 1965 – No programme:
Winston Churchill's funeral was televised instead

6 February 1965 – Division One
Tottenham Hotspur 1-0 Manchester United
Henry

13 February 1965 – Division One
Arsenal 1-2 Leeds United
Eastham   Giles, Weston

20 February 1965 – Division Two
Leyton Orient 2-1 Newcastle United
Elwood (2)   McGarry (pen)

27 February 1965 – Division One
West Ham United 2-1 Liverpool
Hurst, Presland   Hunt

6 March 1965 – Division Two
Charlton Athletic 1-3 Bolton Wanderers
Kenning   Lee (pen), Bromley, Butler

13 March 1965 – Division One
Manchester United 4-0 Chelsea
Herd (2), Best, Law

20 March 1965 – Division One
Leeds United 4-1 Everton
Johanneson (2),   Temple
Bremner, Peacock

27 March 1965 – Division One
West Ham United 2-1 Arsenal
Hurst, Byrne   Baker

3 April 1965 – Division One
Aston Villa 1-0 Tottenham Hotspur
Baker

10 April 1965 – Division Two
Northampton Town 2-2 Derby County
Martin, Brown   Durban (2)

17 April 1965 – Division One
Leeds United 0-1 Manchester United
Connelly

24 April 1965 – Division One
Manchester United 3-0 Liverpool
Law (2), Connelly

The producers

Bryan Cowgill

Bryan Cowgill was the Head of Sport for BBC Television from 1961 to 1974 and he conducted all the negotiations with the Football League that helped to create *Match of the Day*. Having joined the BBC in 1955 Bryan later became Controller of BBC1 before moving to Thames Television in 1978 as their Managing Director. After retiring in 1985 he joined Sky TV as a consultant.

'When BBC2 was launched in 1964 the first controller, Michael Peacock, came to me and asked what sport could do for the channel. What could he expect from us? Well, we already had *Grandstand* on Saturdays and almost every other sport was covered but what I really wanted to do was get football back on Saturday nights, which is where I felt its rightful home was.

BBC2 was supposed to be an innovative new channel and do things that were not covered on BBC1 so we decided to try and secure football highlights that were a decent length. Our previous long-term contract with the Football League cost £7,000 and had run from 1958 to 1961 but it had been for the rights to show only very limited extracts of games.

We had always had a lot of problems with the then Secretary of the Football League, Alan Hardaker, and I thought that BBC2 might be a softly-softly way of working the game back on to television as the channel had so few viewers and was initially only seen in the London area.

In June, I was delighted to hear that the idea of a *Match of the Day* programme appealed in principle to the management committee of the Football League so we set out a statement of proposals. We wanted to select the match four weeks in advance and announce it each week in the *Radio Times* but the clubs unanimously rejected that, a blow to the channel since they were keen to promote it to the public.

In July, an agreement was reached for one season only that saw us pay £20,000 for the rights to show one match a week for 36 weeks in a show that was 55 minutes long. It could go out at any time after 6.30 p.m. on the same evening. We could choose the games but they had to be approved by Alan Hardaker and the Football League. The biggest change, and the thing that made the new programme possible, was that we were now able to record the matches on electronic cameras and beam them back to London where they could be edited into a highlights package.

On 6 August, I requested the games that we wanted to cover including Liverpool against Arsenal for the first show on the 22nd of that month. Our initial choices were all granted and, on the following two weekends, viewers saw Chelsea against Sunderland and Fulham take on Manchester United.

The contract was pretty restrictive as it meant that we had to seek approval from Hardaker every time we wanted to show a game and we were only allowed to show one match a day, hence the name. I always wanted to try and get North versus South or Midlands' games so that it would drive up the audience interest. That was why we chose Liverpool against Arsenal for the first show.

It was a constant battle with Hardaker who would not countenance any control of League football slipping outside of the influence of his office. He wanted to run the whole thing. I wasn't cowed by him, far from it, but I had to watch my step and I didn't want to lose the contract. It was always difficult but with an uneasy respect on both sides.

It used to infuriate him that I had no such problems with the FA who were led by my friend Sir Stanley Rous. Hardaker and Rous didn't get on either which helped to fuel the fire.

Once the contract was signed and the first match selected we had just a couple of weeks to get everything organized. It was very exciting to set up the new show and we had Alan Chivers in charge for the first series, a very skilful and seasoned Outside Broadcast director. Kenneth Wolstenholme was regarded as the voice of football so he was the natural and respected choice to present the BBC's new football show, *Match of the Day*.'

The producers

Alec Weeks

A legendary BBC producer, Alec Weeks directed about 1600 matches between 1959 and 1987 including 15 FA Cup Finals and the 1966 World Cup Final. In addition, Alec worked on eight World Cups and oversaw the BBC's Olympic Games and athletics coverage. In 1977 he won a Bafta for his coverage of the 1976 FA Cup Final. Born in 1927, he joined the BBC as an office boy in 1941. Two years later he became a programme engineer, which involved doing spot effects on shows such as *ITMA*. After three years in the RAF as a Physical Training Instructor where he twice fought Randolph Turpin, he was demobbed in 1948 and rejoined the BBC as a radio studio manager.

'In the pioneering days we got away with murder, were able to experiment a lot and keep pushing the barriers. I had four cameras with each Outside Broadcast unit and knew that only two or three would be working at the end of a match. It was a challenge and in *Match of the Day* we had a new programme on a new channel, which enabled us to train up crews for the World Cup in 1966. Before then they might do opera one night, football the next and then be off on a dog show.

One of the reasons that England was awarded the World Cup was that the BBC had guaranteed that every match would be covered on videotape rather than film. The hope was that in 1966 the new satellites would enable to games to be seen around the world live.

In the first series the director was Alan Chivers, a great professional who had been covering football for many years. I was charged with making VT work before taking over in April 1965. Kenneth Wolstenholme was the main commentator and it was difficult to train others as his contract gave him first call on all soccer on the BBC so he probably did 90 per cent of all games. He had a beautiful voice and was one of the few commentators who could sit at Wembley stadium on World Cup Final day and still have his voice heard above 100,000 chanting fans.

On 30 July 1966 it was like the end of a race. We had been working so hard for the previous two years but had to have a very cold-hearted and dispassionate approach with no emotion to ensure that it would be totally professional coverage. On the day the quietest place in Wembley was probably the scanner. The coverage was all that mattered to us.

We took the cameramen down to the training headquarters before the match and Alf Ramsey let them sit and chat with the players so that they got to be familiar with them ahead of the game. We then looked at tapes of all the German matches as well as photos of the players. It was incredibly professional and I was very proud to be part of that unit. There may have been only two teams on the park but there were three in the stadium that day.

After the World Cup the world of television really sat up and began to take notice of the BBC's sports coverage. Up until then ABC had been regarded as the crack network but now we had teams from all over the world coming to watch our coverage to learn how we produced sport.

We had a marvellous commentary team in the late 1960s with Kenneth, Barry Davies and David Coleman. They were three cracking commentators who each complemented the other. My pick of the commentators would have to be Coleman as on his day he would take some beating. I would have Barry Davies as number two as I think that he is still a very good commentator and Ken in third place since he had such a beautiful voice.

In the early days of colour the lighting was so bad and the cameramen would leave the ground with bloodshot eyes having strained to keep up with play. The equipment wasn't right then and the engineers had their technical books in their hands as they adjusted the colour. We had to persuade clubs to change and improve their lighting for colour transmissions to work so between 1967 and 1969 we had an engineer whose sole job was to advise them for free so that we could move the process on. By the end of the 1960s it all began to click.'

The producers Bryan Cowgill, Alec Weeks **19**

1965–1966

Presenter
Kenneth Wolstenholme

League Champions   Liverpool
FA Cup winners   Everton
League Cup winners   West Bromwich Albion

The show

Despite attempts by some clubs to prevent its return, *Match of the Day* was given a second chance when a new contract was eventually signed between the Football League and the BBC in October 1965, two months after the start of the new season. The cost had increased by 25 per cent to £25,000 although the duration of each programme had been reduced to 45 minutes and it could no longer be broadcast before 10 p.m.

The series was kept on BBC2 as it was still helping to drive acceptance of the new channel, although FA Cup highlights were shown on BBC1 on several Sunday afternoons during the season.

BBC2 was now available to viewers in the North West, and the *Liverpool Daily Post* reported in November that the amazing reaction to the channel was seemingly driven by football. The demand for BBC2 was so great on Merseyside that men were working seven days a week to fit the newly purchased aerials which cost between £5 and £12. The waiting time was several weeks and the reason given by one firm was 'soccer, it's as simple as that. The programme which is really pulling in the viewers is *Match of the Day* on a Saturday night'.

Although arguments with the Football League about the distribution of coverage continued, 28 teams were featured during the season; Manchester United were the most popular side for the editor scoring 19 goals in the seven games in which they featured.

The season

Goals were the story of this season and in the first seven programmes the cameras covered Nottingham Forest beating West Ham 5-0, Arsenal's 6-2 defeat of Sheffield United, Leicester City losing 5-0 at home to Manchester United and Tottenham Hotspur's 5-1 win over Manchester United.

At White Hart Lane, Jimmy Greaves scored one of his greatest solo goals for Spurs as he accelerated past four players to score whilst at the other end viewers saw a classic long range left-footed goal by Bobby Charlton. Two months later the teams met again at Old Trafford, Greaves was missing with hepatitis and the score was reversed, with Manchester United winning 5-1. Charlton was on target again, this time with a right-footed volley from outside the box.

Spurs were also involved in another remarkable high-scoring home game in March when they went 5-1 up against Aston Villa before Tony Hateley scored four times to level the match at 5-5.

Liverpool won the Championship for the second time in three seasons, finishing six points clear of Leeds United who were ahead of Burnley on goal average. Manchester United were fourth and Chelsea fifth.

Match of the Day was at Anfield to see Liverpool beat Chelsea 2-1 in April as the crowd chanted 'we want Shankly' and he reluctantly walked out to accept their applause. Kenneth Wolstenholme remarked that 'not one person from the Spion Kop has invaded the pitch and that should go down as an example to all other supporters'.

Blackburn Rovers finished bottom of Division One after a wretched run that had seen them take just two points from a possible 26 and they were relegated along with Northampton Town whose immediate return to Division Two was a result of their dreadful away form. They conceded 60 goals on their travels as Blackburn, Leeds United, Manchester United and Stoke City all scored six against them.

Opposite **Having beaten four defenders, Tottenham's Jimmy Greaves wheels away in delight after putting his team 3-0 up against Manchester United at White Hart Lane in October 1965. It was one of many classic encounters between Spurs and United that featured on the programme in its early years.**
Above **Bill Shankly and the Liverpool squad look suitably proud of themselves as they show off the silverware won during the 1965–66 season.**

Action replay

Bryan Cowgill was Head of Sport at BBC Television throughout the 1960s and recalls how he brought the replay machine to British television.

'The greatest development for the coverage of sport, and football in particular, was the discovery of the action replay machine. I had produced and directed Wimbledon and had gone to stay in Bel Air with the tennis commentator Jack Kramer in December 1965.

While we were watching American football on CBS I saw a touchdown and about three seconds later saw it again. There it was, on screen again but in slow motion. I was astonished. Jack explained that it was a new replay machine that they had just started experimenting with and, with the 1966 World Cup coming, I just couldn't get it out of my mind as I realized how it could be both revolutionary and revelatory for soccer.

The then head of CBS Sport, Jack Dolph, was a mate so I rang and told him how impressed I was and asked where I could get one. He said that theirs was the prototype – no others existed. When the manufacturers confirmed this I went back to Dolph and asked if we could borrow theirs for the BBC to use in the World Cup. After some negotiations it duly arrived at Heathrow in the spring.

It was seen on-air for the first time in the opening match between England and Uruguay. We were all waiting for the first goal but none came so eventually I decided to use it on a near miss. Everyone was taken aback when it first appeared, including Kenneth Wolstenholme, and the BBC's duty log was besieged by calls from puzzled viewers asking whether the match was live or recorded.

We needed to indicate what was happening so I asked our graphics company, Wurmsers, to devise a caption that explained what it was. They asked me what I wanted it to say and the first words that came out of my mouth were "action replay". It was literally off the cuff but the phrase remains. We then bought the machine off CBS as they were getting another and it became an indispensable part of our football coverage on *Match of the Day* from then on.'

Manchester City's new manager, Joe Mercer, took them straight back into Division One and Southampton also went up for the first time in 81 years having been helped by their 9-3 win against Wolverhampton Wanderers in September.

West Bromwich Albion beat West Ham 5-3 in the two-legged League Cup Final, but it was West Ham's young striker Geoff Hurst who gained most attention during the season and he finished as the top goalscorer in Division One with 38 League and Cup goals to his name. He was coming into form at exactly the right time.

The FA Cup

Although George Best was dominating the football press another teenage star was also emerging, this time in South West London; 18-year-old Peter Osgood was the toast of Stamford Bridge as the Chelsea fans roared 'Osgood is good'.

His first *Match of the Day* goal came in January when the BBC televised highlights of the FA Cup third round match

In 1966 Bobby Charlton was voted European Footballer of the Year. He was only the second Englishman to receive the award; the first was Stanley Matthews in 1956.

Everton's Mike Trebilcock (dark shirt, turning away) strikes the equaliser past the outstretched arm of keeper Ron Springett against Sheffield Wednesday in the 1966 FA Cup Final. Two goals down with 30 minutes left, Trebilcock scored twice in five minutes as Everton came back to win 3-2 with a late winner from Derek Temple.

between Liverpool and Chelsea at Anfield. After Roger Hunt had put the home side in the lead, Osgood's close-range header from a Bobby Tambling corner made it 1-1. Tambling then scored the winner. Having beaten the Cup holders, Chelsea next defeated the runners-up, Leeds United, in the fourth round, a match also featured by the programme.

Their luck in front of the cameras ran out at the semi-final stage, however, when they lost to Sheffield Wednesday at Villa Park. In the other semi-final, Everton beat Manchester United 1-0 at Burnden Park, Bolton. United had been seen on the show in the fifth round defeating Wolverhampton Wanderers 4-2 at Molineux but, just one match from Wembley, they were beaten by a Colin Harvey goal.

In the Final, Sheffield Wednesday looked to have the match sewn up when they took a two-goal lead with just over half an hour remaining. In a tremendous comeback Mike Trebilcock scored twice in five minutes and then Derek Temple hit the winner 10 minutes before the final whistle. It was their first success in the competition for 33 years and made up for a disappointing League season where they finished 11th.

Fact file

Substitutes were allowed for the first time during the season, but only for injured players. Charlton Athletic's inside-forward Keith Peacock made history in a Division Two match against Bolton Wanderers on Saturday 21 August when he ran on in a number 12 shirt and became the first substitute ever to be used in the Football League; 14 were used in total on that day. A second substitute was allowed from 1992 and that was increased to three in the following season.

Footballer of the Year
Bobby Charlton, Manchester United

European Footballer of the Year
Bobby Charlton, Manchester United

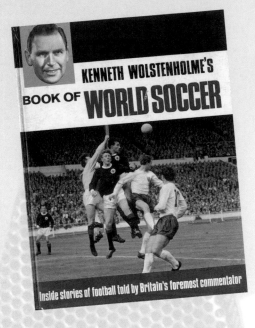

Kenneth Wolstenholme

Kenneth Wolstenholme was the first presenter and commentator on *Match of the Day* and was the leading voice of football for almost two decades on the BBC. Until parting company from the Corporation in 1971, he was television's number one soccer commentator. He commentated on 23 FA Cup Finals, 16 European Cup Finals and five World Cup Finals. In 1966 he produced the most famous line in sports commentating, 'Some people are on the pitch. They think it's all over. It is now' as Geoff Hurst scored England's fourth goal to win the World Cup.

Kenneth Wolstenholme was born to sports fanatic parents in Worsley, a small village near Manchester on 17 July 1920, and was educated at Farnworth Grammar School, near Bolton. On leaving school he began work as a journalist on a local newspaper, but in 1939, as a member of the pre-war RAF Volunteer Reserve, he was mobilised. Ken served throughout the war as a bomber pilot, flying Bristol Blenheims and Mosquitos, firstly on low-level daylight raids and then as a member of the elite Pathfinder Force, which marked the targets for the main force during the

heavy bomber offensive. He completed 100 operations as a bomber pilot and was twice decorated.

After the war Ken started in journalism by writing cricket reports for the *Sunday Empire News* in Lancashire and then began to broadcast regularly in the north of England's Friday night sports programme on the BBC before progressing into the occasional cricket commentary stint.

His main ambition, however, was to replace the BBC's chief sport and football commentator, Raymond Glendenning, and his first football commentary was a Third Division (North) game between York City and Stockport County at Bootham Crescent. The first half was for the British Forces Network but the second was on national radio and Ken was on his way.

In 1948 he wrote to the Head of BBC Outside Broadcasts in London and asked to be considered for a job as a TV football commentator. After an audition at Romford he was offered the chance to demonstrate his skills on a live amateur international trial between the Southern and Northern Counties. That went well and he began to cover football on a regular basis.

Most of the matches that the BBC broadcast in those days were amateur games, apart from the FA Cup Final, but things changed radically when the Head of Sport, Peter Dimmock and his senior Editor, Paul Fox, launched *Sportsview* in 1954 with regular fooball interviews and features as well as brief match highlights.

Ken was a regular contributor to the programme and in the following year when Fox devised two new shows, *Today's Sport* and *Saturday Sports Special*, he was asked to front them both as the main presenter. The first was a short news round-up of that afternoon's results at 7.15 p.m. whilst the second went out after 10 p.m. and featured football action from all around the UK as well as regional sections, interviews with top names and a look at other sports. In addition, Ken was doing almost all the BBC's football commentaries and was a fixture at every main occasion.

Saturday Sports Special ended in 1963 but when League football returned to the screen the following year Ken was the automatic choice to present *Match of the Day*. Bryan Cowgill was Head of Sport at the BBC at the time and recalled: 'Working with Kenneth was always a great pleasure. He will forever be remembered as a highly effective commentator and was largely instrumental in taking the techniques of broadcast commentating from radio on to television. He was one of the first to recognise that the cam-

era was as effective a commentator as he was himself.'

Alec Weeks produced and directed most of the matches that Ken worked on from the early 1960s, including the 1966 World Cup Final. 'We covered all the Cup Finals together from 1965 onwards and all the World Cup matches from Wembley, including the Final on 30 July 1966 when the famous words were uttered. I can guarantee that those words were completely off the cuff. Kenneth had a beautiful voice and the perfect illustration was in 1966. The girders were shaking and Ken's voice cut across the screaming crowds perfectly. You could listen to him for hours. His voice never altered. Quite a man to work with.'

As David Coleman rose to prominence in the 1960s the competition for the top spot was increasing and Ken left the BBC at the end of the 1970–71 season. His last commentary, fittingly, was at Wembley, when Ajax beat Panathinaikos 2-0 in the European Cup Final.

He continued to work as a journalist and then as a commentator on Channel 4's *Football Italia* where he won a new generation of admirers. Kenneth Wolstenholme died in Torquay aged 81 on 25 March 2002 and in November 2003 his daughter, Lena, unveiled a special plaque in his memory at Television Centre. He will always be remembered for his opening words on the first *Match of the Day* and his closing words at Wembley on a July afternoon in 1966.

1966–1967

Presenter
Kenneth Wolstenholme

League Champions   Manchester United
FA Cup winners   Tottenham Hotspur
League Cup winners   Queens Park Rangers

The show

Despite the BBC's acclaimed coverage of the World Cup, the *Match of the Day* contract was far from secure but it was decided that if a small number of clubs did not agree to its terms then coverage would continue without them. The contract was finally signed in mid-August but Liverpool, the Champions, and Everton, the Cup holders, did not endorse it and were subsequently banned by the Football League from being seen either at home or away. Burnley and Bolton Wanderers also refused to sign. Bryan Cowgill remembered that some of the chairmen wanted to break away from the Football League and were reluctant to be bound by the television contract that had been negotiated as they wanted to strike their own individual deals.

'Alan Hardaker was totally against it as he feared that if it was allowed to develop then they might try and break away from the management committee and thereby his control. He told us that he would sort it out and banned them from being televised. It was soon resolved and they were both back on the screens by the end of December.'

This meant that the BBC had to change their plans for the opening show as they had originally intended to be at Anfield to cover Liverpool's match against Leicester City. Instead *Match of the Day* switched to Upton Park where West Ham were playing Chelsea.

The biggest change for the new season was that the programme had now switched to BBC1. David Attenborough, the Controller of BBC2, had initially been keen to keep it on his channel, but Huw Wheldon, the Controller of Programmes, decided to make the switch in response to rumours that ITV were planning to launch a major new football show of their own that would be fronted by the former England captain, Billy Wright.

Michael Peacock was now in charge of BBC1 and he voiced his concerns to Wheldon. He felt that the Billy Wright series 'could well mean that the television public will come to regard ITV as their prime contractor for top class League football... I think that the arguments for transferring *Match of the Day* outweigh the arguments against.'

Wheldon reluctantly agreed and the show moved across to BBC1. The effect was dramatic. By November audiences had risen to almost six million and for the first time the show became a truly national institution.

Under the new contract the BBC paid £33,000 for exclusive rights to Saturday night highlights, while ITV were able to show football on Sundays. It was Alan Hardaker, however, who still had the ultimate power to decide which teams were seen on the two channels and that was to prove an ongoing problem for all three parties.

Secretary of the Football League Alan Hardaker was hugely influential in the adoption of football into the TV schedules. He led the organization from 1957 to 1979.

The season

In the post-World Cup euphoria Kenneth Wolstenholme opened the first show of the new season from Upton Park. 'Welcome to our new viewers, the viewers too who followed us from BBC2 also the new fans who've been won over to soccer by the World Cup. We hope that you'll go along to watch your local team as well as watching *Match of the Day* and, in reply to your many requests, yes, I will explain the more technical parts of the game as we go along.'

Three weeks after Bobby Moore had lifted the Jules Rimet trophy at Wembley the *Match of the Day* cameras were at his home ground to see the three West Ham heroes, Moore, Geoff Hurst and Martin Peters, take a collective bow ahead of the game as a band played on the pitch and the West Ham United and Chelsea fans all applauded. The day ended less cheerfully for the home crowd, however, as goals from John Hollins and Charlie Cooke secured a 2-1 away win. The news round-up for the day recorded that the latest set of Busby Babes had made another fine start to the season as Manchester United beat West Bromwich Albion 5-3.

Below Matt Busby holds up the First Division Championship trophy in front of appreciative team and the *Match of the Day* cameras before Manchester United's final home game of the 1966–67 season against Stoke. The match ended in a 0-0 draw.

Above The BBC team for the World Cup contained some legendary names. Back row (left to right) Frank Bough, Alan Weeks, David Coleman, Walley Barnes; front row Ken Aston, Kenneth Wolstenholme and Arthur Ellis.

1966 World Cup

England's opening match of the World Cup resulted in a 0-0 draw against Uruguay at Wembley, but they beat both Mexico and France 2-0 to top their group and reach the quarter-finals. Geoff Hurst replaced Jimmy Greaves in the England line-up that day and scored the only goal of a bad-tempered match against Argentina, and then two goals from Bobby Charlton against one from Eusebio saw England past Portugal and into the Final.

West Germany took an early lead through Helmut Haller, but Hurst equalized and then his West Ham team-mate, Martin Peters, put England ahead. With less than a minute to go Wolfgang Weber drove the ball past Gordon Banks to level the scores and send the match into extra time. Hurst scored twice more, Kenneth Wolstenholme delivered his immortal lines, England won 4-2 and Bobby Moore walked up the steps to receive the Jules Rimet trophy from the Queen – the most famous moment in English footballing history.

QPR's Mark Lazarus (number 7) turns away after scoring the winning goal in the 1967 League Cup Final against West Bromwich Albion.

There were plenty of goals during the 1966–67 season. Southampton's Ron Davies (above left) scored 37 goals in 41 games, though the only one seen by the cameras came in a 1-0 win over Leeds, while Bobby Tambling (above) scored five in one match as Chelsea crushed Aston Villa 6-2 at Villa Park.

United's fortunes were reversed the following weekend when the programme's cameras saw them lose 3-1 to Leeds United at Elland Road although George Best scored his only goal on *Match of the Day* that season. Despite being their Championship year, they also lost a fortnight later when viewers saw goals by Alan Gilzean and Jimmy Greaves for Spurs cancel out Denis Law's opener, but they recovered their form two weeks after that when the cameras witnessed them demolish Burnley 4-1. In all they appeared on the show eight times that season including an epic encounter with West Bromwich Albion at The Hawthorns in December. A David Herd hat-trick ensured that the match finished 4-3 in United's favour with all seven goals coming in the first half.

There were two other league hat-tricks televised on the show that season. Derek Dougan's helped Wolverhampton Wanderers to a 4-0 victory over Hull in their Division Two encounter in March. It was his debut in front of the cameras. But even that was eclipsed by the astonishing feat of Bobby Tambling when Chelsea travelled to Villa Park in September. He scored two with his left foot and three with his right to complete a staggering five-goal haul as Chelsea beat Aston Villa 6-2. John Boyle scored the sixth. Chelsea were involved in yet another high scoring game when they drew 5-5 with Tottenham Hotspur, although Sheffield Wednesday scored the most goals in a single game, putting seven past Burnley.

The season had begun with Everton breaking the transfer record by signing World Cup hero Alan Ball from Blackpool for £110,000. It was the first six-figure transfer between English clubs but he could only help them to sixth place in the League. Manchester United were Champions with Nottingham Forest and Tottenham Hotspur both four points behind.

Southampton survived their first season in Division One helped by the prolific Welshman Ron Davies who scored 37 goals in 41 League games to finish ahead of Geoff Hurst and Jimmy Greaves in the end-of-season table of leading scorers. *Match of the Day* viewers saw just one of them, however, in October, when the newcomers went to Elland Road and beat Leeds United 1-0. Aston Villa and Blackburn Rovers were relegated while Coventry City and Wolves were promoted from Division Two.

The League Cup was revamped with 90 clubs now taking part. Only Liverpool and Everton decided not to enter. The Final was held at Wembley for the first time and in a dramatic match Queens Park Rangers of Division Three stunned the favourites and holders, West Bromwich Albion, by winning the trophy 3-2. To complete an outstanding season they were later promoted as Division Three Champions.

Sir David Attenborough

Sir David Attenborough is best known for his epic wildlife and natural history shows on the BBC as part of a broadcasting career that began in 1954 when he first introduced *Zoo Quest*. In 1965 he took a break from film-making to become Controller of BBC2 and then Director of Programmes before returning to presentation in 1973.

'In the mid-1960s I had been a television producer for just over ten years, producing mostly travel and animal programmes and then, rather to my surprise, I was made Controller BBC2, when the network was just about 11 months old.

One of the shows I inherited was *Match of the Day* which was one of the great triumphs of BBC2 in that it did get a surprisingly large audience. The football authorities had been extremely wary about allowing any recording of football as they thought it would detract from the crowds and have a bad effect. We managed to persuade them to do it on the grounds that nobody watched BBC2, which was more or less true because it was only visible in a small part of the country, in London and Birmingham, and it had a tiny number of viewers.

You also had to buy a completely new set, a huge great thing with a big clanking switch on it to move from 405 lines to 625 lines.

Then, when it was a big success and it didn't have any particular effect on the crowds, the BBC was faced with a problem as people were asking why they couldn't see this wonderful show. We decided that it ought to go on BBC1, and quite right too, because everybody wanted to see it.

As far as I was concerned as Controller of BBC2 that was fine, because I thought that our policy was to innovate, to bring in new ideas, new programmes, and, indeed, new sports. And so once we'd established the show, it was time to move it over on to the main channel as that gave us a chance to do something new.'

Spurs players (left to right) Terry Venables, Alan Mullery, Dave Mackay and Jimmy Robertson pose happily for the cameras after their victory in the all-London FA Cup Final against Chelsea. Goals from Robertson and Frank Saul gave Spurs a 2-0 lead and a late goal from Chelsea's Bobby Tambling was the Blues' only consolation.

The FA Cup

The ability of television to reflect controversy was evident in the televised highlights of the semi-final at Villa Park between Leeds and Chelsea. With about a minute to go Chelsea were 1-0 ahead and had all 11 players in their box when Leeds were awarded a free-kick. Peter Lorimer rocketed the ball from the edge of the box into the back of the net, but as the Leeds players celebrated, the goal was disallowed. As they stood in horror even the commentator was taken aback and caught up in the emotion. 'He's disallowed it! ...Oh really... and I think you'd have to look through the rule book backwards to find a reason.' In the other semi-final, Spurs beat Nottingham Forest 2-0 at Hillsborough.

Having lost at the semi-final stage in the two previous seasons, Chelsea had finally made it to Wembley where they faced Tottenham Hotspur in the first all-London Final. Jimmy Robertson put Spurs ahead at the end of the first half and Frank Saul added a second before Chelsea made it 2-1 with a goal, inevitably, from Bobby Tambling. It was the third time in seven seasons that Spurs had won the FA Cup.

In an extraordinary season north of the border, Jock Stein managed Celtic to an unprecedented year of success. Having won all three Scottish trophies they then became the first British team to win the European Cup when the 'Lisbon Lions' defeated Italian giants Inter Milan 2-1 in the Final, held in the Portuguese capital.

Footballer of the Year
Jack Charlton, Leeds United

European Footballer of the Year
Florian Albert, Ferencvaros

1967–1968

League Champions   Manchester City

FA Cup winners   West Bromwich Albion

League Cup winners   Leeds United

European Cup winners   Manchester United

Inter-Cities Fairs Cup winners   Leeds United

The show

Once again protracted contract negotiations during the summer ensured the return of the show but the fee had been doubled to £66,000. In order to secure the deal the BBC had to agree to broadcast five matches from Division Two and two from Divisions Three or Four as well as the 23 Division One games that they wanted. The FA Cup coverage was shared between ITV and BBC, with each taking it in turns to have the first choice of matches as well as showing one semi-final each.

The *Radio Times* noted that the BBC2 transmission of Tottenham Hotspur against Manchester United in the Charity Shield on 12 August would be screened in colour from some transmitters and that this would be the first time in Britain that a soccer match had been shown in colour. Another landmark for the programme came on 30 September 1967 when David Coleman presented *Match of the Day* for the first time. On 4 November the show celebrated its 100th edition.

On a stiflingly hot Wembley evening in May 1968 Manchester United won the European Cup for the first time. Bobby Charlton scored two of United's four goals as they crushed Benfica 4-1 after extra time. Here Charlton's first-time looping shot beats keeper Henrique to complete the scoring.

The season

The first *Match of the Day* of the season featured the Charity Shield from Wembley where Tottenham Hotspur's 22-year-old goalkeeper, Pat Jennings, scored after eight minutes. He kicked the ball upfield; it was missed by every player and bounced over the head of his opposite number, Alex Stepney of Manchester United, and into the net. The match ended 3-3 and included two tremendous goals that came from left-foot shots by Bobby Charlton. One of them impressed Kenneth Wolstenholme so much that he said, 'Oh that was a goal good enough to win the League, the Cup, the Charity Shield, the World Cup and even the Grand National.'

The first League weekend saw Everton beat the Champions Manchester United 3-1 at Goodison Park with

One of the programme's matches of the season came on a snowy December afternoon when Manchester City beat Spurs 4-1 at Maine Road. Colin Bell (right) equalised after Jimmy Greaves' opener. City went on to win the 1967–68 Championship, finishing two points ahead of rivals Manchester United.

two goals from Alan Ball. Also on the team sheet that day was Alex Young who was known to supporters as the 'Golden Vision' and was the subject in 1968 of a brilliant BBC film written by Ken Loach.

The other half of Manchester finished the season as Champions, just two points ahead of their illustrious neighbours, although this was not reflected in the on-screen presence of the two clubs. George Best and his team-mates appeared eight times while the City side, which included Mike Summerbee, Colin Bell and Francis Lee, were shown on just three occasions. They were seen losing 1-0 to Arsenal in September and 2-0 to Leeds United in March, but in between they secured a cracking 4-1 victory over Spurs at Maine Road on a snow-covered, icy pitch.

West Bromwich Albion recorded the biggest win of the year when they beat Burnley 8-1, although West Ham came close when they defeated Fulham 7-2. Seven goals were also scored in October when Chelsea conceded all of them to Leeds United at Elland Road. The match was played a day after their manager, Tommy Docherty, resigned having received a month-long FA suspension following an incident during Chelsea's close-season tour to Bermuda. He was succeeded by Dave Sexton.

At the end of the season, with the two Manchester teams level, the *Match of the Day* cameras were at Old Trafford to see the defending Champions lose 2-1 to Sunderland as, despite another goal from Best, strikes by Colin Suggett and George Mulhall denied them the vital win. City, meanwhile, travelled

Frank Bough

Frank Bough was an occasional presenter or commentator on several editions of *Match of the Day* in its first three seasons. He had been a useful footballer and played at Wembley for Oxford University in the 1954 Varsity match as a right-half. After National Service in the Royal Tank Regiment, where Gerald Sinstadt gave him his first broadcasting opportunity on British Forces radio, Frank moved to the north-east and joined ICI at Billingham in 1957. Five years later a career in broadcasting looked more attractive than life in industry and he became presenter of *Look North*.

His first football commentary had been at Darlington in 1962 for radio but in August 1964, after Frank moved to London to take over from Peter Dimmock as the presenter of *Sportsview*, Dimmock sent a memo to the rest of the sports unit asking them to try him on a few *Match of the Day*s. This was partly to have a reserve in place behind Kenneth Wolstenholme and partly with a view to using him on the World Cup a couple of years later. He made his first appearance on 9 January 1965 to introduce Everton's 2-2 draw with Sheffield Wednesday in the FA Cup and the Division Four match between Oxford United and Tranmere Rovers. During the World Cup, he was sent to his old stomping ground in the north-east to cover group matches in Sunderland, Middlesbrough and Newcastle.

to Newcastle United where they clinched the title with a 4-3 win to finish two points ahead of their neighbours.

Sheffield United and Fulham were relegated while Ipswich Town and Queens Park Rangers – who had completed the journey from the Third to First in successive seasons – replaced them. After consistently coming second, Leeds United finally won some trophies under Don Revie. They beat Arsenal 1-0 in the League Cup Final and then added the European Inter-Cities Fairs Cup beating Ferencvaros of Hungary by a single goal over two legs.

The FA Cup

The third-round coverage saw Chelsea beat Ipswich 3-0 while in the fourth round two goals from Jimmy Greaves

and one from Martin Chivers meant that the Cup holders Tottenham Hotspur progressed at the expense of Preston North End. In January, Chivers had become the most expensive British footballer when he moved from Southampton to Spurs for £125,000. By the semi-finals, both London clubs had fallen by the wayside and *Match of the Day*'s cameras were at Villa Park to see West Bromwich Albion beat local rivals Birmingham City thanks to goals by Jeff Astle and Tony Brown. At Old Trafford, Everton beat Leeds United 1-0.

Unfortunately it wasn't one of the classic Finals and at full-time the score was 0-0. Three minutes later the deadlock was broken when Astle's goal completed an astonishing run that had seen him score in every round of that season's competition. It was West Brom's fifth FA Cup win and their first since 1954.

Jeff Astle (left) and Bobby Hope celebrate as West Bromwich Albion win the FA Cup for the first time since 1954. Astle scored in every round of the competition including the only goal of the Final three minutes into extra time.

The most famous win of this season came on 29 May when Matt Busby finally achieved his lifetime's ambition and Manchester United won the European Cup. It had already been a vintage season for George Best whose 28 League goals had made him the joint leading scorer in Division One, and he and Bobby Charlton inspired United to victory against Benfica at Wembley. The match went into extra-time before the British side finished as 4-1 winners.

Footballer of the Year
George Best, Manchester United (right)

European Footballer of the Year
George Best, Manchester United

David Coleman

David Coleman was born in 1926 and, after playing a few matches for Stockport County reserves, became a reporter on the *Stockport Express*. In 1953, he started freelancing on radio in Manchester and the following year joined the BBC in Birmingham. He made his debut as a reporter on *Sportsview* on the night that Roger Bannister ran the first sub-four-minute mile. When *Grandstand* launched in 1958 David was the main presenter from the second show onwards, and for the next decade, he combined presentation with commentary work on both football and athletics.

During the 1960s, David Coleman embodied sport on the BBC and dominated coverage in a way that is unlikely ever to be repeated. During almost ten years as the presenter of *Grandstand* he set the standards and devised a style of broadcasting and professionalism that has been emulated by almost every presenter who has followed. He presented the first live coverage of the Grand National, linked from the Five Nations and, commentated on football for two decades and athletics for almost 40 years. His versatility was legendary and ranged from famously interviewing the Beatles on *Grandstand* in 1964, following their triumphant return from America, to the extraordinary reports from Munich in 1972 after the tragic murder of the Israeli athletes.

Bryan Cowgill was the Head of Sport throughout the 1960s and remembers that when the decision to change the look of *Match of the Day* was made, the choice of presenter was an easy one. 'David took over as he was the best-known face of BBC TV Sport. He fronted *Grandstand* and *Sportsnight with Coleman* and wanted to get more involved with football and he was a respected and authoritative presence on screen.'

Colourful, slick, smartly dressed and robust in his views, he was the man who brought *Match of the Day* into the modern era when he presented it from 1969 to 1973, at the same time that he was also fronting the midweek show, *Sportsnight with Coleman*. However, it is the enthusiastic and minimalist approach to his football commentaries that resonates most with football fans and he rarely wasted words when a goal was scored, 'one-nil' summing up what had happened.

His producer in the 1970s was John Shrewsbury who

recalls that David took the same approach to presenting, especially as he used to commentate on the main match and was then flown or driven back to the studio in London. 'David used to turn up about three minutes before transmission, rattle off the opening link, wait until they were in VT then go off to his dressing room and just come back for the next link.'

But as well as football, over the years David's voice has become closely associated with athletics. From Rome in 1960 to Sydney in 2000 his is the voice on all the classic athletic triumphs of the past 40 years: from Packer, Hemery and Peters, through Coe, Ovett and Wells to Cram, Christie and Gunnell.

He has also become the most celebrated and mimicked of all sports presenters and his distinctive voice ensured that he made regular appearances on shows such as *Spitting Image* while *Private Eye* immortalized many of his phrases, both real and imagined, in their 'Colemanballs' books. As well as live commentary, David Coleman presented 376 editions of *A Question of Sport*. In many respects his career mirrors the history of televised sport. He retired in 2000 after the Sydney Olympics.

1968–1969

League Champions Leeds United

FA Cup winners Manchester City

League Cup winners Swindon Town

Inter-Cities Fairs Cup winners Newcastle United

The show

This was the season that David Coleman began to stamp his authority on the BBC's football coverage. Having presented *Grandstand* for most of the previous decade he handed that show over to Frank Bough and took on the midweek slot. *Sportsview* was renamed *Sportsnight with Coleman* and the new format began on 12 September at 9.05 p.m. on BBC1.

Although Kenneth Wolstenholme presented the Charity Shield from Maine Road, the changeover was beginning and Coleman hosted most of the shows that season. He was away in Mexico City during October, however, to commentate on the Olympic athletics and with more coverage of the event on the BBC than ever before, the *Match of the Day* programmes during that period shared their transmission spots with the action from the games and were billed as *Olympic Grandstand with Match of the Day*.

On 26 October, Kenneth Wolstenholme was also in Mexico to commentate on the Final of the Olympic football tournament so Radio Sport's Maurice Edelston, who had helped out with the occasional *Match of the Day* commentary in the past, presented that night's edition.

The following week saw another experimental colour transmission on BBC2 when Chelsea beat Manchester City 2-0 and on 1 January 1969 the television licence fee was increased from £5 to £6 to help pay for the conversion to colour. At that time BBC2 was still only available to about 70 per cent of the population.

Swindon Town's two-goal hero Don Rogers can't let go of the League Cup while watching the highlights of his team's shock 3-1 victory over Arsenal in the Final.

The season

David Coleman didn't have far to go to commentate on the first featured League match of the season as it was just around the corner from Television Centre at Loftus Road where newly promoted QPR took on Leicester City. Leicester included the most expensive player in the history of the Football League, Allan Clarke, who had moved from Fulham in the summer for £150,000. His brother, Frank, was leading the QPR attack. Wearing number eight Allan scored the first goal, a poacher's effort inside the box, before a member of another famous footballing family, Les Allen, equalised.

Only six of that season's editions featured four or more goals as defences tightened. A Martin Peters hat-trick saw West Ham United beat West Bromwich Albion 4-1 in August but it wasn't until February, when Cardiff City beat Oxford United 5-0 in their Division Two clash, that the viewers saw more than three goals in a match.

Away from the cameras though, there were still a few high-scoring games. West Ham put eight past Sunderland, QPR lost 8-1 to Manchester United, Everton beat Leicester 7-1 and Burnley conceded seven against both Tottenham Hotspur and Manchester City. Jimmy Greaves was once again leading the Spurs' attack and had a terrific season, finishing as the

Opposite **Don Revie and his players celebrate with champagne and cigars after winning the First Division Championship. They suffered only two defeats during the season and set a record of 67 points.**

League's leading goalscorer. His 36 League and Cup goals included four in their 5-1 home win against Sunderland.

The nucleus of Derby County's future Championship-winning side was seen in March in another Division Two game when goals by Roy McFarland, John O'Hare and Alan Hinton saw them to a 3-2 away win at Blackpool. Managed by Brian Clough and Peter Taylor, Derby were promoted alongside Crystal Palace.

After their early optimism, QPR went straight back to Division Two having won just four League matches. Leicester were also relegated. QPR's situation hadn't been helped by their managerial merry-go-round. After a poor start Bill Dodgin was replaced by Tommy Docherty, the Rotherham United manager. Docherty resigned after a month complaining that there was no money for him to buy new players and Les Allen took over. Docherty resurfaced a few weeks later as the new manager of Aston Villa.

Don Revie finally managed Leeds United to the Division One Championship having been close in the four previous seasons. They only made four appearances on the show but won all of the matches: against Arsenal, Everton, Chelsea and Leicester. Leeds achieved a record 67 points with Liverpool in second place on 61.

As with QPR in the previous year, Third Division Swindon Town won both promotion and the League Cup. They defeated Arsenal 3-1 in the Final on a pitch that was more mud than grass in the biggest shock of the season. Two

Commentators' competition

Throughout the season BBC Sport held a competition to find a new football commentator ahead of the 1970 World Cup. The final took place on *Sportsnight with Coleman* on 22 May after the 10,000 entries had been whittled down to the last six. The judging panel was Sir Alf Ramsey, Denis Howell MP and Minister for Sport, Peter Black from the *Daily Mail*, Manchester City's captain Tony Book and the Head of BBC Sport, Bryan Cowgill. The six finalists had been recorded at Wembley commentating on the Home International between England and Wales and were awarded marks based on their voice, identification of players, knowledge of the game, use of language and presentational flair. The winner was Idwal Robling (right), a sales manager for a packaging company, and he subsequently went on to make a number of appearances on *Match of the Day*. Liverpool player Ian St. John was runner-up and he and the remaining four all went on to have distinguished broadcasting careers. Gerry Harrison came third, Larry Canning was fourth, Radio One DJ Ed Stewart finished fifth and Tony Adamson sixth.

goals in extra-time from Don Rogers sealed a famous victory.

Joe Harvey managed Newcastle United to their first European success when they beat Ujpest Dozsa of Hungary 6-2 on aggregate across the two legs of the Fairs Cup Final.

The FA Cup

Only six FA Cup matches were seen on *Match of the Day* before the Final on 26 April between Manchester City and Leicester City. It had already been a mixed season for Joe Mercer's Mancunians. They had started well, beating West Bromwich Albion 6-1 in the Charity Shield, but went out in the first round of the European Cup against Fenerbahce and managed only 13th place in the League as defending Champions. Both semi-finals were settled with a single goal against the previous year's finalists. Leicester overcame West Brom at Villa Park while City beat Everton at Hillsborough.

David Coleman presented *Grandstand* on BBC1 with the full FA Cup Final build-up from 11.25 a.m. to 5.15 p.m. but the match made history by being broadcast simultaneously on BBC2 in colour for the very first time. Referee George McCabe used the first ever 50 pence piece for the toss, some six months before they went into circulation.

The Final was very entertaining but the only goal came in the 24th minute when Neil Young's shot beat a young Peter Shilton to give Manchester City the FA Cup for the fourth time. It was their first success in the competition since 1956, but for Leicester it was a third Cup Final defeat in nine seasons, and to complete their gloom they were also relegated three weeks later.

1968 European Nations Cup

The host nation, Italy, beat Yugoslavia 2-0 in the Final replay having drawn the original match 1-1. Goals from Bobby Charlton and Geoff Hurst gave England third place after they won the play off 2-0 against USSR. All four Home Nations had originally been placed in the same qualifying group and played each other between 1966 and 1968. Only eight teams qualified for the knockout stages in Italy.

Fact file

The BBC's national monopoly on football highlights was threatened when ITV launched their new Sunday afternoon football show, *The Big Match*. Although some other regions previously had their own football coverage, this was the first programme to make a major impact. Devised by the hugely influential figure of John Bromley and hosted by Brian Moore, it also gave a regular spot to LWT's Head of Sport, Jimmy Hill, as an analyst. The competition intensified still further with the introduction of Saturday lunchtime shows on both channels. Brian Moore presented 'On the Ball' on ITV while Sam Leitch (right) fronted the weekly 'Football Preview' in *Grandstand*.

Footballer of the Year
Tony Book, Manchester City and
Dave Mackay, Derby County (shared)

European Footballer of the Year
Gianni Rivera, AC Milan

1969–1970

Presenter
David Coleman

League Champions   Everton

FA Cup winners   Chelsea

League Cup winners   Manchester City

European Cup-Winners' Cup winners
Manchester City

Inter-Cities Fairs Cup winners   Arsenal

The show

With a new contract that had cost £100,000 for the season the BBC decided to make some radical changes to the programme. David Coleman took over as the main presenter, the show became live and studio-based rather than pre-recorded at the ground of the featured match, and there were now two games shown each week.

As well as the main game there were also regional opt outs towards the end of each programme with six regions each allowed to show a maximum of 10 minutes of their games. This meant that the BBC now had cameras at seven matches each Saturday.

It also meant a major headache for the production teams around the UK with the increased cost of the additional staff, equipment and studios and resulted, at times, in a number of very inexperienced people putting the show together in the regions. The viewers didn't seem to object though and by November the regular audience was up to almost ten million. Jonathan Martin was the new studio director at the time and he remembered the dangers that the new format brought.

'David Coleman was still commentating on the main games and he would sometimes arrive at the studio just five minutes before transmission so there was very limited studio analysis. We'd show 30 minutes of the game and then do a round-up of news, results, tables and interviews for about eight minutes. A caption was then put up, usually a League table, and held for about seven seconds so that the regions could opt out.

Some regions produced good shows but there would be occasions when others would pre-record their section and run it in regardless of the duration. That lasted for one season but it did mean that in 1970–71 we got what we really wanted, two games per show.'

Everton's Sandy Brown looks ruefully at the camera after putting through his own net in the Merseyside derby. His shame was compounded when locally an own goal became known as a 'Sandy Brown'.

The season

On the first Saturday of the League season the main game was Crystal Palace's 2-2 draw with Manchester United, while around the regions viewers saw Leeds beat Spurs 3-1, Wolves defeat Stoke City by the same score, Exeter City lose 3-0 to Wrexham and Southampton beaten 2-0 at home by West Bromwich Albion.

On 15 November Liverpool beat West Ham United 2-0 on the weekend that BBC1 began to transmit in colour which helped to give the show a new vibrancy and edge. Three weekends later Liverpool were again seen winning, this time in the Merseyside derby when the unlucky Sandy Brown scored one of the greatest own goals of all time in front of the Goodison crowd.

Although the viewers were possibly overwhelmed by the Everton outfit of blue shirts, white shorts and orange socks, nothing was going to dissuade the Everton number three from throwing himself at the ball as it crossed his goal-mouth and pulling off a stunning diving header into the net and past a slightly irritated goalkeeper.

The following week saw a major reversal for Shankly's men as they were on the receiving end of a 4-1 pasting by Manchester United at Anfield. It was a match that saw yet another classic strike by Bobby Charlton, this time into the top right-hand corner.

The defending Champions, Leeds United, were the featured team in the programme that ended the 1960s and the one that began the 1970s. On 27 December, two goals from Mick Jones saw them to a 2-1 home win over Everton, and then on 10 January they travelled to Stamford Bridge for what was arguably the match of the season. With sideburns that looked far more impressive in colour, John Hollins and Peter Osgood scored for the home team as they went 2-1 up at half-time, Allan Clarke scoring for Leeds; Terry Cooper, Johnny Giles, Peter Lorimer and Mick Jones replied in the second half to secure a 5-2 away win.

The biggest away win on *Match of the Day* that season came in March when Jimmy Greaves made his debut for West Ham against Manchester City at Maine Road having left Tottenham Hotspur in part exchange for Martin Peters. Greaves kept up his astonishing record of scoring on his debut for every one of the ten teams he represented, ranging from Chelsea reserves, to England, AC Milan, Spurs and now West Ham.

He scored twice through the mud that passed as a pitch as West Ham won 5-1, a great improvement on their previous

Everton's Alan Ball strides purposefully to the Goodison Park dressing room with the First Division Championship trophy tucked safely under his arm.

Kop choir competition

After the success of the previous year's commentators competition, the BBC chose to switch their attention to the fans. In conjunction with the Football League Review and *Match of the Day*, a kop choir competition was broadcast on *Sportsnight with Coleman* in the week before the FA Cup Final. The screens were filled with images of rattles and rosettes, duffle coats, parkas, kids in bobble hats and seas of scarves – with not a replica shirt in sight. The supporters of Liverpool, Newport County, Rotherham United, Southampton, Tottenham Hotspur and Wolverhampton Wanderers were all filmed as they demonstrated their top kop tunes.

Sadly these didn't extend much beyond 'United' or 'County' alongside the inevitable 'We'll support you ever more' and 'You'll never walk alone'. As the six kop leaders sat silently in the studio, looking like slightly scarier versions of *University Challenge* contestants, the judging panel consulted.

Alan Hardaker, Bob Wilson and referee Roger Kirkpatrick decided that the fans of Third Division Rotherham United were the karaoke kings and they were left to work out how to split the prize of 30 places at the European Cup Final in Italy and one Ford Cortina.

Peter Osgood dives to head Chelsea's equaliser against Leeds in the FA Cup Final replay at Old Trafford in 1970. Chelsea went on to win 2-1 with a goal in extra time.

visit to the city in front of the cameras when Manchester United had beaten them 5-2 in September. In joining Spurs as part of the same deal, Martin Peters became the first British player to cost £200,000.

Harry Catterick managed Everton to the title for the second time in eight seasons, and their seventh Championship in total. They were nine points ahead of second-placed Leeds United and were helped by their miserly defence who conceded just 34 goals in the entire campaign. Chelsea were third and Brian Clough led Derby County into fourth spot in their first season in Division One.

Huddersfield Town and Blackpool were promoted from

Division Two while Sunderland and Sheffield Wednesday were relegated. The biggest fall from grace was that of Aston Villa. Having signed Tommy Docherty in the hope that he would manage them out of Division Two, their supporters were a little surprised when he did just that, but in the wrong direction.

One manager who was very popular with the fans was Manchester City's Joe Mercer as he and their coach, Malcolm Allison, led the side to a Cup double. They beat West Bromwich Albion 2-1 in the League Cup Final before becoming only the third British side to win the European Cup-Winners' Cup. They defeated Polish club Gornik Zabrze 2-1 in the Final in Vienna.

It was an outstanding European season for English clubs as Arsenal beat Anderlecht 4-3 across the two legs of the Fairs Cup Final. Celtic came close to completing a British hat-trick when they beat Leeds United in the semi-finals of the European Cup but lost the Final 2-1 to Feyenoord after extra time.

The FA Cup

This season *Match of the Day* was able to show the highlights of three matches from the third round onwards. The high-est scoring game came in the fourth found when four goals by Allan Clarke and two by Peter Lorimer saw Leeds United to a 6-0 win at non-League Sutton United. The biggest shock came in the sixth round when Barry Endean's solitary goal for Watford was enough to dump Liverpool out of the Cup and prompt Bill Shankly to rebuild his side.

The BBC had the unlucky draw in the semi-finals as ITV viewers saw Chelsea beat Watford 5-1 while it took Leeds United and Manchester United three games just to score a single goal. Billy Bremner finally broke the deadlock with the winner at Burnden Park in the second replay

The Final also went to a replay when the first match ended 2-2 after extra-time. In an aggressive match Leeds twice took the lead through Jack Charlton and Mick Jones but Peter Houseman and Ian Hutchinson equalized before the final whistle and no further goals were added in extra time. It was Wembley's first drawn FA Cup Final and one that started a deep rivalry between players and supporters of both clubs.

The teams met again 18 days later at Old Trafford and, once again, Leeds took the lead through Mick Jones. But Peter Osgood and David Webb both scored to enable Ron Harris to become the first Chelsea skipper ever to lift the FA Cup.

A *Question of Sport* began its long run on BBC1 at 6.20 p.m. on Monday 5 January 1970. David Vine (right) was the host, Cliff Morgan and Henry Cooper the captains and their guests were George Best, Lillian Board, Ray Illingworth and Tom Finney. Among the show's captains have been Emlyn Hughes and Ally McCoist, while few would have envisaged in 1970 that the *Match of the Day* frontman, David Coleman, would later present 376 editions of the quiz.

Footballer of the Year
Billy Bremner, Leeds United

European Footballer of the Year
Gerd Müller, Bayern Munich

Barry Davies

Barry Davies was born in 1937. After a spell at the Royal Dental Hospital he joined the army and served in Germany rising to the rank of Lieutenant and broadcasting on the British Forces radio. A stint on BBC Radio and several years writing for *The Times* followed before Barry became one of ITV's football commentators when they recruited new voices to work on the 1966 World Cup. Having been based in the north-east during the tournament he stood behind ITV's Hugh Johns at Wembley to watch the Final but three years later joined Kenneth Wolstenholme as one of the BBC's regular commentary team.

'Although I'd enjoyed my time with ITV I always knew that I needed to move channels if I was to make a success of the job and I felt that I was a BBC-type person. My first *Match of the Day* experience was a strange one though, as things didn't quite go to plan. It was the opening weekend of the 1969 season and I was expecting to work on Leeds against Spurs, but on the day before the show David Coleman lost his voice so I was suddenly whisked back to London. I had to commentate on Crystal Palace's 2-2 draw with Manchester United and then present the show, live, in the evening. It was very daunting but also enjoyable and although I did occasionally fill in for David down the years I would loved to have presented more shows.

I have always felt very privileged to have the opportunity to talk about something I enjoy and I've never felt especially pressured by the job. I like the fact that I turn up at a match without knowing in advance what is going to happen and have always had a very open approach to my commentary. I don't call up the managers on the night before a game to find out their tactics as I don't what to be told what to look for. I just try to add words to what I see in front of me.

I always fully prepare with notes, facts and history, but am no longer as desperate to add the facts in as I used to be when I was younger. I don't like forcing something in unless I feel that the match has lost the attention of the viewers. Some of my best commentaries have probably been at big tournaments when I was slightly unprepared because we hadn't had access to the training grounds. After 35 years my pre-match homework follows a pattern now but the notes I make would win no artistic prizes as they are scribbled in private shorthand that has developed over the seasons.

No matter how well prepared a commentator is, they can't get it right all the time. I've made two howlers when I called the goalscorer wrongly. The first came when I totally misidentified a Bristol City player and gave a goal to Gerry Gow instead of Geoff Merrick. I didn't find out until after the game so in order to correct it for *Match of the Day* I had to go and stand in the middle of the pitch with a microphone and try and recreate the commentary. The second time was on a recent live match when I thought that Michael Owen had scored but it was actually Bruno Cheyrou. They both had crew cuts, but I didn't realize that I had got them muddled until I saw Mark Lawrenson grimacing at me so I corrected it immediately.

There have been a lot of changes to the way that television covers football in the past three decades and most of them have improved it, but I think that there is a tendency for some commentators to talk too much and introduce predetermined lines. In Kenneth Wolstenholme's day there were far more pauses and silences so that the viewers could see the action for themselves. As the years have gone by the style has become more and more like a radio commentary, but that is something that I try to resist. Something else that has changed is the relationship that we have with the players as it used to be much easier to talk to them. I've had a very good rapport with most players and managers, but because I try to tell the truth as I see it I've sometimes been slightly on the edge.

Once, after I had been critical of Rodney Marsh when he was playing for England, Don Revie told me that he agreed with my first two points but was praying that I wouldn't make the third as, by then, I was telling an international player how to play the game. Another time, after he felt that I had been critical of him, Revie simply refused to be interviewed by me which was a pity as there was a lot about him that I admired.

Because we have both been commentating on *Match of the Day* for more than 30 years John Motson and I have become very closely associated in the public eye and I think that something we agree on is that our differing styles and personalities have been good for each other and for the programme. We're not especially close friends but are colleagues who do the same job and I have a great deal of respect for him. The thing that people forget is that although we both appear on the same show we rarely meet as by definition if one of us is at a game the other isn't. There has never been any animosity between us though, we've always shared information at the big tournaments and there is always camaraderie between us.

There are times when I wonder if I should have done something else with my life but I have had a wonderful time with the BBC. Of course, I would have liked to have commentated on more of the big finals but I have great memories of the 1994 World Cup Final and two FA Cup Finals as well as numerous European ones. Liverpool's first European Cup in 1977 was one of the great nights of my career.

I've had a job that has taken me all over the world and has included ten Olympic Games, and ten World Cups as well as Wimbledon, ice skating and more than 20 other sports plus, of course, *Match of the Day*. I've had a great career and it has been privilege to watch so much superb sport and work with so many wonderful colleagues.'

1970–1971

Presenter
David Coleman

League Champions Arsenal

FA Cup winners Arsenal

League Cup winners Tottenham Hotspur

European Cup-Winners' Cup winners Chelsea

Inter-Cities Fairs Cup winners Leeds United

The show

The new decade saw the traditional *Match of the Day* format finally established. The regional opt outs had been axed and instead there were two matches per show with new title music and 'news, views, analysis and action'.

David Coleman introduced the first show. 'Good evening, we hope you like the new music and we hope too that you like the new programme.' He was in a studio behind a desk with a massive microphone attached to his tie. Behind him on the set, either side of his head, were the badges of the featured teams, so to introduce the individual matches the director had to ask the main camera to go in closer and lose the non-relevant badges.

The new format saw the introduction of the Goal of the Month competition that led to tens of thousands of postcards being sent to the BBC. Mick Jones of Leeds was adjudged the first winner for his goal against Manchester United in their opening match of the season.

The season

The first show of the new season saw Manchester United lose 1-0 at home to Leeds United whilst a brace from Ian Hutchinson secured a 2-1 win at Stamford Bridge for Chelsea over Derby County.

Arsenal were featured in week two as they put four past Manchester United, thanks to a hat-trick by John Radford. It was the start of a year of turmoil for United that would see Sir Matt Busby return in January as manager and George Best suspended for regularly missing trains to matches.

The Londoners made 12 League and Cup appearances on *Match of the Day* this season and several more in the mid-week *Sportsnight with Coleman*. Most were wins but the cameras did also capture their surprise 5-0 loss at Stoke City in late September. That was one of only six occasions when a side scored five goals in one game. The noticeable drop in the number of goals being scored was reflected on the terraces where the attendance figures were dropping for most clubs. By coincidence both teams featured in other high-scoring games when West Bromwich Albion beat Stoke 5-2 but then went on to lose 6-2 to Arsenal.

The weekend after Stoke's rout of the future Champions the *Match of the Day* audience was treated to a goal that was so cheeky and unusual it became the mainstay of many music items. Coventry were at home against Everton and after the Sky Blues had been awarded a free kick on the edge of their visitors' box Willie Carr stood over the ball, trapped it between both feet and leapt into the air. As he did so, he flicked the ball backwards for Ernie Hunt to volley into the top right hand corner of the goal past a diving keeper and a startled wall. It became known as a 'donkey kick'.

One of the best matches of the season came on Boxing Day when the Baseball Ground crowd saw Derby County and Manchester United share eight goals. Dave Mackay and Frank Wignall put the home team two ahead, the visitors then scored three goals in four minutes with two from Denis Law and one by George Best before Kevin Hector equalised in front of goal. Archie Gemmill squeezed the ball inside the right post and Brian Kidd headed the final goal of the game from a Bobby Charlton corner. Two days later Wilf McGuinness was replaced as manager of United by the man he had succeeded, Sir Matt Busby.

Manchester United were featured eight times on *Match of the Day* that season, behind the twelve Arsenal appearances, eleven by Leeds and ten by Liverpool. The new format meant that 43 different teams appeared in League or Cup.

Leeds had another controversial season and their reputation for aggression was enhanced on 17 April when they met West Bromwich Albion in a crucial league match at Elland Road. The home team were a goal down in the final quarter of the game when they all stopped after the linesman waved for offside against Colin Suggett. The referee, Ray Tinkler, waved play on and with a two-to-one advantage Jeff Astle easily scored.

Don Revie's players angrily surrounded the referee, dozens of fans ran on to protest and it took the police several minutes to regain order. They went on to lose their seven-point lead over Arsenal in the title race and as punishment for the pitch invasion were forced to play the first four games of the following season at neutral grounds.

Arsenal clinched the title with a win at Tottenham Hotspur but the cameras were not present as it was a Monday evening. It marked the start of a remarkable week for their captain, Frank McLintock, who collected the Footballer of the Year award on Thursday and lifted the FA Cup on Saturday.

Leeds United were second for the fourth time in seven seasons but had the consolation of winning the European

Arsenal manager Bertie Mee with the spoils of the Londoners' double-winning season.

Referee Ray Tinkler is protected from angry Leeds players after he'd allowed a Jeff Astle goal for West Bromwich to stand despite an offside flag. Leeds lost the match and subsequently the Championship by a single point.

Colchester's Ray Crawford steers the ball past Leeds goalkeeper Gary Sprake to give his side a 2-0 lead. In one of the biggest ever FA Cup shocks, Fourth Division Colchester put Leeds out in the Fifth Round, eventually winning the match 3-2.

Inter-Cities Fairs Cup for the second time in four years, beating Juventus on away goals.

Chelsea were also successful on the continent and won the European Cup-Winners Cup when they beat Real Madrid 2-1 in Athens. They needed extra time of the replay to do so, just as they did in the FA Cup Final in the previous year.

The third domestic trophy was also claimed by a London club when Tottenham Hotspur beat Aston Villa 2-0 to win the League Cup.

Leicester City and Sheffield United won promotion from Division Two, replacing relegated Burnley and Blackpool.

The FA Cup

Once again the highlights of three FA Cup matches were shown in each round and the cameras always seemed to be in the right place to record the big upsets. In the third round Blackpool beat West Ham United 4-0 and in the fifth it was the turn of Leeds United to suffer humiliation.

On 13 February they had to travel to Colchester United of Division Four and were left reeling when the home team

went 3-0 up thanks to a brace by Ray Crawford and one by David Simmons. Norman Hunter and Johnny Giles replied for Leeds but that was not enough to avoid one of the most famous of all FA Cup upsets. Colchester's celebrations lasted just three weeks, however, until Everton put five past them in the next round at Goodison Park.

Match of the Day's semi-final featured Liverpool beating Everton 2-1 at Old Trafford and in the other tie Arsenal were two down at half time to Stoke City but recovered to draw before winning the replay 2-0.

With increasing competition from ITV the build up to kick-off on *Cup Final Grandstand* lasted three-and-a-quarter hours and included the debut of 'It's a Cup Final Knockout'. David Vine and Eddie Waring hosted the special competition between surviving members of the 1950 FA Cup Final Arsenal and Liverpool sides.

When the match got under way Kenneth Wolstenholme was commentating on his 23rd and last FA Cup Final on a very hot afternoon in North London but there were no goals for him to call in the first 90 minutes.

Two minutes into extra time, however, Liverpool took the lead when Steve Heighway put the ball past Bob Wilson. Nine minutes later Eddie Kelly equalised and then with just nine minutes remaining Charlie George drove the ball past Ray Clemence to win the match, the Cup and the double for Arsenal. As he lay down on the Wembley turf, arms aloft to celebrate, he could scarcely have known that he was creating one of the competition's most iconic images.

1970 World Cup

The finals were staged in Mexico and England got through to the quarter-finals having finished second in their qualifying group. They beat Romania and Czechoslovakia 1-0 but lost by the same score to Brazil in one of the best matches of the competition. Franz Beckenbauer's West Germany gained revenge for 1966 when they won 3-2 after extra time in the next round although only five of the men who won at Wembley took part in the match. Moore, Ball, Hurst, Peters and Bobby Charlton were the only survivers from the 1966 Final. The 1970 Final was possibly the greatest ever as goals by Pele, Gerson, Jairzinho and Carlos Alberto secured a 4-1 win for Brazil over Italy.

Charlie George lies flat on the Wembley pitch after giving Arsenal the lead in the FA Cup final against Liverpool. His goal won the match, the Cup and the double for the Londoners.

1971–1972

Presenter
David Coleman

League Champions   Derby County

FA Cup winners   Leeds United

League Cup winners   Stoke City

European Cup-Winners' Cup winners
Glasgow Rangers

UEFA Cup winners   Tottenham Hotspur

The show

Match of the Day returned in July featuring the Watney Cup, a short-lived competition that saw the highest scoring sides from all four divisions take part in a knock-out tournament spread across a couple of weekends.

When the league action began the BBC were still not allowed to mention the matches they were covering in advance. All the *Radio Times* could do was describe the rough location and reputation of the grounds and the approximate league positions of the teams.

On 9 October another landmark in the history of *Match of the Day* was reached with the first mention of a young commentator named John Motson in the billings. He and Barry Davies covered both matches that afternoon and their classic commentary partnership – the Starsky and Hutch of football – was in place.

Barry also adopted another role that season and presented a number of programmes as the popularity of the show increased and audiences began to regularly hit 12 million.

George Best's twinkling feet are too much for the lunging John McCormick of Crystal Palace.

The season

In the first full League programme the defending Champions Arsenal defeated Chelsea 3-0 at Highbury, while Liverpool beat Nottingham Forest 3-1. That game that saw a 20-year-old player named Kevin Keegan turn and score in the box on his debut. Alan Ball was another player in the spotlight when he was transferred from Everton to Arsenal for a record fee of £220,000.

The eventual Champions, Derby County, made their first appearance at the end of August when they were seen drawing 2-2 with Southampton. They were only featured in five more programmes that season.

Southampton may have managed a draw in that game at the Baseball Ground but their defence was cruelly exposed later in the campaign.

In November a hat-trick by George Best helped Manchester United to a 5-2 away win at The Dell, but worse was to come in March when a rampant Leeds United turned in one of the all-time classic *Match of the Day* performances.

Not only did their seven goals include a Peter Lorimer hat-trick but towards the end of the game they toyed with their opponents, putting together a string of 25 passes as the crowd cheered and Barry Davies remarked that it was almost cruel. Just a fortnight before, Leeds had beaten Manchester United 5-1 and while the Dutch were on their way to developing Total Football, in early 1972 it looked as though Leeds United had developed total domination.

Manchester United were shown on 13 weekends that season and one of their earliest appearances featured one of George Best's greatest goals. Towards the end of a still goalless game against Sheffield United, Best collected the ball, with his shirt outside his shorts, long hair flowing and sideburns like a couple of beer mats stuck on the sides of his face. He ran to the right, beating four defenders, before slotting the ball inside the far post and past keeper John Hope.

It was a mixed season for Best who was sent off against Chelsea, prevented by Manchester United for playing for Northern Ireland against Spain in Belfast because of death threats, dropped by his club in January for not turning up in training and ordered by new manager Frank O'Farrell to live in 'digs' and concentrate on getting fit.

The Championship race was one of the closest for many seasons and at the start of the final week four clubs still had a chance. Manchester City were the first to fall away,

Brian Clough (left) and Peter Taylor show off the League Championship trophy to Derby fans at the Baseball Ground.

finishing on 57 points and Derby County ended their campaign with a 1-0 win against Liverpool that left them with 58 points.

Having won the FA Cup on the Saturday, Leeds United had to play Wolverhampton Wanderers two days later, needing just a draw to clinch the double. Incredibly they lost, while Liverpool could only finish 0-0 at Arsenal. This left both clubs stranded on 57 points and meant that Derby County, whose players were relaxing on the beaches of Majorca, were Champions for the first time.

Nottingham Forest and Huddersfield Town were relegated, with Birmingham City and Norwich City winning promotion from Division Two. There was more success for British clubs in Europe when, in the first all-British European final, Tottenham Hotspur beat Wolverhampton Wanderers 3-2 over two legs to lift the first UEFA Cup and Rangers beat Dynamo Moscow 3-2 to win the Cup-Winners' Cup. The season's other trophy, the League Cup, had been won by Stoke City who beat Chelsea 2-1 in the Final.

Alan Weeks

One of the occasional voices heard on *Match of the Day* was the veteran commentator Alan Weeks. As well as commentating on midweek matches and many of the games shown on *Saturday Sport Special*, Alan was probably the most versatile of all of the great BBC Sport voices.

Born in Bristol, Alan began at the BBC in 1951 when Peter Dimmock heard him on the public address system at the Brighton Ice Rink. He went on to cover more than 30 different sports and work on seven Winter Olympics, five Olympic Games, four World Cups and five Commonwealth Games. His was the voice that was heard as John Curry, Robin Cousins and Torvill and Dean all won Olympic Gold. Alan retired in 1996 and sadly died in May of the same year aged 72.

The FA Cup

As usual, *Match of the Day's* coverage of the FA Cup began with the third round, but earlier in the competition Ted MacDougall of Bournemouth had placed himself in the record books by scoring nine goals as they beat Margate 11-0 in the FA Cup in November. Astonishingly only one was a penalty.

Perhaps the biggest shock of the 1971–72 season came on 5 February when Colin Addison's Southern League Hereford United took on the mighty Newcastle United in an FA Cup third round replay. Having already drawn at St James' Park this match produced what is possibly the most shown and most famous *Match of the Day* goal ever. Malcolm Macdonald put the visitors ahead before Ronnie Radford unleashed his 40-yard shot that ensured sporting immortality for both him, and the BBC's new young commentator, John Motson.

'Radford again ... oh what a goal, what a goal, Radford the scorer, Ronnie Radford, and the crowd, the crowd are invading the pitch and now it will take some time to clear the pitch.'

As the police tried to clear the biggest collection of green parkas outside of a mod rally in Brighton, Motty and Hereford composed themselves for the start of extra time.

Substitute Ricky George then turned and shot the winner past Newcastle's Captain Bobby Moncur, low into the goal and the crowd once again invaded. Radford's effort was voted Goal of the Season while George enjoyed a second moment of great success in 1998 as part owner of Earth Summit, the winner of that year's Grand National. In the next round Hereford lost to West Ham in a replay at Upton Park.

In the semi-finals, *Match of the Day* featured Leeds United's 3-0 win against Birmingham City at Hillsborough. Two goals from Mick Jones and one from Peter Lorimer took Don Revie's team to Wembley for the third time in eight years. The other game was a repeat of the previous season's semi-final, as once again Arsenal squeezed past Stoke City, this time after a replay.

The FA Cup Final was celebrating its centenary year and it saw a fiercely competitive match between two strong rivals. Just one goal separated the teams when Allan Clarke's diving headed met a cross from Mick Jones to score in the 54th minute and take the trophy back to Leeds for the first time.

Ronnie Radford shoots from 40 yards out.

The ball beats Newcastle keeper Willie McFaul.

Radford celebrates the Goal of the Season with the Hereford United fans.

Goals from Radford (top left) and Ricky George (centre left) ensured that the cameras captured one of the greatest days in Hereford United's history.

Chelsea opened their defence of the European Cup-Winners' Cup with an extraordinary encounter against Hautcharage from Luxembourg. They won the away leg 8-0 which included a hat-trick by Peter Osgood. Two weeks later, at Stamford Bridge, Osgood added another five as Chelsea won 13-0. In the next round they were eliminated by the Swedish side, Atvidaberg.

In January, disaster struck at Ibrox during a match between Rangers and Celtic. When Rangers scored a last-minute equalizer, scores of fans who were already leaving the ground tried to turn back to see what was happening but were engulfed by those who were still going the other way. With neither group aware of the problem they surged against each other causing barriers to collapse – 66 people were killed in the crush.

Goal of the Season
Ronnie Radford for Hereford against Newcastle, FA Cup, February 1972

Footballer of the Year
Gordon Banks, Stoke City

European Footballer of the Year
Franz Beckenbauer, Bayern Munich

John Shrewsbury

John Shrewsbury started his working life as an office boy for *The Eagle* comic in 1955 before moving to Hayters News Agency as a runner. He wrote *Bobby Charlton's Football Book* and the *Grandstand* and *Sportsview* annuals before taking the FA preliminary coaching badge and referees' paper at the same time as Jimmy Hill and Bertie Mee.

He joined the BBC in May 1968, and between November 1971 and December 2000 directed almost 600 football matches including 13 FA Cup Finals and two replays. John was the Executive Producer of football from 1984 to 1997.

'My happiest memories were on *Match of the Day* and working on it was, for me, the best achievement of my career. I loved it and am very proud of the fact that I directed football having been taken by my Dad to my first match when I was about five years old.

The first game I directed was West Ham against Manchester City in 1971. I was an assistant producer at the time, working on *Match of the Day* and *Sportsnight*. As the two shows had just combined, David Coleman wanted to get his own team around him and told me that for my debut I would get the best match, crew and camera positions and "I'll come and commentate to keep you out of trouble". He kept his word and got me the Cup Final crew.

My second game was Cardiff City against Leeds United and my third was Hereford United against Newcastle United in the third round of the FA Cup. It was my first match with Motty who had only recently joined the BBC, and they sent us to the game as a couple of raw youngsters as it was expected to only be a short edit. When Newcastle were knocked out it became the main game on that night's show and the reaction to the match kicked off both our careers.

Things do go wrong sometimes, especially in the early 1970s when the technology was far more basic. There was one famous edition of *Match of the Day* that David Coleman presented with Bryan Cowgill producing in the gallery. I was in VT at the time but fortunately had nothing to do with the incident as it unfolded.

A junior assistant producer, who shall remain nameless, was editing a match that had three goals in it. In those days, in order to show replays you had to transfer the goal into a special machine that would slow it down and then edit the new tape back onto the main recording. Unfortunately on this occasion the AP got a little muddled.

David was sitting in the studio watching the edit being broadcast when the first goal went out. It was a 30-yard shot, but the replay was of a header from a corner. Only David spotted it, and he yelled at the gallery "F*** – did you see that – it's the wrong f*****g replay! It's the replay of the wrong goal!!".

We all sat and waited and sure enough, the second headed goal was followed by a replay of the ball dribbling over the line while for the third the viewers were finally treated to another view of the long-range shot that had made it 1-0.

Needless to say there was a lot of shouting and that particular producer didn't work on *Match of the Day* again.

Mistakes can happen to anyone though and a producer once did a *Match of the Day* edit that elicited another major flurry of expletives from David Coleman, as he announced to the gallery, "Brian Kidd has just thrown the ball to himself. Kidd to Kidd".

David was probably the best sports broadcaster ever and I also worked with him for ten years on athletics. He could crystallize what was going on in a single sentence. On his day he was the best ever. I also loved working with Barry Davies and John Motson who are wonderful and I could never separate them.

I worked with so many great people at the BBC with all the production teams, commentators, pundits, presenters and technical crews. I have been very fortunate, been in the right place at the right time and had a charmed life.'

The directors

Alan Griffiths

For BBC Sport's senior Match Director, Alan Griffiths, the return of *Match of the Day* has particular resonance. As a nine-year-old boy he had been taken by his father to watch Liverpool play Arsenal on 22 August 1964, the first game ever to be featured on the show. He still has the match day programme from that afternoon and can recall how vivid the noise was even though memories of the action have faded. Alan has directed the last three FA Cup Finals as well as more than 300 matches since 1985. He also directed the BBC's Test cricket coverage from 1985–99.

'Football coverage has changed immensely across the course of the 300 or so matches that I have directed. My earliest memory of televised football was the 1962 FA Cup Final and that was probably the game that made me a sports fan. When I was a lad I used to think that Kenneth Wolstenholme operated the camera as well as commentating so it came as quite a shock to discover that wasn't the case.

Other than that, the obvious change is that we have far more cameras now in response to the way that Sky developed their coverage. When I directed my first match between QPR and Spurs in 1985 I had four cameras, now there are 15 or 16 for a live match and more than 20 at a cup final. That game ended 2-2 and all I can remember is that I was very nervous.

I was fortunate when I started out to be working alongside some outstanding directors in Alec Weeks, Fred Viner and John Shrewsbury but even so, every match and ground is different and the nerves are still always there. My next game remains as the highest scoring one that I have covered as it finished 4-4 between Sheffield Wednesday Chelsea. It was quite a baptism.

The pace of the game also used to be far slower and that was reflected in the coverage. The ball is hardly ever dead now; especially as the goalkeeper can no longer hold the ball from a back pass. Along with every director I just have great admiration for all the incredible work that the cameraman, sound staff and engineers do in order to bring the games to the screens. There is so much that goes on behind the scenes, regardless of the weather or conditions, and they are the really unsung heroes of *Match of the Day*.

I generally know which match I'm going to direct about three weeks in advance and organize planning meetings at the ground with the Stadium Manager and Safety Officer of the club that we are visiting. We'll work out camera positions, parking, passes, access and cabling, although most Premiership clubs now have permanent cables which make a big difference.

The vans usually arrive on the Friday to start putting in the equipment and I'll get there for a rehearsal and technical check early on Saturday. We have about 40 people on site for each game so everyone has to know their role. After filming interviews for 'Football Focus' the crew break for lunch, then it is one final check of the equipment at about 2.30 and we wait for kick-off. Every Director relies heavily on their Production Assistants and I have been lucky to have worked with some terrific ones including Barbara Berry and Judy Jones who, between them, were with me for at least 80 per cent of the matches I have directed.

My first match for the new season was between two of the newly promoted teams, Norwich City and Crystal Palace. It finished 1-1, they made us feel very welcome and it was good to be back.'

1972–1973

Presenter
David Coleman

League Champions   Liverpool

FA Cup winners   Sunderland

League Cup winners   Tottenham Hotspur

UEFA Cup winners   Liverpool

The show

The programme continued in a very settled routine in this season although it was to be David Coleman's last as presenter. The BBC's football portfolio was the strongest it had ever been and included the highlights of two League games a week, the FA Cup, League Cup and Home Internationals.

   The contractual arrangement still gave the editors difficulties, however, and on five evenings the show was obliged to lead with a Division Two fixture, and twice with a match from Division Three.

The season

In the first League weekend Liverpool beat Manchester City 2-0. They were seen ten times in all and featured in the highest scoring match on the programme that season when they beat Birmingham City 4-3 in December, having recovered from 3-1 down.

   Leeds United featured most frequently with 13 appearances, while Leicester City with three and Birmingham City with just two were the least fancied sides by the editors.

   It proved to be a low-scoring season for the show and teams who scored three or more goals in a game were

Birmingham's John Roberts beats Manchester United's Jim Holton in the air. Birmingham only appeared on the show twice during the season, once against Liverpool when they lost 4-3 and in this match in March when they won 3-1 at St Andrews.

featured on just 14 of the 43 League, Cup and International weekends.

In October the scoring was dominated by World Cup heroes when Tottenham Hotspur went to Manchester United. Unfortunately for the Old Trafford faithful their medal winner, Bobby Charlton, got just the one, while Martin Peters scored four. A few weeks later Frank O'Farrell was sacked as United's manager and replaced by Tommy Docherty while George Best, who had been suspended by the club, announced his retirement just weeks after signing a new six-year contract.

Emlyn Hughes captained Liverpool to the Championship at the start of an incredible 19-year run which would see them finish outside of the top two on just one occasion: 1981. They finished three points ahead of Arsenal with Leeds United third and Bobby Robson's emerging Ipswich Town in fourth place. Hughes also led Bill Shankly's Reds to their first European trophy, the UEFA Cup. They defeated Germany's Borussia Mönchengladbach 3-2 in the two-legged Final.

The defending Champions, Derby County, came seventh but managed to reach the semi-final of the European Cup where they lost to Juventus. In August they had broken the British transfer record by signing David Nish from Leicester City for £250,000.

Leeds added to their impressive list of second placings by losing the European Cup-Winners' Cup final to A C Milan.

Tottenham Hotspur qualified for Europe by winning the League Cup for the second time in three years when Ralph Coates' goal was enough to see them defeat Norwich City in a dull Final at Wembley.

After brief spells in Division Two, Burnley and Queens Park Rangers were promoted, their places being taken by the relegated Crystal Palace and West Bromwich Albion.

The final televised League match of the season came from Stamford Bridge where Chelsea met Manchester United. It was a somewhat strange spectacle as the ground was undergoing a major refurbishment and the whole of one side of the ground – the one facing the cameras – was

Liverpool's Larry Lloyd (left) and Tommy Smith hold the Premiership trophy – it was the first of many League titles for a club that dominated English football for the next 20 years.

Steve Cram

Steve Cram is one of Britain's most successful athletes. During his long career he won World, European and Commonwealth gold medals and broke numerous world records. Born in 1960, Steve is also a lifelong Sunderland supporter who has strong recollections of watching *Match of the Day* as a child.

'In our house I remember my Dad letting me watch *Match of the Day* as a reward for making sure my younger brother Kevin went to sleep early on Saturday nights. We had to share a bedroom and the deal was that if Kevin was asleep then I could see the show. I can vividly recall silently climbing out of bed, crawling across the floor, trying to open the door without letting too much light in and then scampering downstairs when I heard the programme starting.

Sunderland were rarely on the show in those days and my first memory of seeing them is from the end of the 1967–68 season when they went to Old Trafford and beat Manchester United 2-1 just before United won the European Cup. For us that was an epic game.

As I grew older and was spending a lot of time training, *Match of the Day* was the one show each week I really wanted to watch. We had a family connection as well because my uncle, Bobby Cram, who had played for West Bromwich Albion, was the captain of Colchester United when they pulled off their famous FA Cup win against Leeds United on the show in 1971.

We used to live in a police house on an estate that had a special area where we could play football. After Sunderland's great FA Cup victory in 1973 all the kids ran out to recreate the winning goal. Everyone had to take it in turns to be either Ian Porterfield scoring or David Coleman commentating, so the back square was full of youngsters excitedly yelling "Porterfield, one nil".'

a building site. The players had to change in a series of portacabins in the corner of the stadium. But the most significant thing about the match was that it was Bobby Charlton's 754th and last game for United. A fitting presentation took place before kick-off and everyone in the stadium gave him a standing ovation as he left the field. In the event, Chelsea's Peter Osgood scored the only goal of the game.

Crystal Palace's Don Rogers (centre) lifts the ball over Everton goalkeeper David Lawson to score his first goal for the club on his debut appearance.

The *Match of the Day* cameras witnessed a cracking match in February when Manchester City visited Tottenham. Despite two goals from in-form Spurs striker Martin Chivers, City won 3-2 with two goals from Francis Lee and one from Rodney March. Here Spurs' Alan Gilzean gets his header away despite the presence of City's Colin Bell.

Sunderland's Jim Montgomery pulls off the second part of an incredible double save as he pushes Peter Lorimer's shot on to the crossbar. A goal in the 32nd minute from Ian Porterfield had given the Second Division team the lead, Montgomery's save ensured they held on and the cup found its way to Roker Park.

Celebrity football

In the 1970s and 1980s *Match of the Day* was often associated with celebrity football teams who travelled the country playing charity matches.

There were two teams: Tony Gubba organized one side that included John Motson, Bob Wilson, Alan Parry and members of the production team. Their goalkeeper, Chris Lewis, was then the Floor Manager on the show, and in 1974 he launched another side with his friend Dennis Waterman. Many members of the *Match of the Day* team also played alongside them with their biggest crowd coming at Craven Cottage when a showbiz XI took on Malcolm Macdonald's XI in front of some 25,000 spectators to raise money for the victims of the Harrods bomb blast.

The Dennis Waterman XI poses before a game: (left to right, back row) Teddy Maybank, ex-Fulham and PSV; Danny Rioch (brother of Bruce) Aston Villa, Chris Lewis, manager and goalkeeper; Martin Peters, OBE; Jan Webster, England scrum half, (front row) Bobby Gould, ex-Arsenal, Wolves; John Taylor, Captain of Wales, British Lions; Dennis Waterman, captain; Sir Geoff Hurst, Tony Osoba, *Porridge*; and Robin Asquith of *Confessions* fame.

The FA Cup

The sixth round produced the Goal of the Season when Peter Osgood volleyed the ball into the Arsenal net at Stamford Bridge as part of their 2-2 draw. Arsenal then went on to win the replay at Highbury to secure a semi-final spot for the third successive year.

When Arsenal went to Hillsborough they faced Sunderland of the Second Division, a side whose only previous Wembley visit had come in 1937 when they won the Cup. This time they were the undoubted underdogs but produced a shock result by winning 2-1.

Match of the Day was at Maine Road to see a goal from Billy Bremner secure Cup holders Leeds United the chance to retain their title. They went into the Final safe in the knowledge that no Division Two team had won the trophy for 42 years.

As Bob Stokoe and Don Revie led their teams out on to the pitch on 5 May few, if any, neutral fans thought that Sunderland had a chance against a side packed with ten international players.

The match was decided by two key moments. In the 32nd minute, Ian Porterfield put Sunderland ahead, and then in the 70th minute, Jim Montgomery pulled off a sensational double save. He deflected shots from Trevor Cherry and Peter Lorimer, the second on to the underside of the bar, and convinced fans who had travelled down from the north-east that this was going to be their day.

As Sunderland's captain, Bobby Kerr, held the trophy aloft it was in the knowledge that his side had produced the greatest Cup Final upset in the history of the competition. They later collected a second trophy when Sir Stanley Rous presented Sunderland with the Team of the Year award at the BBC's *Sports Review of the Year*. As they received the award, they could easily have been given a third one for the thickest sideburns and fattest tie knots – an accurate reflection of the fashion statements footballers were making in the early 1970s.

1972 European Championship

West Germany beat USSR in the Final held in Brussels. England had earlier lost 3-1 to them in the two-legged quarter-final at Wembley and in Berlin. Only the last four countries went to the finals in Belgium in this season.

Fact file

Jack and Bobby Charlton (above) both retired on 28 April 1973 to move into management. Jack took over at Middlesbrough and Bobby at Preston North End. Another England legend Bobby Moore edged towards the end of his career, beating Bobby Charlton's record to become England's most capped player.

Goal of the Season
Peter Osgood for Chelsea against Arsenal, FA Cup, March 1973

Footballer of the Year
Pat Jennings, Tottenham Hotspur

European Footballer of the Year
Johan Cruyff, Barcelona

The commentators

Tony Gubba

Tony Gubba was born in Moss Side, Manchester in 1943. He went to Blackpool Grammar school and worked on various newspapers before joining Southern TV at Southampton and then moving to Liverpool as the BBC's North of England news correspondent.

'Although I worked in news I had always loved sport, especially football, and used to watch *Match of the Day* thinking it must be the greatest job on Earth to be David Coleman commentating at Wembley.

In 1973 I was asked by *Grandstand* to cover a local horse called Red Rum on the day of the Grand National. I was up at the crack of dawn to report live into *Grandstand* from Southport where the horse was based, but when Red Rum won my report suddenly became a major feature for the Grand National highlights show. In those days, the highlights were run as part of a special *Match of the Day*.

Sam Leitch, the editor, decided that he wanted to use my feature first and then show the race. The only problem was that no-one had recorded the sound, so I was flown to London, sat next to David Coleman and had to revoice the package "live" as it went out on the show. That was my somewhat unconventional *Match of the Day* debut and 31 years later it is still fantastic to be part of the programme.

Following the Red Rum feature I got a call asking if I would like to join BBC Sport as a presenter and interviewer, and I hosted *Sportsnight* for a year or so before Harry Carpenter took it on. I then began to do commentary and cut my teeth on table tennis and bobsleigh before being invited to have a go at a game for *Match of the Day*.

When I started out David Coleman was still the number one, and I think that he is the most professional broadcaster I have ever worked with. He is the Dimbleby of sports broadcasting: he always had a great eye for a story and when the opportunity came always had the right words. His famous commentary style was to say "one nil" and I used to think that he knew which team had scored but not which player!

David represents a time when all the great commentators and presenters were also journalists and I think that has changed a lot recently, and not necessarily for the better. Television now employs people for what they have done in the past rather than what they can do now.

Another thing that's changed is the way the games are edited. When I started out the matches were recorded on two-inch tape and everything was very basic. The tape had to be cut and glued together and the process was sometimes like watching a decorator at work. This meant that unlike today's digital era the VT editors couldn't separate the sound from the pictures meaning we all had to be very disciplined. We couldn't talk over certain things such as goal kicks or throw ins as they were potential cutting points that might be used later to help move the action to another period in the match. As a result we tended to commentate in packages and on small sections that were self-contained.

One of the most exciting matches I commentated on came when I got a call on a Tuesday from *Sportsnight* in early 1985. They asked me to go in to the studio the following evening to voice a couple of minutes of a League Cup quarter-final replay between Sheffield Wednesday and Chelsea.

I wasn't too comfortable with that so offered to go to the ground instead. I got there early the next morning to watch Sheffield Wednesday train and then it was back to the hotel to do my notes on both teams. This usually takes an afternoon, although if a team I don't know very well is involved, it can take a couple of days to visit the training ground and finish the research. On this occasion I prepared to put on a full match commentary and was mightily relieved that I had, as an astonishing game unfolded.

By half-time the home team were leading 3-0 but by late in the second half it was 3-3, before Chelsea finally took the lead. Doug Rougvie then gave away a last-minute penalty and the game ended 4-4. In all, 35 minutes of the match were shown and I was very pleased that I had decided to go to Hillsborough.

If that was one of the best games, then two of the greatest players that I have been lucky enough to watch and describe are Gianfranco Zola and Eric Cantona. Both of them were able to do things on the pitch that took your breath away, and sometimes left me almost speechless. I would have loved to have had the chance to describe some of Cantona's predecessors at Old Trafford. I always wanted to swap places with Kenneth Wolstenholme when he was commentating on Best, Charlton, Law and Crerand.

One of the trickiest matches I had to commentate on featured the Romanian team in the 1998 World Cup. When they met Tunisia, the Romanians ran out with identical haircuts: cropped short and dyed blonde. They were a nightmare to identify!

The greatest thing about being a commentator is that you feel involved in the game – almost as much as the players. After you've done all the preparation and sit there at five-to-three with the notes in front of you and the microphone in hand, you feel as involved as you can be without actually running out onto the pitch. Even now the buzz is fantastic.'

1973–1974

Presenter
Jimmy Hill

League Champions   Leeds United
FA Cup winners   Liverpool
League Cup winners   Wolverhampton Wanderers

The show

'Good evening and welcome to *Match of the Day* for the start of the 1973–74 season, a vital season for British football as England, Scotland and Wales desperately fight to qualify for the World Cup.'

Those were the opening words of *Match of the Day's* new presenter, Jimmy Hill who had just been signed from LWT. Jimmy revolutionised the presentation of football on television and was the first person both to present the show and offer expert analysis. He was joined in each programme by a co-host who would read a news round-up, usually Tony Gubba or Bob Wilson.

The cover of *Radio Times* heralds a new format for the programme, one that remained the same for 15 years.

The *Radio Times* ran the news on its front cover under the heading 'Catch of the Year', and described Jimmy as 'belonging in the classic mould of those sporting heroes beloved of boys' comics like *Wizard* and *Hotspur*'. The BBC were clearly happy to have him.

The first match of the season was used to demonstrate some of the changes on *Match of the Day*. Barry Davies had been at the Baseball Ground to commentate on Derby County's 1-0 victory over Chelsea.

He was invited into the studio, which had a second set next to the main desk, where he was asked to comment on his commentary. Barry felt that he had slightly undersold Derby's performance but pointed out that 90 minutes of commentary had been edited into a 30-minute package. He then discussed the game, his role and reviewed the contentious points.

The new-style analysis continued, as Jimmy then reviewed the match and ended the section by offering his opinion, thereby establishing a pattern that was to continue for years. He forcefully expressed his annoyance that Derby kept the ball in the corner at one point and he also strongly condemned the crowd violence at the end of the game.

With Jimmy Hill presenting, John Motson and Barry Davies commentating and the theme tune becoming increasingly familiar, the classic *Match of the Day* line-up was in place, and would remain so for the next 15 years.

Above Cyril Knowles scores for Spurs in their 2-0 win over Manchester United at White Hart Lane.

The season

It may have been a new look but it was not a vintage season for football fans tuning in for goals on *Match of the Day*. In 32 of the 42 weekends, no team scored more than two goals and the paying spectators were staying away as well. In just two seasons gates had dropped by three and a half million people. A combination of unadventurous football, the rise of hooliganism, the three-day week and power shortages all contributed to the drop, but the result was simply that far fewer people were going to watch their teams play.

One of the rare occasions when a team scored three in front of the BBC's cameras came on the first weekend of the League season when Manchester City's new acquisition, Denis Law, scored twice in their 3-1 win over Birmingham City.

Across the city Law's former team mates were having a torrid time and at the end of the season it would be his goal in the Manchester derby that would condemn them to the Second Division.

This seemed an impossible situation when Tommy Docherty's team made their first appearance of the season on the show in mid-September. On that occasion they comfortably beat West Ham United 3-1 at Old Trafford, but two months later the signs were ominous as they lost 2-1 away to Tottenham Hotspur. It was Bill Nicholson's 16th and final season in charge at White Hart Lane but the

Below Wolves skipper Mike Bailey holds up the trophy after their 2-1 win over Manchester City in the League Cup Final. It was Wolves first ever victory in the competition.

match will mainly be remembered (in *Match of the Day* terms anyway) for being the last time that George Best featured on the show scoring a goal for Manchester United. He had first scored in front of the cameras back in March 1965 as part of their 4-0 win over Chelsea, but in this season he played just 12 games before Docherty dropped him.

Leeds won their second Championship under Don Revie, led by the tenacious Billy Bremner. Their dominance was shown by the fact that they lost just one of their nine televised league matches that season, and that was at Anfield in March when Steve Heighway scored the only goal of their match against Liverpool.

They had previously gone 29 games unbeaten before losing 3-2 to Stoke City, having been 2-0 in the lead. It was a great season for their captain, Billy Bremner who scored ten goals, lifted the Championship trophy and led Scotland in the World Cup finals.

Liverpool came second, five points behind Leeds with Derby County in third place despite having lost their managing partnership of Brian Clough and Peter Taylor. They resigned after a fall-out with the chairman, Sam Longson, in October and despite strike threats from the players, were replaced by Dave Mackay. Clough and Taylor later joined Division Three side Brighton and Hove Albion.

After almost 80 seasons new rules were introduced to govern promotion and relegation and the principle of 'three up and three down' became part of League football's way of life. Norwich City, Southampton and, sensationally, Manchester United were replaced in Division One by Middlesbrough, Luton Town and Carlisle United.

The League Cup Final was a listless affair between two teams stuck in the middle of Division One as Wolverhampton Wanderers beat Manchester City 2-1 at Wembley.

Superstars

In 1973 David Vine presented the first edition of *Superstars* on BBC1. The classic series saw sportsmen from many different disciplines compete against each other across two days of competition. It ran for 12 years, featured almost 200 competitors, and footballers regularly took part – Bobby Moore was in the initial line-up on the first show. They tended to be good sprinters and in 1975 there was an epic 100 metres final between Mick Channon and Malcolm Macdonald that the latter won in an amazing time of 10.9 seconds.

The most famous event to involve a soccer player came the following year in a *European Superstars* heat held at Bracknell in Berkshire. Liverpool's Kevin Keegan fell badly onto cinders at the first bend of the cycling competition and was badly bruised and cut. He got back up, finished the race, competed in the steeplechase and won the competition.

Superstars was resurrected in 2002 as part of Sport Relief.

Kevin Keegan gives it his all on the parallel bars. Keegan suffered even more in 1975 when he fell off his bike on to a cinder track. But he got up, dusted himself off, got back on his bike and went on to win the competition.

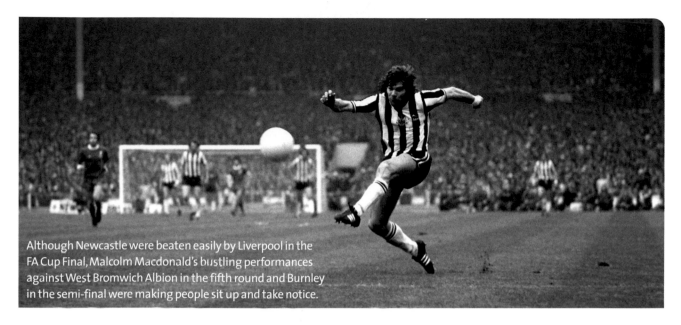

Although Newcastle were beaten easily by Liverpool in the FA Cup Final, Malcolm Macdonald's bustling performances against West Bromwich Albion in the fifth round and Burnley in the semi-final were making people sit up and take notice.

The FA Cup

Malcolm Macdonald scored twice for Newcastle in their semi-final at Hillsborough as Burnley lost 2-0, while *Match of the Day* witnessed a 0-0 draw between Leicester City and Liverpool at Old Trafford. Liverpool won the replay 3-1 at Villa Park four days later.

Cup Final Grandstand began even earlier this year as Frank Bough opened the show from Wembley at 11.15 a.m, Mike Yarwood was among the special guests, the winner of the Goal of the Season was announced, Ken Dodd was one of those taking part in 'It's a Cup Final Knockout' and Brendan Foster headed a field of International athletes in a special 3000 metres race around the Wembley pitch. Bruce Forsyth led the crowd in the pre-match singing before Bill Shankly and Joe Harvey led Liverpool and Newcastle United out onto the pitch.

Liverpool were looking for their first win since 1965 although Newcastle's memories had to reach back a decade further. Kevin Keegan put Shankly's team ahead 13 minutes into the second half, Steve Heighway added a second in the 75th minute, and then, just before the final whistle, Liverpool's total dominance saw them put together 11 consecutive passes before Keegan made it 3-0. Jimmy Hill brought a new style of coverage to the *Cup Final Match of the Day* celebrations later that evening on BBC1. He reviewed and analysed the game surrounded by the Liverpool side at their post-match party.

Fact file

Sir Alf Ramsey was sacked as England manager after winning 69 and losing just 17 out of 113 matches between 1963 and 1974. Having won the 1966 World Cup he was knighted in the following year but lost the confidence of the FA in this season after England failed to qualify for the 1974 World Cup finals. Needing a win they could only draw 1-1 with Poland at Wembley thanks to the goalkeeping skills of Jan Tomaszewski.

Joe Mercer acted as caretaker manager for seven matches before Don Revie was appointed on a full-time basis.

Goal of the Season
Alan Mullery for Fulham against Leicester, FA Cup, January 1974

Footballer of the Year
Ian Callaghan, Liverpool

European Footballer of the Year
Johan Cruyff, Ajax

PFA Player of the Year
Norman Hunter, Leeds United

PFA Young Player of the Year
Kevin Beattie, Ipswich Town

MATCH OF THE DAY

The presenters

Jimmy Hill

Jimmy Hill was born in Balham on 22 July 1928 and in the 1950s played for Brentford and Fulham and qualified as a coach by the age of 24. As chairman of the old Players Union he fought for freedom of contracts and the abolition of the maximum wage, and as the innovative manager of Coventry City (1961–67) he took them from Division Three to Division One.

Jimmy resigned from the club in October 1967 to become head of sport at the newly formed London Weekend Television. He re-launched the former ABC show *World of Sport*, *The Big Match* and 'On The Ball'; poached Brian Moore from BBC radio to become their main commentator; and persuaded a young presenter named Richard Davies to adopt the name 'Dickie' as it sounded warmer!

He later had spells as the managing director of Coventry City, director at Charlton Athletic and chairman of Fulham as well as ventures of varying success in Saudi Arabia and America. When he was back at Coventry, he introduced its all-seater stadium, half-price tickets for the jobless and campaigned for three points for a win.

As well as all those roles Jimmy has found time to become an accomplished rider, tennis player, and golfer. He once acted as a stand-in linesman at Highbury during an Arsenal v Liverpool match, when Denis Drewitt tore a thigh muscle and there was no replacement. After the crowd were asked if anyone was qualified, Jimmy borrowed kit and jogged out to help referee Pat Partridge.

In September 1973 he moved to the BBC where he could reach a national audience hosting *Match of the Day*. He pre-sented the show until 1989 when the BBC lost the League contract and Desmond Lynam took over to front The Road to Wembley. However, Jimmy remained a regular pundit for another decade, and had many verbal jousts with Alan Hanson and Terry Venables. Jimmy left the BBC and joined Sky after the 1998 World Cup.

'One of the biggest changes I found when I joined the BBC was autocue. Everything I'd done on-screen at LWT had been as a pundit and I was able to speak off the top of my head. I used it for the first time on my very first show but I was never a great script reader. Before, I'd been an ad-libber and just hoped what I said was alright. To suddenly read out loud was difficult at first but I soon got used to it and was professionally adequate in a short space of time. Mind you, there were times when I still misread it and one Saturday night I inadvertently closed a show with "just to remind you, before you go to sleep don't forget to put your cocks back".

The new-look *Match of the Day* was developed when the head of sport Sam Leitch took the programme's director Jonathan Martin and myself to lunch in Notting Hill. After seven hours and many bottles of wine Sam had explained his philosophy for the show. We developed the plan for me to both present and analyze, something that had never been done before. It wasn't an approach I had thought about, but Jonathan pointed out that it would be unique.

Sam was so open minded to new ideas – such as having Barry Davies on the first show analyzing his own performance as a commentator – and between the three of us we changed the style. It was great fun and proved to be a critical lunch that helped us really get to know each other. Jonathan

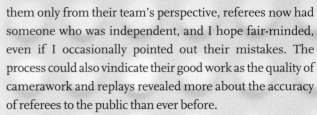

them only from their team's perspective, referees now had someone who was independent, and I hope fair-minded, even if I occasionally pointed out their mistakes. The process could also vindicate their good work as the quality of camerawork and replays revealed more about the accuracy of referees to the public than ever before.

We had a tremendous postbag, especially from Australia, one of the many countries the show was sold to. I think we got a reaction because for the first time we gave our opinions by looking straight into the camera and talking directly to the public.

I'm often asked who my favourite players are and I have to say that although some stand out such as Law, Osgood and Charlton, I loved them all and they were all my heroes. That has remained the same from when I was a kid on the terraces, through my playing and broadcasting career, and I still have an almost childish enthusiasm for players today. I have never lost that wide-eyed attraction to those who play the game professionally and still look upon them with awe.

I loved being part of *Match of the Day* and am proud that by using my experience to give it a special perspective I was able to help bring something unique to the screen. For me it is a British institution without which Saturday nights are never the same.'

was last seen that evening clinging to a lamp-post in southwest London.

We also thought it was essential for me to attend a match before I analyzed it – too risky to pass judgment on a game that I hadn't been at. If it was within driving distance of London that was easy and I was able to watch the whole game and get back in time, but I sometimes had to fly around the country in order to get back in time for the show.

When we began with the new-look *Match of the Day* the reaction from the players wasn't too bad, as I was able to bring a professional view to an incident. As I had been a player, coach, manager and chairman, I had the talent and knowledge to be accurate. I was a senior FA coach, knew the laws of the game and had a background of authority so was unlikely to make a mistake.

Referees were not too happy as their mistakes were highlighted, but whereas supporters at the ground would judge

1974–1975

Presenter
Jimmy Hill

League Champions   Derby County
FA Cup winners   West Ham United
League Cup winners   Aston Villa

The show

After 16 months of negotiations, the secretary of the Football League, Alan Hardaker, finally called the editor of *Match of the Day*, Sam Leitch, on 17 July to confirm the League were prepared to sign a three-year contract.

As Sam wrote in the *Radio Times*, 'it had been a very difficult process. Some of the clubs were still convinced they were getting a raw deal from television, despite an increase of 53 per cent in fees. They also added a number of new clauses including one which banned pre-match interviews in *Grandstand* and they maintained their insistence that no publicity be allowed until the featured matches had begun the second halves of their games.'

As the profile of the show grew, so did the demands of the audiences but the technology was still very old-fashioned and often restrictive. John Rowlinson was an assistant producer who later became the director of *Match of the Day*.

'One of my earliest jobs with the football unit was to go into the office on a Monday after the show and put the goals and any interesting features onto a compilation reel. It was too expensive to keep and store everything, so most match recordings were wiped and often the match edits themselves as well. No one foresaw the video and DVD explosion. We kept a few outstanding matches but not that many.'

The season

The opening match of the season saw two managers at the opposite ends of their careers lead their teams out for the Charity Shield. Bill Shankly, having announced his retirement, led Liverpool out for the last time, and Brian Clough, the newly appointed manager of Leeds United, walked alongside him.

The match ended 1-1 before Liverpool won 6-5 on penalties, but the game is mainly remembered for Kevin Keegan and Billy Bremner being sent off for fighting. At a time when hooliganism and violence were tightening their grip on the sport, two of the biggest names in football scrapping at a showpiece occasion was not the image that the authorities wanted to project. They were both suspended for 11 games.

The first League weekend saw newly promoted Carlisle United surprise Chelsea with a 2-0 win at Stamford Bridge. One of the teams that replaced them in Division Two, Manchester United, were featured five times during the

Referee Reg Matthewson sends off Leeds United's Billy Bremner (left) and Liverpool's Kevin Keegan after they traded punches during the Charity Shield at Wembley.

Though largely ignored by the *Match of the Day* cameras, Derby County won their second league title in four years, this time under Dave Mackay. Here County's Kevin Hector (left) goes past Carlisle United's Bobby Parker.

season as they bounced straight back to the top flight as champions. Interest in them was so great that in one epic match against Sunderland 60,000 turned out to watch them win at Old Trafford.

The highest scoring match on the programme that season came on 8 February when Liverpool beat Ipswich Town 5-2. Ipswich themselves put five past Newcastle United when they beat them 5-4 in an incredible match at Portman Road although Wolverhampton Wanderers posted the record score for the campaign when they demolished a hapless Chelsea 7-1.

Dave Mackay had managed to restore harmony at Derby County following the acrimonious departure of Brian Clough and he took them to their second title in four years. They were, however, all but ignored by the cameras and featuring on only four League weekends that season and only once in the final four months of the campaign.

Brian Clough, meanwhile, resigned from Leeds United after just 44 days and joined Nottingham Forest in Division Two. He was succeeded at Elland Road by Jimmy Armfield who took the club to the European Cup Final where they were defeated 2-0 by Bayern Munich. After the game the Yorkshire club's supporters rioted through Paris causing

mayhem and bringing yet more shame to English football after a year that had seen many hundreds of arrests.

At Wembley, Aston Villa beat Norwich City 1-0 in the League Cup Final and capped a great season by being promoted to Division One for the first time since 1967. They were joined by Norwich City and a rejuvenated Manchester United who returned as champions. Luton Town, Carlisle United and Chelsea were relegated.

The FA Cup

In the sixth round a scrawny, long haired, 21-year-old striker called Alan Taylor first came to the nation's attention when he scored both of West Ham's goals against Arsenal at Highbury. He had only joined the club earlier that season from Fourth Division Rochdale but proved to be a great investment by also scoring twice in their 2-1 victory over Ipswich Town in the semi-final replay at Stamford Bridge.

The second semi-final also went to a replay before Fulham overcame Birmingham City at Maine Road. John Mitchell scored the only goal to enable two of football's most respected elder statesmen, Alan Mullery and Bobby Moore, to make one last appearance at Wembley.

Twenty three years separated the ages of the men who led the teams out for the Final on 3 May. Alec Stock of Fulham had been in management with various clubs since 1946 and already enjoyed Wembley success as an underdog when he took Queens Park Rangers to a shock victory against West Bromwich Albion in the 1967 League Cup Final.

West Ham's John Lyall had recently become only the fourth post-war manager of the club when Ron Greenwood moved up to become general manager, but his side were to dominate a slightly disappointing match. The game turned in a four-minute spell 15 minutes into the second half when Alan Taylor scored twice to secure his side the FA Cup for the first time since 1964. Bobby Moore, who had received the trophy on that occasion, had to be content with a runners-up medal this time as he watched his successor as captain, Billy Bonds, collect the FA Cup.

Above In the traditional *Match of the Day* end-of-season matches, the Home Internationals, England thrashed Scotland 5-1 at Wembley. Gerry Francis celebrates one of his brace of goals. The other scores came from Kevin Beattie, Colin Bell and David Johnson, while Bruce Rioch scored from the spot for Scotland.

Above right West Ham's Trevor Brooking celebrates victory over London rivals Fulham in the FA Cup Final. The Hammers' Alan Taylor scored twice to take the cup back to Upton Park for the first time since 1964.

Far right Sheffield United's Tony Currie had a superb season for the Yorkshire club who finished a creditable 6th in the First Division. His strength, passing ability and goals lit up many a *Match of the Day* during the season and the commentator called his goal against West Ham in March 'a quality goal by a quality player'.

1974 World Cup

Hosts West Germany beat Holland 2-1 in the Final after the English referee, Jack Tayor, had given the Dutchmen a penalty in the first minute of the game. Johan Cruyff scored but 25 minutes later Paul Breitner equalized, also from the penalty spot. Just before half time Gerd Müller scored the winning goal. Scotland were the only British team to reach the final stages but failed to progress from their group having beaten Zaire and drawn with Brazil and Yugoslavia.

Bob Wilson had retired as Arsenal's goal-keeper at the end of the previous season and now took over as host of the Saturday morning football preview spot within *Grandstand*. It was renamed 'Football Focus' and Bob hosted it for almost two decades before being succeeded by Gary Lineker, Ray Stubbs and now Manish Bhasin. Initially a short preview of the matches to be played that day, it gradually expanded to become the stand-alone show that exists today.

Goal of the Season
Mickey Walsh for Blackpool against Sunderland, Division Two, February 1975

Footballer of the Year
Alan Mullery, Fulham

European Footballer of the Year
Oleg Blokhin, Dynamo Kiev

PFA Player of the Year
Colin Todd, Derby County

PFA Young Player of the Year
Mervyn Day, West Ham United

Bob Wilson

Bob was born in Chesterfield in 1941, and joined Arsenal in 1963. He soon established himself as their first-choice goalkeeper and won the European Fairs Cup in 1970 and the League and FA Cup double in 1971. Having been a BBC pundit during the 1970 World Cup finals, Bob became a regular analyst and was told by the BBC Head of Sport, Sam Leitch, that when his playing career finished, he wanted him to join the BBC. Bob retired from Arsenal in 1974 and decided to take up the offer.

'I began presenting 'Football Preview' in 1974 when it was renamed 'Football Focus', and remained with the show for 20 years. I've also presented more than 200 editions of *Grandstand*, many *Sportsnights* and a variety of events including the London marathon. *Match of the Day*, however, was the one I always wanted to work on, and because I was the first footballer to be hired by the BBC to present a show, I was immensely proud.

I remember that among the players, *Match of the Day* was the definitive programme. *The Big Match* built up a good reputation but the joy of *Match of the Day* was the immediacy of seeing it on a Saturday night. It was compulsive viewing at 10 p.m. and the huge audiences reflected that. It was, and is, a national institution.

As players, we used to make sure we were all back at home in time to see the programme in the evening and I remember one occasion in particular during our double-winning season. It was still in August but we had beaten Manchester United 4-0 at Highbury, and I had made a great save from George Best when I took it off his feet. I had to make sure that I was home to see the show, as there were no repeats.

It certainly helped me because I went from being a relative unknown with Arsenal to being regarded as one of the best goalkeepers in the First Division. This is largely because I had been seen so many times on the show and people could see I had a very dramatic style.

Sadly, because of the expense of keeping film and tapes in those days, many of the games were junked. Often, the only records kept were the goals, not the great saves, so I don't have too many examples of goalkeeping from that time to use when I coach young keepers today.

In the 1970 World Cup, I asked Bryan Cowgill if I could pull together some montages to demonstrate the individual skills of players and the different tactics that teams were employing. I would start going through the tapes at 10 a.m. and we'd not finish until late afternoon. This kind of analysis is standard now, but it just wasn't done then and we were able to give viewers in-depth pieces on Pele's skills and Peru's tactics, for example.

After Sam Leitch offered me the chance to host the lunchtime show I knew that it was a huge risk as no player had ever before gone straight into presenting. Even Jimmy had been an analyst first. It was an achievement that I was very proud of and I loved the two decades I spent at the BBC.

'Football Focus' was a real challenge as I suddenly had to cope with remembering links, conducting interviews and listening to the producer and editor in my ear. It was very demanding and it was a real credit to the BBC that they stuck with me early on when I faced criticism. Being a recent former player helped enormously as I was able to get access to the teams, but I admit that it was often difficult to ask tough questions of people I knew well.

As well as presenting many editions of the show and umpteen World Cup and European Championship programmes, I spent ten years working on *Match of the Day* from the mid-1970s alongside Jimmy Hill. I loved doing the round-ups in the evening with him as we were always waiting for the next drama.

I love Jimmy very much and have huge respect for all he has achieved, but he had an extraordinary ego and he would often come out with something outrageous. He was hated for a while when I was still at Arsenal because of some comments that he made about Peter Storey, although at least he had the guts to say what he felt.

On one occasion during a show, fire alarms rang out all around us. Jimmy looked at me and asked what I thought we should do. When I replied that we ought to get the f*** out of there he looked bemused and said, "no, no, the nation needs us", and he meant it!

Being new to broadcasting could be scary and I would often go off to watch a match in the afternoon but have to rush back to do a live report for *Grandstand*. I once had to leave Fulham when they were leading 2-0 with about 20 minutes to go. The car had no radio and I was stunned when I got to the Lime Grove studio and Frank Bough, who was presenting, told me that it had ended 5-2.

I went into a panic as I had missed five of the goals, but Albert Sewell, our resident statistician, calmed me down, advised me to just give the gist of the game and then handed me a list of all the goals, their times and scorers.

He saved me on so many occasions and was always at the end of a phone when I needed a statistic. All the football presenters from David Coleman through to Gary Lineker have relied on Albert. Des made him famous with his many on-air references to 'Our Man Albert' and he was essential to all of us.

As a presenter, *Grandstand* is the ultimate challenge as it is a five-hour live show with no autocue. It's amazing how professional Steve Rider is, as he never seems to make a mistake. Being a football man though, the supreme show was, and still is, *Match of the Day*. Of all the things I did, my ambition was to be the programme's main presenter, and when I was asked to front ITV's football coverage in 1994, I told the BBC I would stay if I could be the main anchor.

Sadly that wasn't possible so I moved across to ITV, but *Match of the Day* remains very close to my heart. I love the fact that the title has been kept, even in the lean years, and that the great music is still the same.'

1975–1976

Presenter
Jimmy Hill

League Champions   Liverpool

FA Cup winners   Southampton

League Cup winners   Manchester City

UEFA Cup winners   Liverpool

The show

This season saw the appearance of special celebrity judges to choose the winners of the Goal of the Month competitions. They included Nat Lofthouse, Jackie Milburn, John Charles, Denis Law, Tom Finney and Danny Blanchflower.

The show was regularly combined with other major sporting events and the title *Match of the Day Special* was used so often it almost became a sub brand in its own right. Show jumping, European and World ice-skating, the Winter Olympic Games, athletics, the Grand National and boxing were all featured.

10.10 Match of the Day
Introduced by Jimmy Hill. Action, news, interviews, analysis. Coverage of two of today's important First Division matches. Match No 1 comes from the Midlands. Commentator BARRY DAVIES Match No 2 comes from the North. Commentator JOHN MOTSON

Football TV presentation by ALEC WEEKS and JOHN McGONAGLE *Match of the Day* presented by MARTIN HOPKINS Editor JONATHAN MARTIN

11.10 Parkinson
Michael Parkinson and his guests of the week
Bette Davis
Ron Moody

Production team:

Kevin Keegan leads the celebrations as he scores Liverpool's third goal against Wolves to clinch the Championship – their first under Bob Paisley.

The season

Yet another slump in support for football saw the game record its lowest set of attendances since the war. With just under 25 million paying spectators the game had lost 5 million since 1968.

The opening day had been optimistic, however, and saw Gerry Francis of Queens Park Rangers score a fantastic goal that took the ball from one penalty area to the other in four moves. It was adjudged Goal of the Season as QPR beat Liverpool 2-0. Two goals from Malcolm Macdonald made the other headlines on that show as Newcastle United won 3-0 away to Ipswich Town.

Liverpool got off to a slow start when the BBC cameras were present and failed to score in their first three televised matches, but they later made up for it with results that included a 3-1 win over Manchester United at Anfield, 2-0 revenge against QPR in December and a John Toshack hat-trick as West Ham United were demolished 4-0 at Upton Park.

For QPR it was a season where their manager Terry Venables so nearly turned a cult side into a legendary one. Francis was made England's captain and their side also boasted the flair and talent of players such as Stan Bowles, Dave Webb, John Hollins and Frank McLintock.

Goals once again flowed on Saturday nights. High-scoring

This year's Goal of the Season came at Loftus Road on the first day when Gerry Francis, seen here getting away from Phil Thompson, scored in the Londoners' 2-0 win against Liverpool. QPR finished the season in second place, one point behind the Reds.

games included Stoke City beating Leeds 3-2; Birmingham City putting four past Burnley with Alan Campbell, Peter Withe, Howard Kendall and Trevor Francis on the score sheet and Wolverhampton Wanderers beating Newcastle 5-0 in April, thanks in part to a John Richards hat-trick.

Lawrie McMenemy's experienced Southampton side were showing form in Division Two as well as the FA Cup. Two goals by Mick Channon helped them to a 4-1 win over Chelsea in October and six weeks later a brace from Peter Osgood led the way as they beat Sunderland 4-0 at The Dell.

Liverpool's first Championship under Bob Paisley was hard fought and they needed nine victories in their last ten matches to win it. Their last home game was an eight-goal thriller, which Liverpool had to win as QPR breathed down their necks. The Merseysiders hammered Stoke City 5-3 including an outstanding goal by Emlyn Hughes after he played a one-two with Kevin Keegan.

Clive Thomas

Clive Thomas was probably the most famous and controversial referee in Britain during the first two decades of *Match of the Day*. Born in Wales in 1936 he was on the ground staff of Norwich City when an ankle injury cut short his career aged just 16. Having a handkerchief and basic knowledge of the game, Clive's career began as a linesman during a local match and from that moment fame and infamy beckoned along with the ultimate accolade of being selected to referee in the 1974 and 1978 World Cup finals.

'I was the youngest referee in the UK when I began as a 17-year-old in Wales – a year below the official limit. As they were short on officials they let me carry on and progress through the ranks until I became a Football League referee when I was 28 at about the same time as *Match of the Day* began. I have to confess, however, that I was never actually asked to take a single refereeing test or qualification in my entire career but was just in the right place at the right time. I grew up as a referee with *Match of the Day* and was regularly featured on the show. I loved cameras being at games in which I was officiating and the buzz it gave me. Some referees hated seeing the BBC vans arriving at a ground but I thrived on it and definitely refereed differently when I knew I was on. I knew I had to be on my toes and would go to great lengths to ensure that every decision I gave was the right one.

I've always maintained that the officials are part of the entertainment as they are essential to every game and should have the right to express comments and be honest when they get things wrong. When action replays were introduced I always spoke up in their favour. I believe that the spectators at the ground and at home want to see the right decision being made, even if I did wince many times when I sat at home and saw I had made the wrong decision.

I still watch the show from a referee's perspective and think that the presentation of it is superb. I would absolutely endorse the use of an extra official to decide on crucial incidents that involve goals, especially now the technology is so quick. I'm all in favour of it as everyone just wants to know that the right decision has been made.

Although I often had issues with Jimmy Hill he was always about 20 years ahead of the game with his thoughts and ideas. He and *Match of the Day* helped my career as I became known throughout the UK and around the world. People still stop me at airports and ask about decisions I made 30 years ago!'

Liverpool finished just one point ahead of QPR with Manchester United in third place and Derby County fourth having also reached the semi-final stages of the European and FA Cups. At the other end of the table Wolverhampton Wanderers, Burnley and Sheffield United were replaced by Sunderland, Bristol City and West Bromwich Albion.

Liverpool also won the UEFA Cup with a 4-3 aggregate win over FC Bruges, West Ham United were the losing finalists in the European Cup-Winners' Cup when they lost 4-2 to Anderlecht and Manchester City beat Newcastle United 2-1 in the League Cup Final.

The FA Cup

The holders, West Ham United went out at the first hurdle when they lost at home to Liverpool on *Match of the Day*. They in turn were knocked out by Derby County who made it to the semi-final at Hillsborough where they lost 2-0 to Manchester United. Their new star youngster, Gordon Hill, scored both goals in front of the cameras as they reached the Final for the first time in 13 years.

At Wembley, Manchester United faced Second Division Southampton who were playing in the stadium for the first time. Southampton had beaten Aston Villa, Blackpool, West Bromwich Albion, Bradford City and Crystal Palace on their way to the Final and secured their first major trophy when Bobby Stokes scored the only goal of the match with just seven minutes left.

Southampton's Mick Channon (left) and David Peach hold the FA Cup after their 1-0 victory over Manchester United in the Final.

Fact file

A new schedule started on 18 October that proved to be one of the classic Saturday line-ups on BBC1. After *Grandstand* came *The Basil Brush Show* with Roy North, *Dr Who* starring Tom Baker, *Bruce Forsyth and The Generation Game*, *The Dick Emery Show*, *Kojak*, *Match of the Day* and *Parkinson* featuring Bette Davis and Ron Moody.

Goal of the Season
Gerry Francis for QPR against Liverpool, Division One, August 1975

Footballer of the Year
Kevin Keegan, Liverpool

European Footballer of the Year
Franz Beckenbauer, Bayern Munich

PFA Player of the Year
Pat Jennings, Tottenham Hotspur

PFA Young Player of the Year
Peter Barnes, Manchester City

1976–1977

Presenter
Jimmy Hill

League Champions   Liverpool

FA Cup winners   Manchester United

League Cup winners   Aston Villa

European Cup winners   Liverpool

The show

With the show settled into an established Saturday night schedule, the format barely changed throughout the season. Gerry Francis was a studio guest for the first League programme where he collected the Goal of the Season award for the previous campaign.

The Grand National, show jumping and gymnastics were all combined with various editions and the programme also followed the progress of Britain's new young ice-skating hope, Robin Cousins. Bob Wilson presented some of the shows in January.

Genesis reached number 14 in the singles chart in March with their *Spot the Pigeon* EP which contained a football related track called 'Match of the Day'.

GENESIS
Spot The Pigeon

Match Of The Day
Pigeons
Inside And Out

The cover of the Genesis EP *Spot the Pigeon* on which they claimed, 'Yes, *Match of the Day's* the only way to spend your Saturday'.

The season

This was the year of the striker and Jimmy Hill had no shortage of goals to analyze as they exploded on to the screens almost every weekend.

The opening League programme set the tone as Everton depressed the previous season's runners-up by putting four past Queens Park Rangers at Loftus Road. Leeds United and West Bromwich Albion drew 2-2.

Although they were later relegated, Tottenham Hotspur gave false hope to their supporters with a 3-2 win against Manchester United at Old Trafford in early September and Liverpool demonstrated their Championship-retaining intentions on the fourth weekend of the season when they beat Derby County 3-2.

Brighton set a then record for the most goals by one team on *Match of the Day* when they demolished York City 7-2 at the Goldstone Ground on 18 September in their Division Three encounter. Peter Ward and Ian Mellor led the way with two goals each. The following month saw Ward score four and Mellor three as they put seven more past Walsall.

The highest-scoring weekend came on 4 December when *Match of the Day* viewers were treated to 16 goals in the two featured games. A Kenny Burns hat-trick helped Birmingham City to a 6-2 away win against hapless Leicester City, while at Highbury Malcolm Macdonald was facing his old club, Newcastle, for the first time. In an epic match the Gunners ran out 5-3 winners thanks to a near inevitable hat-trick from Supermac. When he headed in his third he simply walked away, arms aloft, gum chewing, knowing he had proven a point to his former manager, Gordon Lee.

Liverpool clinched the Championship when they drew 0-0 with West Ham United on the final Saturday of the season. They lost the FA Cup Final to Manchester United but recovered to beat Borussia Mönchengladbach 3-1 in Rome

to win the European Cup for the first time. They were the first British winners since Manchester United nine years before. In June Kevin Keegan left them and joined SV Hamburg for a new British transfer record fee of £500,000.

Manchester City were second in the League, just one point behind Liverpool, with Ipswich Town third and Aston Villa fourth. Villa won the League Cup but needed two replays before finally beating Everton 3-2. Sunderland, Stoke City and Tottenham Hotspur were relegated. They were replaced by Wolverhampton Wanderers, Chelsea and Brian Clough's Nottingham Forest.

The most bizarre moment of the season came when a groundsman had to re-paint the penalty spot before Gerry Daly took the kick that ensured First Division survival for one of Clough's old clubs, Derby County.

Top Liverpool skipper Emlyn Hughes doffs his hat in celebration as the Merseysiders win the European Cup for the first time in the club's history.

Right Kenny Burns, a stalwart of the classic years of *Match of the Day*, scored a hat-trick in front of the cameras as Birmingham City beat Leicester 6-2 in December.

Martin Hopkins

Martin Hopkins was in charge of *Grandstand* and *Sports Personality of the Year* for more than two decades from the mid 1970s. As the man behind the BBC's coverage of countless Grand Nationals, Wimbledon Championships, Commonwealth Games and Olympic Games he developed a reputation as one of the world's finest producers. He was also in charge of *Match of the Day* for three seasons and directed what was probably the most famous set of opening titles in television sport.

'I wanted something different and decided to find a designer who knew nothing about football to see what they came up with. I was advised to speak to Pauline Talbot who loved the thought of the crowd at a match acting as a single emotional unit. She had been inspired by an image from years before of thousands of children in China holding up cards of Chairman Mao.

Initially I approached the army and police to see if they could provide the disciplined people who would be needed, but they both thought that it was impractical so I decided to ask some of the local schools to see if they could help.

I addressed the assemblies of the Hammersmith County Girls' School and the Christopher Wren Boys' school and hated every minute of it. I knew that I wasn't cut out for teaching. Once the schools had agreed we'd ask QPR if we could use their ground as it is right next to Television Centre. On the afternoon of filming there were two immense lines of schoolchildren snaking their way through west London, and both schools told me they had record attendance figures that day.

Because *Match of the Day* was getting ten or twelve million viewers then and they knew that they would be seen on BBC 1 every Saturday night for a whole year, every kid wanted to be in it. I had special badges made to give them at the end that said "See me on *Match of the Day*" and they were all desperate to have one.

Giant pictures of Jimmy Hill, *Match of the Day's* logo and match action had been cut into squares, each of the 2000 cards numbered and the exact location noted on a huge graph. That meant that we could call the number through the microphone if any of the cards fell out of place.

I sat with a megaphone in the stand opposite and got the children to practice a few times so that they could get the inevitable mischief out of their systems. Then, when it came to record, I became much sterner and they responded fantastically. The whole shoot was very straightforward, the children behaved themselves and thanks to Pauline's ideas the title sequence became a television legend.'

The most famous title sequence in the history of the programme featured Jimmy Hill's face and the programme logo on cards held up by the schoolchildren of Shepherd's Bush.

Manager Tommy Docherty (centre) leads the celebrations as Manchester United beat Liverpool 2-1 to win the FA Cup for the first time in 14 years. It was his last match in charge of the club.

The FA Cup

The Goal of the Season went to Terry McDermott's opening goal against Everton in Liverpool's semi-final at Maine Road. There was also controversy in that match, when the teams were level at 2-2 and Brian Hamilton had appeared to score the winning goal for Everton with just three minutes remaining.

Referee Clive Thomas disallowed it, saying that there had been an infringement, but no amount of post-match analysis by Jimmy was able to discover why. Liverpool won the replay 3-0. In the other semi-final, at Hillsborough, Manchester United reached Wembley for the second year in a row by beating Leeds United 2-1.

With John Motson commentating on the Final for the first time, all three goals came during a five-minute spell early in the second half. Stuart Pearson scored for United in the 51st minute, Jimmy Case equalized and the winner went in off a Jimmy Greenhoff deflection to give United the Cup for the first time since 1963.

1976 European Championship

Czechoslovakia won the Championship by beating West Germany 5-3 on penalties after the Final finished 2-2. The best-performing team in the UK were Wales who lost their two-legged quarter final 3-1 on aggregate against Yugoslavia. During the qualifying rounds, Malcolm Macdonald created history by scoring five headed goals for England against Cyprus at Wembley.

1977–1978

Presenter
Jimmy Hill

League Champions   Nottingham Forest

FA Cup winners   Ipswich Town

League Cup winners   Nottingham Forest

UEFA Cup winners   Liverpool

The show

This season saw *Match of the Day* celebrate its 500th edition. It was marked with a special *Radio Times* cover and a new set of opening titles with hundreds of schoolchildren holding up cards that depicted Jimmy Hill's face and the *Match of the Day* logo. After a short break David Coleman resumed commentary duties alongside John Motson and Barry Davies while Alan Weeks and Tony Gubba also featured intermittently on the show. On 14 January, Coleman was in Buenos Aires to send a live report from the 1978 World Cup draw and the season was rounded off by the Home Internationals that took on a greater importance than usual with England and Scotland about to leave for Argentina.

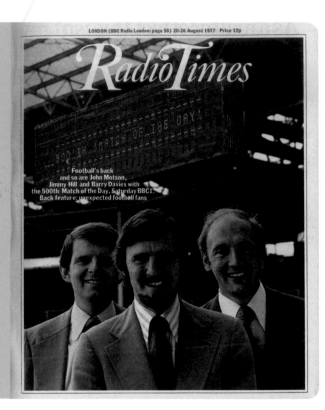

LONDON (BBC Radio London: page 56) 20-26 August 1977   Price 12p

RadioTimes

Football's back and so are John Motson, Jimmy Hill and Barry Davies with the 500th Match of the Day, Saturday BBC1. Back feature: unexpected football fans

The season

Kenny Dalglish set a new transfer record between two British clubs when he moved from Celtic to Liverpool for £440,000. He scored after seven minutes of his League debut as they drew 1-1 at Middlesbrough.

Although Nottingham Forest made an instant impact on the fourth show of the new League season when they beat Wolverhampton Wanderers 3-2 at Molineux, *Match of the Day* viewers saw only four more of their games as they sped towards the Championship in their first season in Division One.

The biggest win of the season, and a new programme record came on 22 October when the cameras visited White Hart Lane to see how Tottenham Hotspur were

doing in their fight to bounce straight back out of Division Two. They struck lucky as Bristol Rovers were on the end of a record drubbing.

New boy Colin Lee had just been signed for £60,000 from Torquay United and made quite a debut. He scored four times as Spurs put nine past the Rovers goalkeeper, 18-year-old Glyn Jones, who was playing only his third first-team match. Ian Moores also scored a hat-trick and there were goals too from Peter Taylor and Glenn Hoddle. Nine days later Jones was back playing Spurs in a reserve team game. This time it ended 1-1.

The team to follow if you wanted to see goals was undoubtedly Chelsea. Away from home they had the leakiest defence of the season and conceded 49. They did manage to go to Birmingham City and win 5-4 but lost 5-1 at Coventry City, 6-0 at Everton and 6-2 to Manchester City.

Nottingham Forest won the Championship at their first attempt, finishing seven points ahead of Liverpool and losing just three League matches. Brian Clough became only the second English manager after Herbert Chapman to take different clubs to the title. Liverpool were second, just ahead of Everton, Arsenal and Manchester City.

Forest also beat Liverpool 1-0 to win the League Cup.

Below left Tottenham's Colin Lee heads one of his four goals on his debut as Spurs put nine goals past Bristol Rovers in their Division Two match.

Below Liverpool finished the season as runners-up in the League Championship and the League Cup, but there was consolation for Merseysiders in the European Cup Final where a single goal from Kenny Dalglish against Bruges was enough to retain the trophy.

Brian Clough (right) and Peter Taylor (third left) have to enlist some help in showing off the silverware that Nottingham Forest won during an incredibly successful season for the club.

Jonathan Martin

Jonathan Martin first worked on *Match of the Day* in the late 1960s and edited the show for most of the 1970s. He was Head of BBC Sport from 1981 to 1998.

'*Match of the Day* was probably the biggest misnomer of any programme title because it frequently wasn't the best match of the day. Throughout the 1970s the selection process was hideous and we were heavily restricted by the Football League and their anti-television approach. We had to pick the games that we wanted to cover five weeks in advance, so had to guess who was going to be on form and playing well. We were also contractually obliged to show up to 20 Division Two matches a season, with eight of them placed as the main game, as well as four Division Three fixtures with a couple of them placed as the main match.

These restrictions made it very difficult, especially as, although we had the exclusive contract to broadcast highlights on Saturdays, ITV had the same arrangement for Sundays. As they were divided into regions it added to the complications. We used to take it in turns to decide who would cover which matches.

The way that it worked was that if we had first choice we would pick the first game, ITV would then pick the next three to cover Granada, Midlands and London, and we would then take our second choice, which was effectively the fifth.

It was even worse when they had first choice, as we ended up with the second and sixth preference games. It was pure luck if we ended up with the game that everyone wanted to see that night. We were very lucky and although there were a number of weekends when there would be only one goal for us to show, it wasn't until April 1978 that we had our first goalless edition.

My greatest personal memory of the programme concerned another match in the 1977–78 season when Tottenham Hotspur beat Bristol Rovers 9-0. In those days we tended to choose Liverpool against Everton whenever they clashed but we knew that there was always a high risk of it ending up 0-0.

I remember making the selection for the second game for that show and seeing that in Division Two Spurs were due to play Bristol Rovers who were languishing towards the bottom of the table. I used to check the goals columns to see who had the leaky defenses as part of my never ending quest for goals and they looked like a good bet to let a few in.

At the end of this particular edition in October the Merseyside derby had indeed finished 0-0 but we struck gold with our second choice as Spurs set a new *Match of the Day* goalscoring record and won 9-0.

My father was a great Spurs supporter so I drove home that night thinking that he must have really enjoyed the show. The next morning, however, I learned he had passed away during the night which meant that almost the last thing he would have seen in his life was his club's amazing performance on the show. That has made it a very poignant memory for me.'

It was the first time either club had reached the Final of this competition and it was finally settled by a John Robertson penalty in the second half of the replay at Old Trafford after the first game at Wembley had finished 0-0.

Consolation came for Liverpool back at Wembley when they reached their second successive European Cup Final and became the first British club to retain the trophy when they beat FC Bruges 1-0. Kenny Dalglish scored the only goal of the game.

It was also a good season for Bolton Wanderers, Southampton and Tottenham Hotspur who all returned to Division One. West Ham United, Newcastle United and Leicester City went the other way.

The FA Cup

Cup holders Manchester United were knocked out by West Bromwich Albion in a fourth round replay and the Midlands side then went on to defeat Derby County and Nottingham Forest before succumbing to Ipswich Town in a classic and bruising semi-final at Highbury.

Ipswich Town's goalscorer Roger Osborne is congratulated on his FA Cup-winning strike by John Wark (number 8) and a smiling Mick Mills.

In the fifth round, Wrexham of Division Three, who had previously beaten Newcastle United, were taken to a replay by non-League Blyth Spartans. Having overcome them 2-1 the Welsh team lost 3-2 to Arsenal in the quarter-finals. They in turn beat Leyton Orient 3-0 in the semi-final at Stamford Bridge.

Arsenal had finished fifth in Division One and took on underdogs Ipswich Town who were 13 places below them in the final table. Bobby Robson's Suffolk side dominated the game and scored the only goal. In the 77th minute, Roger Osborne beat Pat Jennings, collapsed from exhaustion and was immediately substituted but he had done enough to secure their first ever FA Cup success.

The commentators

John Motson

John Motson was born in Salford in 1945 and joined the *Barnet Press*, a weekly paper in Hertfordshire, when he was 18. Four years later he moved to Sheffield to join the *Morning Telegraph* as a sports reporter and sub-editor and he began his broadcasting doing short reports with BBC Radio Sheffield. In December 1969 John voiced his first football commentary for Radio 2, the second half of Everton against Derby County. In October 1971 he made his *Match of the Day* debut on Liverpool's 0–0 draw with Chelsea. He has subsequently commentated on hundreds of matches, including a record 25 FA Cup Finals.

'I clearly remember watching the first programme in August 1964. I was 19 years old, and working at the *Barnet Press*. I'd just come back from covering Finchley in the Athenian League and we didn't have BBC2 at our house so I went to see it on a friend's television. I don't know whether we realized then we were witnessing something that was going become an institution, but certainly I remember us being very excited.

My own introduction to the programme came when I was with BBC radio and at the 1971 FA Cup Final to do the interviews. David Coleman came round the corner and didn't stop but just said "I've recommended you to Sam Leitch". I was bewildered as I'd never met David before, but a week later, Sam, who was editor of *Match of the Day*, phoned me and said he wanted to try me out as a television commentator. It was all very secretive, and I wasn't supposed to tell anybody, but they sent me to Leeds to do a UEFA Cup tie, and I got offered a year's trial on the show.

If it didn't work out, I knew I had to go back to my old job in radio, but I didn't make the best of starts. To be honest my first two or three League match commentaries were, to say the least, a bit fitful. I remember Malcolm Allison having a go at me at Derby after they played Manchester City because he thought my report was rubbish. Then the first cup tie I got was a much-delayed replay between Hereford and Newcastle.

I got sent there on the basis that Newcastle would probably coast through and it would make three minutes at the end of the show. I drove down with Ricky George, who's still a friend of mine and was the Hereford substitute. He got the winning goal but the thing that sticks in everybody's mind is the Ronnie Radford goal, five minutes from the end.

Newcastle were leading 1–0 and suddenly the ball popped up on that very muddy surface and Ronnie hit a shot that was just out of this world. It was an incredible goal and that's what I think propelled that cup tie into FA Cup folklore.

They promoted that match to the top of the programme and featured about 40 minutes of it. I was used to getting the five-minute last match slot, but I think it convinced people that I could handle a big game. As the season wore on I got a bit more confidence and was rewarded with a permanent contract with *Match of the Day*.

Working with Jimmy Hill was both stimulating and a bit scary. There was an arrangement in those days that when the presenter had to go to a match out of London a small four-seater plane was hired by the BBC to transport presenter, commentator and producer to the game. On one particular occasion Jimmy and I were going to Everton and as we approached Merseyside the plane got caught in a terrible gale and we were swaying all over the place and nearly came down in the Mersey.

When we landed Jimmy insisted we got a couple of port and lemons down us to steady our stomachs and that was the only time in those days that I ever drank before a game. When the programme started later that evening, Jimmy's first words were, "Well you won't believe the day I've had today, my tummy's still upside down..."

Of course, he hadn't considered the current three-day week and that there was a petrol strike going on. The BBC's duty office was absolutely inundated with calls from people complaining that the BBC could afford to hire a private plane for Jimmy Hill and John Motson when they couldn't get petrol for their cars. The BBC plane was banned and never appeared again.

I've always believed in getting to the game three hours before the kick-off. I do my homework on the Friday and draw up my commentary board which I still do with felt tip pens, and stick it on a piece of card. I've never got into the computer era I'm afraid. I like to get there early as I think you can sometimes pick up information from people who are drifting around. I try to ring managers and club employees the day before to get a bit of an insight into who might be playing, then at about two o'clock I get myself down to the dressing room corridor. I'll check the teams when they go in to the referee, then go upstairs to the commentary position. At the end of the match I get myself to the nearest bar.

The first sheepskin coat I ever bought was in the seventies and it started a bit of a cult. It really reached a climax at Wycombe in 1990 with the image that everybody remembers of me in the snow. Since then of course I've changed them several times but if you walk into a big retail store in London you'd find it very difficult to buy a full-length sheepskin coat.

For a long time there was a lad in Essex who made them to measure, but then he disappeared and I had to look elsewhere. I got one from a firm in Borehamwood that was going export it to Russia, and just recently I've had two strokes of luck. I met two chaps at Tottenham who work on Saville Row and they offered to make me a coat, which God bless them, they did. It arrived on Christmas Day.

David Coleman once said to me it's about survival and I'm just lucky I've survived this long. After I'd been in the job about ten or twelve years I remember saying to myself, "Make sure your voice comes up after the music as long as you possibly can because the day it doesn't is the day your career will end." I've been lucky really to have been around all these years.'

1978–1979

Presenter
Jimmy Hill

League Champions Liverpool

FA Cup winners Arsenal

League Cup winners Nottingham Forest

European Cup winners Nottingham Forest

The show

In November ITV signed a secret three-year, £5 million deal with the Football League to show edited highlights on Saturday nights instead of Sundays in an attempt to break away from the joint negotiating strategy and replace *Match of the Day*. The previous deal had been worth £420,000 a season but Michael Grade and John Bromley outflanked the BBC to announce the new package.

The BBC were furious and the battle between the two companies took place on the front pages of the national newspapers under the headline 'Snatch of the Day'. Jimmy Hill claimed that the Football League lacked integrity, while Alec Weeks, the producer of football, declared, 'We are not downhearted and we are not beaten yet.'

Indeed they weren't and a ruling by the Office of Fair Trading prevented ITV's exclusive contract being signed. For the duration of the next four-year contract, it was agreed that the BBC and ITV would have to alternate their programme coverage, with *Match of the Day* switching to Sunday afternoons for the 1980–81 and 1982–83 seasons.

The season

Liverpool started their pursuit of the Championship in fine style with a 4-1 win over Manchester City in front of the cameras at Maine Road. A fortnight later the top-scoring game came from Second Division Burnley as they beat West Ham United 3-2.

The highest-scoring matches to be filmed came on consecutive weekends in December, courtesy of the previous season's FA Cup finalists. On 23 December, Tottenham Hotspur fans were left demoralised after Arsenal's visit to White Hart Lane when they went away 5-0 winners, thanks to an Alan Sunderland hat-trick and others by Liam Brady and Frank Stapleton. Although Spurs were featured six times there were no goals from their new star signings, Argentinians Osvaldo Ardiles and Ricky Villa.

The following weekend it was the turn of Ipswich Town to shine. They entertained Chelsea at Portman Road and

Tottenham manager Keith Burkinshaw shows off his new Argentinian stars Ricky Villa (left) and Osvaldo Ardiles fresh from their World Cup exploits during the summer.

In a season of firsts for Nottingham Forest: Brian Clough was the first manager to pay £1 million for a player when he bought Trevor Francis (left); and Viv Anderson became the first black player to appear for England in November 1978.

beat them 5-1. It was another bad season for Chelsea who won only five matches, conceded 92 goals and finished in bottom place. As well as their East Anglian embarrassment, Middlesbrough beat them 7-2 and Nottingham Forest put six past their defence.

The first domestic £500,000 transfer saw David Mills move from Middlesbrough to West Bromwich Albion in January, and he helped them to third place in the League. A month later Brian Clough doubled that fee and made front page headlines by purchasing Trevor Francis from Birmingham City for £1 million. It put a great deal of pressure on the 24-year-old but he repaid Clough's faith by helping Forest to second place in Division One and scoring the winning goal in the European Cup Final.

It was also his European debut, and when Forest beat Malmo 1-0 in Munich it meant that the trophy stayed in England for a third consecutive year and confirmed

Clough's status as one of the great managers.

Forest also became the first club to retain the League Cup when they beat Southampton 3-2 at Wembley. Clough asked his assistant, Peter Taylor, to lead the team out and then celebrated their win in his own unique style. While the players went to a nightclub the Clough family went home, bought fish and chips, put the cup on top of the TV set and watched *Match of the Day*.

Bob Paisley was an equally satisfied manager as he saw Liverpool regain the Division One Championship with a record 68 points, having lost only four games. They managed it by scoring 85 goals, conceding only 16, and using just 15 players.

Chelsea were joined in the drop to Division Two by Birmingham City and Queens Park Rangers. Crystal Palace, Brighton & Hove Albion and Stoke City won promotion.

Billy Connolly

The set formula of *Match of the Day* meant there was rarely room for a non-footballing guest but on one show this season the editor, Jonathan Martin, made an exception. Alongside Jimmy Hill and Tony Gubba was a rising star of British comedy, Billy Connolly, who described himself as a Celtic supporter with Partick Thistle sympathies. Connolly was in London to play in a five-a-side competition at the Empire Pool Wembley where his team-mates were Elton John, Rod Stewart, Bill Oddie and Dennis Waterman.

Scotland manager Ally MacLeod tries to explain how his team lost to Peru, drew with Iran and then beat Holland. Despite Archie Gemmill's famous goal against the eventual runners-up, Scotland failed to get past the first round.

The FA Cup

There was very little FA Cup action seen as *Match of the Day* only covered two games from each of the third and fourth rounds this season. The cameras were, however, at Villa Park in March to see last year's losing finalists, Arsenal, return to Wembley. They defeated Wolverhampton Wanderers 2-0 with goals by Frank Stapleton and Alan Sunderland.

Manchester United beat Liverpool 1-0 in the other semi-final after a replay at Goodison Park having drawn the original match at Maine Road 2-2.

In the Final, Brian Talbot, who had helped Ipswich to win the Cup the previous year, opened the scoring for Arsenal in the 12th minute, and just before half-time they added a second when Liam Brady's cross was headed home by Frank Stapleton. The trophy looked certain to return to Highbury as the score was still 2-0 with just four minutes left on referee Challis's watch, when suddenly the match exploded into life. Gordon McQueen's close-range shot

In one of the most exciting FA Cup Finals for many years, Arsenal were 2-0 up at half time, Manchester United scored twice in two minutes to bring the scores level and then a minute later Arsenal's Alan Sunderland (right) met a cross from Graham Rix to make the final score 3-2.

pulled a goal back to give Manchester United hope and then two minutes later the Arsenal side was thrown into turmoil when Sammy McIlroy put the ball past Pat Jennings to equalize.

Liam Brady, who had been involved in both Arsenal goals, led one final surge forward and sent the ball out to Graham Rix on the left. His cross was met by Alan Sunderland who scored the winning goal – the third in three minutes – to secure an incredible victory for the north Londoners.

1978 World Cup

The only British representatives were Scotland, managed by the wildly over-optimistic Ally MacLeod. Although they beat Holland, one of the favourites, they failed to get past the first round by losing to Peru and drawing with Iran. A thrilling Final saw the host nation, Argentina, beat Holland 3-1, with Mario Kempes scoring twice.

1979–1980

Presenter
Jimmy Hill

League Champions Liverpool

FA Cup winners West Ham United

League Cup winners Wolverhampton Wanderers

European Cup winners Nottingham Forest

The show

Mike Murphy was the new editor of *Match of the Day* having originally begun his career as Jimmy Hill's junior assistant at LWT. He tried to introduce a re-mixed version of the theme tune but hadn't reckoned on the good-natured hostility to it from Jimmy and Bob Wilson, who campaigned on air for viewers to write in and complain.

For the first time *Match of the Day* was allowed to screen additional games, and on 13 weekends there were highlights from three different matches. Bob Wilson and Tony Gubba were still presenting the news round-ups – Bob presented the occasional show as well – and David Coleman also made a few appearances during the season as a commentator. The one new name on the rota was that of Desmond Lynam from Radio Sport and he presented several of the news slots early in 1980.

The season

As the new footballing decade arrived transfer fees began to spiral out of control. Manchester City continued the trend in September when they broke the record and paid Wolverhampton Wanderers £1.4 million for Steve Daley. Wolves then in turn paid Aston Villa £1.5 million for Andy Gray while later in the season, Kevin Reeves became Manchester City's second million pound man.

Match of the Day's season began in style with the Charity Shield, when Liverpool beat Arsenal 3-1. Terry McDermott scored twice and Kenny Dalglish added the third.

On 27 October, 19-year-old Billy O'Rourke made his goalkeeping debut for Burnley at Loftus Road in front of the *Match of the Day* cameras. After slipping to let in the first goal he must have thought that things would improve. They didn't and he conceded six more as QPR won their Second Division game 7-0. Also on the show that night was Manchester City's 4-0 home defeat to Liverpool.

The match of the season came in February when Liverpool travelled to Carrow Road. David Fairclough, who was usually referred to as their 'super-sub' began the game against Norwich City and scored a hat-trick, which on any other weekend would have made the headlines.

Justin Fashanu stole his thunder, however, when he flipped the ball up, turned and sent an exquisite left-footed volley into the top left corner of the net, past a diving Ray Clemence. It was voted Goal of the Season but didn't affect the result. With the game tied at 3-3, Kenny Dalglish and Jimmy Case scored two late goals to keep Liverpool on top of the table.

The only other hat-trick on the show that season came in April from Andy Ritchie when Manchester United beat

Wolverhampton Wanderers' winning goalscorer Andy Gray celebrates with the League Cup.

Tottenham Hotspur 4-1 at Old Trafford. Ray Wilkins completed the scoring with Ossie Ardiles replying for Spurs. Manchester United could field a side that was packed with internationals, and they performed strongly on the programme winning five and drawing two of the games in their nine appearances.

It wasn't enough to catch Liverpool, however, who retained the title with 60 points, two ahead of Manchester United. Ipswich Town came third and Arsenal fourth. The final *Match of the Day* of the League season featured both the crucial games as Manchester United lost 2-0 at Leeds United and Liverpool clinched the Championship at Anfield by beating Aston Villa 4-1.

Above Norwich City's Justin Fashanu spins, shoots and scores *Match of the Day's* Goal of the Season against Liverpool in February. Unfortunately for the Canaries, Liverpool's David Fairclough scored a hat-trick and goals from Dalglish and Case saw the Reds run out 5-3 winners.

Below Nottingham Forest's Trevor Francis (left) is tracked by Liverpool's Alan Hansen. These two teams dominated British football during the late 1970s and early 80s and produced several classic encounters for the cameras over the years.

Nottingham Forest finished fifth in the League but retained the European Cup by beating Kevin Keegan's SV Hamburg 1-0 on an emotional night in Madrid. John Robertson scored the only goal to ensure that the trophy would be returning to the City Ground.

Arsenal were not so fortunate in the European Cup-Winners' Cup Final. Having lost the FA Cup Final to West Ham United just four days earlier, they were beaten by Valencia in Brussels. The match was still goalless after extra time but the Spaniards won the penalty shoot-out 5-4.

One trophy that Forest failed to retain was the League Cup. They did manage to reach their third successive Final but lost 1-0 to Wolverhampton Wanderers. A mistake by Peter Shilton gave Andy Gray an easy chance to score.

Having won two League Championships in the 1970s Derby County found themselves starting the new decade in Division Two alongside Bolton Wanderers and Bristol City. There were celebrations, though, at Leicester City, Birmingham City and Sunderland who all returned to the top division.

Right Martin O'Neill's performances played a major part in Nottingham Forest's success in both domestic and European competitions under Brian Clough.

Spin-offs

To celebrate the 30th anniversary of the show John Motson produced a special book that listed the complete record of all the matches broadcast on *Match of the Day* to that point.

With the increased success of the show the inevitable spin-offs began and in this decade that meant an annual. The *Match of the Day* annuals ran from 1979 to 1982 with a brief revival in 2001, linked into the monthly magazine of the same name that ran for several years in the late 1990s.

The annuals followed the standard format of presenter and commentator interviews, player profiles, club features, quizzes and of course, many pages of photos. Many other branded items have appeared over the years including board games, diaries, photo sets and even a *Match of the Day* piggy bank.

The most successful offshoots were the videos that have focused on the many great moments shown across the years. They have come out in multiple formats based around clubs, players and decades.

Trevor Brooking (left, on the ground) heads the only goal of the FA Cup Final for Second Division West Ham against Arsenal. They became the lowest-placed team to collect the trophy since Wolves in 1908.

The FA Cup

Arsenal became the first side since Blackburn Rovers in 1886 to reach the FA Cup Final for a third successive year but they did it the hard way taking an energy-sapping four attempts to get past Liverpool in the semi-final. They drew 0-0, 1-1 and 1-1 before a Brian Talbot goal finally separated the teams at the end of the third replay, just nine days before the Final itself.

At Wembley, Arsenal met West Ham United who had also needed a replay to get past Everton in their semi-final. The Hammers had finished seventh in Division Two and when a famously rare header from Trevor Brooking proved to be the only goal of the match they became the lowest-placed club to collect the trophy since Wolverhampton Wanderers in 1908. It was their second win in five years and one of their team, Paul Allen, was just 17 years and 256 days old when he collected his medal.

Alan Hardaker retired as secretary of the Football League after a 22-year reign. Although he supported the concept of televised football he had proven himself to be a very tough and often difficult negotiator, as the many memos and letters in the BBC archive confirm. As secretary since 1957 he oversaw the creation of *Match of the Day* and devised the League Cup competition. He once said that if the FA Cup Final was football's equivalent of Royal Ascot then the League Cup Final was its Derby day.

Goal of the Season
Justin Fashanu for Norwich against Liverpool, Division One, February 1980

Footballer of the Year
Terry McDermott, Liverpool

European Footballer of the Year
Karl-Heinz Rummenigge, Bayern Munich

PFA Player of the Year
Terry McDermott, Liverpool

PFA Young Player of the Year
Glenn Hoddle, Tottenham Hotspur

1980–1981

Presenter
Jimmy Hill

League Champions   Aston Villa

FA Cup winners   Tottenham Hotspur

League Cup winners   Liverpool

European Cup winners   Liverpool

UEFA Cup winners   Ipswich Town

The show

After 16 seasons in the Saturday night slot, *Match of the Day* moved to Sunday afternoons with Jimmy Hill and Bob Wilson presenting from a blue and yellow set. With new titles, short-sleeved, open-necked shirts and a 5 p.m. start the programme worked in the same way but felt very different.

Jimmy, for one, enjoyed the new routine as it reminded him of his previous role working on LWT's *The Big Match* when he would finish the show and go for a Guinness by the river with Brian Moore. For the production team it was a nuisance as they had to work for the whole of the weekend and try to develop a different style. Bob Wilson remembered that the editor, Mike Murphy, deliberately started looking for news stories that would be ahead of the Monday papers, rather than just reflecting on the stories that had appeared in the Sunday papers.

Steve Archibald (left) and Garth Crooks combine to set up another chance for Tottenham against Arsenal. The pair scored 47 times between them during a prolific season at Spurs.

The season

The opening programme saw Tottenham Hotspur beat the European Champions, Nottingham Forest 2-0, after Glenn Hoddle's penalty sent Peter Shilton the wrong way and Garth Crooks showed great solo skill in the box. It was the first of 47 goals that he and strike partner Steve Archibald were to score in a prolific season for the pair.

There were now highlights of three games every weekend and although the majority, 64, were from Division One there were also 19 from Division Two, eight from Division Three and two from Division Four.

One of the Division Two games was arguably the match of the season and came in October when Chelsea beat Newcastle United 6-0. Colin Lee, who had scored four goals on his Spurs debut three years before, completed a hat-trick but Chelsea managed just 40 goals in their other 41 matches and finished mid-table. Their manager, Geoff Hurst, was sacked and replaced by John Neal.

Kevin Keegan returned to England to prepare for the 1982 World Cup and joined the growing army of veteran players at Southampton. With Alan Ball, Dave Watson, Mick Channon, Charlie George and Chris Nicholl, manager Lawrie McMenemy had assembled one of the most experienced teams in the country and they had a good season, finishing in sixth place.

Bryan Robson was leading the way at West Bromwich Albion who won 3-2 at Spurs and beat Manchester United 3-1 at The Hawthorns. They, along with Liverpool, Ipswich Town and Aston Villa, were the leading teams throughout the season and all regularly featured on the show.

At Christmas, Liverpool and Aston Villa were level on 34 points with Ipswich in third place on 33, although Bob Paisley's team had played two more games. Aston Villa then had a crucial week in early January. They lost to Ipswich in the FA Cup but beat Liverpool 2-0 in the League, with goals by Peter Withe and Dennis Mortimer. Unlike his rival managers, Ron Saunders now had no cup distractions and could focus his team solely on the League.

Villa beat Middlesbrough 3-0 to set up an amazing final few days as they had 60 points from 41 games while Ipswich had 56 from 40.

On the final full weekend Saunders knew that unless Ipswich won it was all over. Aston Villa lost 2-0 to Arsenal but to John Motson's amazement, the Villa fans began cheering and celebrating. They had heard Middlesbrough had beaten Ipswich meaning that Villa were Champions for the first time since 1910.

Ipswich were runners-up, but beat AZ 67 Alkmaar 5-4 on aggregate to lift the UEFA Cup, largely thanks to 14 goals from their Scottish midfielder John Wark. Other League placings saw Arsenal come third and WBA fourth, with Liverpool taking fifth place.

It was the first time in nine seasons that Liverpool had finished outside of the top two but the club still collected two major trophies. The first came in March when they beat West Ham United 2-1 to win the League Cup after a replay, but the European Cup was the main prize. Liverpool won it for the third time in their history when Alan Kennedy scored the only goal in the match as they beat Real Madrid 1-0 in Paris.

Aston Villa players celebrate their title victory despite losing 2-0 at Highbury on the season's final day.

The FA Cup

For BBC viewers the FA Cup began earlier than ever before: the *Match of the Day* cameras were at Harlow Town to see them lose 2-0 in their first round match against Charlton Athletic.

Manchester City had installed John Bond as their new manager and in the fourth round he saw them put six goals past his old club Norwich City. Appearing on *Match of the Day* proved to be a lucky omen and with the cameras present each time, they beat Peterborough United and Everton in the next two rounds and Ipswich Town in the semi-final at Villa Park.

Meeting them at Wembley were Tottenham Hotspur who had needed a replay to get past Wolverhampton Wanderers in their semi-final. With two Argentinians in the Spurs side the media focus during the pre-match build-

Clive Allen

It was an extraordinary year for Clive Allen who had ended the previous season with Queens Park Rangers as the League's top goalscorer. In June he became the first million-pound teenager when Arsenal paid £1.2 million for the 19-year-old. However, he was then sold for the same fee to Crystal Palace just a few weeks later where he joined Terry Venables.

During the course of the season, Allen played under four managers as Venables was succeeded by Ernie Walley, Malcolm Allison and Dario Gradi.

None of them could halt Palace's terrible form and they were relegated as the bottom club, having won only six games and claiming just 19 points. Allen scored only nine League goals but he was at the centre of a famous incident that resulted in goal nets being redesigned.

Palace were playing Coventry City at Highfield Road in September on their first appearance of the season on *Match of the Day*. Allen clearly scored from a free-kick, but as the ball went into the net it bounced back off the stanchion. It was so fast that the officials thought it had hit the bar, so no goal was given, despite the entire Palace team's protest. Jimmy Hill, who was also the Coventry chairman, proved it to be a goal in the analysis that evening, but by then Palace had already lost 3-1.

Ipswich Town's John Wark(left) heads the only goal of the UEFA Cup semi-final against Cologne. Wark's 14 goals in the competition were largely responsible for the East Anglian club's European triumph.

up had mainly been on Osvaldo Ardiles, especially after the obligatory Cup Final single was released.

'Ossie's Dream', recorded with Chas and Dave, proved to be one of the most successful football records of all time, reaching number five in the charts and earning the entire squad an unforgettable place on *Top of the Pops*. On the day of the Final the family of the new singing sensation, and that of his team mate Ricky Villa, were interviewed live by Barry Davies as part of the build-up. Few guessed it would be Villa who would leave the biggest mark on the competition.

John Bond and Keith Burkinshaw led their teams out twice as the first match ended 1-1 after extra time, meaning that in the year of the hundredth Final, a replay was needed. It was a reprieve for two men in particular. Manchester City's Tommy Hutchison had opened the scoring with a diving header, but was later in despair after being credited with an own goal when the ball was deflected by his shoulder past Joe Corrigan to bring the scores level. Ricky Villa had trudged disconsolately away from the first game, having been substituted but when the match was replayed five days later he scored twice to give his adopted north London fans their first FA Cup celebration party since 1967.

The replay produced five goals, with two of them coming in the opening ten minutes when Villa put Spurs ahead

and Steve Mackenzie levelled with an outstanding volley. In the second half Kevin Reeves scored from the penalty spot for Manchester City before Garth Crooks equalised in the seventieth minute.

Seven minutes later Ricky Villa won Spurs the Cup and secured his place in FA Cup history. He weaved through the Manchester City defence to score a brilliant solo goal and enable Steve Perryman to climb the steps and lift the trophy.

1980 European Championship

England reached the finals by winning seven and drawing one of their eight qualifying matches. They scored 22 goals with Kevin Keegan and Bob Latchford responsible for half of them, but were unable to make it past the group stage in Italy. In the Final, West Germany beat Belgium 2-1.

Fact file

Ron Saunders famously used only 14 players all season as Aston Villa won the League Championship. Des Bremner, Gordon Cowans, Ken McNaught, Tony Morley, Dennis Mortimer, Jimmy Rimmer and Kenny Swain played in all 42 games. The other seven were Gary Shaw (40) Allan Evans (39) Peter Withe (36) Gary Williams (21) Colin Gibson (19) David Geddis (8) and Eamonn Deacy (5).

Goal of the Season
Tony Morley for Aston Villa against Everton, Division One, February 1981

Footballer of the Year
Frans Thijssen, Ipswich Town

European Footballer of the Year
Karl-Heinz Rummenigge, Bayern Munich

PFA Player of the Year
John Wark, Ipswich Town

PFA Young Player of the Year
Gary Shaw, Aston Villa

Tottenham's Ricky Villa rounds off his brilliant run in the FA Cup Final replay against Manchester City by slipping the ball past City keeper Joe Corrigan to score the winning goal.

1981–1982

Presenter
Jimmy Hill

League Champions   Liverpool

FA Cup winners   Tottenham Hotspur

League Cup winners   Liverpool

European Cup winners   Aston Villa

The show

The programme returned to its rightful place in the Saturday night schedules for the 1981–82 season. Only two games per show were allowed, but a wide spread of teams were covered. In all 49 different League clubs were seen in action. Liverpool were featured most often and appeared ten times. Manchester City were seen on nine occasions, Manchester United on eight and Swansea City on seven.

The fans of Brighton and Hove Albion had to wait until 27 February to see their side, while Coventry City, despite the presence of Jimmy Hill on the programme, appeared just once.

The season

John Toshack had taken Swansea City from Division Four to Division One in just five seasons and they were featured on the first *Match of the Day* of the series. Bob Latchford was a recent signing from Everton and he scored three as the Welsh side beat Leeds United 5-1. They were also on the following week's show but this time lost 4-1 to West Bromwich Albion following a brilliant hat-trick by Cyrille Regis.

Swansea's Bob Latchford (number 10) scores one of his three goals as the Swans beat Leeds 5-1 on the first day of the season.

Kenny Dalglish raises his arms in celebration as Mark Lawrenson scores for Liverpool against Spurs at Anfield. Liverpool's 3-1 win clinched their fifth Championship in seven years.

At Manchester United, Ron Atkinson was given access to the Old Trafford cheque book as the club tried to restore some of its former glory. Frank Stapleton was bought from Arsenal for £1.1 million in August and in October, Bryan Robson moved to United for a new British record fee of £1.5 million. Brian Clough was also dealing in seven-figure sums at Nottingham Forest, taking Justin Fashanu to the City Ground for £1 million and then selling Trevor Francis to Manchester City for the same amount.

At Christmas Swansea were top, just ahead of Manchester United and Ipswich, with Liverpool languishing in 12th place, nine points behind the leaders. On Boxing Day they were beaten 3-1 at Anfield by Manchester City and their season looked to be over. The same could be said for any potential singing career that Jimmy Hill and Bob Wilson had in mind when they ended the show surrounded by a school choir and singing specially written lyrics to the *Match of the Day* theme tune. It wasn't a hit.

That game did, however, prove to be a turning point for Bob Paisley's side and having beaten Swansea 4-0 a week later in the FA Cup third round, they embarked on an astonishing period of League success, losing only two of their remaining 25 matches.

Everything hinged on the final weekend and the *Match of the Day* cameras were at both of the vital games. Peter Davenport's hat-trick condemned Ipswich to a 3-1 home defeat against Forest while goals from Mark Lawrenson, Kenny Dalglish and Ronnie Whelan helped Liverpool to a 3-1 win against Spurs to clinch the title four points ahead of Ipswich with Manchester United third.

Liverpool had taken 63 out of a possible 75 points to charge up the table and win the Championship for the fifth time in seven seasons. Swansea finished a respectable sixth.

At the bottom of Division One it was a bad season for Middlesbrough, Wolverhampton Wanderers and Leeds United who were all relegated. It seemed incredible that Leeds and Derby County, who had been Champions in 1974 and 1975 respectively, would now be meeting each other in Division Two. Promoted in their place were Luton Town, Watford and Norwich City. Martin O'Neill had captained the Canaries to ten wins in their final eleven games to just scrape into the top three.

Liverpool won a second trophy by successfully defending the League Cup in its first season as the Milk Cup. They beat Spurs 3-1, but only made it as far as the quarter-finals in the European Cup. That trophy did, however, stay in England for a sixth consecutive season when Aston Villa beat Bayern Munich 1-0 in the Final. Ron Saunders had resigned as manager earlier in the campaign because he felt that there was too much interference in his running of the club. Tony Barton had been promoted from chief scout to take his place.

Striking for soccer

When three points were introduced for a win this season it was the culmination of a long campaign by Jimmy Hill. As well as introducing many innovations at the various clubs he was involved with Jimmy had made a number of suggestions that proved to be well ahead of their time.

In his book *Striking for Soccer*, which was published in 1961, he advocated major changes to the game calling for smaller divisions and a Super League to feature the greatest players.

He also suggested a winter break, and argued that in the future, clubs would have to be run as businesses while the matches would need to be presented rather than just staged. He also recommended that all managers and referees should go on training courses and gain specialist qualifications to help improve the game.

As for television, Jimmy wrote that he wanted to see one game brought forward to the Friday night and televised; that seats, restaurants and bars should be put into grounds and that floodlights should be used to stage midweek evening games. All of this was eventually implemented.

STRIKING FOR SOCCER by Jimmy Hill

21-year-old Gary Lineker scored Leicester City's fifth goal as they beat Shrewsbury Town 5-2 in the FA Cup sixth round.

Villa's triumph in Rotterdam was largely thanks to the heroics of the reserve goalkeeper Nigel Spink. The former Chelmsford City player had made only one first-team appearance when he came on in the tenth minute of the Final to replace the injured Jimmy Rimmer. He kept a clean sheet while Peter Withe, who had previously won the competition with Nottingham Forest, scored the only goal of the game.

The FA Cup

In the sixth round Leicester City against Shrewsbury Town produced seven goals and yet two goalkeepers kept clean sheets. After Shrewsbury took a 2-1 lead, injured Leicester goalkeeper Mark Wallington was replaced by striker Alan Young. After the home team equalised, Young was involved in a collision and had to hand the keeper's jersey to winger Steve Lynex. Ten minutes later Young felt fit enough to resume, Lynex set up the third Leicester goal and they went on to win the match 5-2. The final goal was scored by a new 21-year-old striker called Gary Lineker.

That proved to be the end of their Cup success that season, however, as they lost the semi-final 2-0 to Spurs at Villa Park. In the other game Terry Venables led Queens Park Rangers to their first ever FA Cup Final when they beat West Bromwich Albion 1-0 at Highbury.

West Bromwich Albion's Cyrille Regis, seen here in action against Manchester United, scored this year's Goal of the Season in the FA Cup fifth round tie against Norwich City.

For the second year running the Final went to a replay and Spurs emerged the winners. Terry Fenwick and Glenn Hoddle were the scorers in the first game and Hoddle added a second in the replay when his sixth-minute penalty sent Peter Hucker the wrong way to enable Spurs to retain the trophy. It was their seventh FA Cup win.

The big difference this time was that Osvaldo Ardiles and Ricky Villa were missing from the Spurs line-up because of the Falklands conflict. Ardiles had returned to Argentina having been booed during the semi-final, and Keith Burkinshaw decided not to play Villa even though he had stayed with the club.

1982–1983

Presenter
Jimmy Hill

League Champions   Liverpool

FA Cup winners   Manchester United

League Cup winners   Liverpool

European Cup-Winners' Cup winners   Aberdeen

The show

Match of the Day was back on Sundays, but with only two matches per programme as they entered the third year of the contract with the Football League. A new area of contention came with the issue of shirt sponsorship, which gave both the BBC and ITV a major problem. Up until that point only two-and-a-half square inches had been allowed for a sponsor's logo.

With football entering an increasingly commercial age and the clubs desperate to obtain more money from their sponsors, the broadcasters relented and eventually a deal was done. Under the new agreement they could have up to 16 square inches on each shirt but with the lettering restricted to no more than two inches in height. The days of the classic sponsor-free strips were gone forever.

Liverpool manager Bob Paisley retired at the end of the season. With 13 major trophies in nine years, Paisley was one of the most successful managers in the history of English football.

The season

Kevin Keegan needed a new challenge and moved down a division from Southampton to Newcastle United. On his first appearance in front of *Match of the Day* cameras he scored four as they went to Rotherham United and won 5-1. Two weeks later they were featured again but saw the scoreline reversed when they met Fulham at St James' Park.

Ian Rush was the new goalscoring hero at Anfield and ten of Liverpool's games were televised during the season. These included their demolition of Everton at Goodison Park in November when Rush scored four in their 5-0 win. It was the first Merseyside derby hat-trick since 1935. In the same match Glenn Keeley was sent off on his Everton debut after just 32 minutes for a professional foul on Kenny Dalglish and never played for the club again.

Watford were also going well in their first season in Division One and were seen on *Match of the Day* two weeks later when two penalties by Luther Blissett and goals from John Barnes and Les Taylor saw them defeat Brighton and Hove Albion 4-1. Interviewed after the game their manager Graham Taylor said that he was proud that his team had an old fashioned and unsophisticated style. He denied that there was anything 'kick and rush' about them. At the end of the year Liverpool were on 40 points, five ahead of Manchester United and Nottingham Forest, with Watford in fourth place.

Liverpool won their third consecutive League Cup when they beat Manchester United 2-1 after extra time in the Final. Alan Kennedy and Norman Whiteside had made it 1-1 when Ronnie Whelan's brilliant curling shot secured victory. An emotional Bob Paisley, who had announced his retirement at the end of the season, was told by his team to go and collect the trophy which he did with a scarf draped around his neck.

David Pleat leaps from the dugout at the start of his famous run onto the Maine Road pitch as Luton's last day victory against Manchester City kept them up in the top flight.

In the League, Liverpool stormed away from the pack and won the title with five games to go. They finished 11 points clear of Watford, and the *Match of the Day* cameras followed Paisley onto the pitch as Graeme Souness held the championship trophy up to the crowd and handed it over to his manager. Paisley had won 13 major trophies in nine years, including six Championships and three European Cups.

It was an amazing season for Watford, run by Graham Taylor and Elton John, who were runners-up. In 1976 when Elton took over as chairman they had been mid-table in Division Four. Behind them were Manchester United, Tottenham Hotspur and Nottingham Forest. Watford striker Luther Blissett finished as the season's leading goalscorer with 27 in the League.

The other end of the table produced an incredible climax to the season. Luton, in their first year after promotion, went to Maine Road knowing that they had to win to stay up. Manchester City were also in danger of relegation, but a draw would see them safe. With less than five minutes to go, and the score still 0-0, Luton boss David Pleat sent on substitute Raddy Antic who promptly scored. At the final whistle, Pleat ran leaping and clapping across the pitch in a brown suit with light brown shoes, pausing briefly only to button his jacket.

Manchester City, despite their big money signings, were relegated with Brighton and Swansea. Wolverhampton Wanderers returned at their first attempt and were joined by Queens Park Rangers and Leicester City.

The only British success in Europe came when Aberdeen beat Real Madrid 2-1 in extra time to win the European Cup-Winners' Cup.

The FA Cup

Manchester United reached the Final after beating Arsenal 2-1 at Villa Park. At Wembley they met Brighton and Hove Albion, who had already been relegated from Division One and were looking to salvage something out of a wretched season by reaching their first ever Final.

Led by manager Jimmy Melia they had won their semi-final 2-1 against Sheffield Wednesday at Highbury, and with a dramatic flourish, flew to Wembley in a helicopter on the morning of the Final.

Perhaps this season is best remembered at Watford where, under the guidance of chairman Elton John and manager Graham Taylor, the team finished as Division One runners-up with Luther Blissett as top scorer with 27 goals.

Although Manchester United won the FA Cup beating Brighton 4-0 in a replay, this year's competition is probably more famous for Gordon Smith's point blank miss in extra time of the first match. With the score 2-2 and just the keeper to beat Smith (centre) fluffed his chance and Brighton's titanic efforts seemed to go to waste.

After 14 minutes Gordon Smith headed the underdogs into a surprise lead but that was wiped out early in the second half by Frank Stapleton, who, following his transfer from Arsenal, became the first player to score in the FA Cup Final for two different clubs.

Ray Wilkins's goal gave Manchester United the advantage and they looked set for victory, but just three minutes from the end Gary Stevens equalized to force extra time. In the final minute of the additional half hour Brighton had a chance to write themselves into FA Cup history. But Smith, with just the goalkeeper to beat and right in front of the goal, blew his chance and both teams returned five days later for the replay.

United totally dominated the second encounter and won the match 4-0. Their captain, Bryan Robson, scored twice while Norman Whiteside and Arnold Muhren added the others. Such was the confidence of the United team that they let the Dutchman score from a penalty when he had never taken one for them or indeed for his previous club, Ipswich Town.

1982 World Cup

England made a dream start to their World Cup campaign when Bryan Robson scored against France after just 27 seconds and they easily qualified for the second stage. Having drawn 0-0 with West Germany they needed to beat Spain 2-0 to reach the semi-finals. Despite bringing on Trevor Brooking and the previously injured Kevin Keegan, the match ended goalless and England went out of the tournament unbeaten. Northern Ireland, surprisingly, topped their group in the first stage but Scotland failed to reach the second round. Italy won their third World Cup when they beat West Germany 3-1 in the Final in Madrid. Paolo Rossi was their star player, scoring six goals in the finals.

Newcastle United try to take advantage of the new TV guidelines on shirt sponsorship as Kevin Keegan sports a new 16 square inch sponsor's logo for a famous local brewery.

The pundits

Garth Crooks

Garth Crooks was born in 1958 and played for Stoke City before moving to Tottenham Hotspur in 1980. There, he built a reputation as a prolific goalscorer, winning two FA Cups and the UEFA Cup. After a brief spell with Manchester United he spent two seasons at West Bromwich Albion and three with Charlton Athletic before retiring in 1990. He was Chairman of the PFA from 1988 to 1990. Since joining the BBC in 1990 Garth has worked on *Match of the Day* and 'Football Focus' as well as many other major sporting events.

'As a boy my early memories of *Match of the Day* are heart-breaking, having to watch Stoke City twice being beaten in the semi-finals of the FA Cup. I always longed to be associated with the competition and I finally got the chance in my first season with Spurs in 1981. We reached the semi-final against Wolves and were leading 2-1 when Kenny Hibbitt dived and Clive Thomas gave a penalty. It was like being a kid again as I relived the nightmare and was convinced that the curse of Stoke had struck. We drew 2-2, but I couldn't watch the show that night. We won the replay four days later, however, and I scored twice which meant I was

I try not to stitch them up but I also have to remember that I am a journalist and make sense of what is happening at the ground and in the changing rooms so that I can convey that to the viewers. It means that I sometimes have to decide what was on and what was off the record as sometimes players take me so much into their confidence that I have to make a judgement on their behalf.

What is special about the BBC is that they respect that. The Sports Department have an approach, almost an unwritten rule, that you are expected to respect the interviewee and give them the BBC treatment.

In my playing days, I always used to watch the show on a Saturday night before going out. To score when the *Match of the Day* cameras were there was great, and to be Goal of the Month was a big deal. I remember being so envious when Justin Fashanu got the award. I won it twice and it was very special. The first was a volley against Everton and the second was a header against Wolves, both at White Hart Lane. Overall, the best memory for me would be the 1981 Cup Final replay when we beat Manchester City 3-2 and I scored the second goal. I know the show wasn't called *Match of the Day* that night, but it was the same show in spirit, and for me that took some beating.'

interviewed by Bob Wilson. It was the first time I had been on, but there was a freezing wind that made my eyes water and as I was trying to talk I kept worrying that everyone would think I was crying! That was my debut on the show.

When I moved to London I started working with Capital Radio, and when I was left out of the 1982 World Cup squad, the BBC asked if I'd join their panel. I worked with David Coleman, Lou Macari and Lawrie McMenemy, which was a great experience. It was a fantastic introduction to TV and the editor, Mike Murphy, gave me a great deal of help and advice. It was a tough baptism but even at the age of 22, it left me in no doubt that I wanted my future to lie in television as a reporter.

When I first began in that role I used to get very nervous, and it's only recently that I have conquered this. Coming to terms with the nerves, especially at press conferences, was a battle but I just love being involved and being at the grounds with the teams before, during and after the games. It is such a privilege to be able to share those moments with the players. Nothing can replace playing but this comes very close, especially when the guys confide in you. *Match of the Day* is still a special show to so many of them, exactly as it was when I was playing.

1983–1984

Presenter
Jimmy Hill

League Champions   Liverpool

FA Cup winners   Everton

League Cup winners   Liverpool

European Cup winners   Liverpool

UEFA Cup winners   Tottenham Hostspur

The show

Match of the Day was back on Saturday nights as a highlights show, but was supplemented by live matches on Friday evenings. The BBC and ITV had been allocated seven games each with the commercial channel choosing to broadcast theirs on Sunday afternoons.

It was a radical change in strategy by all involved, as prior to this new two-year contract the only regular live football had been the FA Cup Final, England playing Scotland and the European Cup Final.

Times were changing though and a new brand of younger businessmen were getting involved with the top sides. Tottenham Hotspur became the first British club to float on the Stock Exchange when they were valued at just over £9 million. The shares were four times oversubscribed and the process wiped out the club's debt, to the delight of their new chairman, Irving Scholar.

Match of the Day was cancelled from 15 October to 19 November because of strike action at the BBC.

The season

The first League afternoon of the new season was warm, sunny and full of goals. *Match of the Day* featured Aston Villa beating West Bromwich Albion 4-3 and newly promoted Queens Park Rangers losing 3-1 at Manchester United.

Arsenal's new young star was a 21-year-old Scot called Charlie Nicholas who had joined them from Celtic amid massive publicity. Viewers saw him for the first time on 10 September when, despite the hype, Arsenal were beaten 2-0 by Liverpool at Highbury with goals by Kenny Dalglish and Craig Johnston.

One of the surprises of the season came when manager Bobby Gould brought in the English Dance Theatre to help Coventry City's players with mobility and balance. It seemed to pay off when they beat Liverpool 4-0 at home in December, with a hat-trick from Terry Gibson past a bearded Bruce Grobbelaar.

The same weekend saw another manager fail to dance his way out of trouble when West Ham United beat Arsenal 3-1. After seven years in charge at Highbury, Terry Neill was sacked and replaced by Don Howe.

Yet again Ian Rush produced a great performance for *Match of the Day* when his hat-trick secured victory for Liverpool at Aston Villa during a live match in January. Liverpool were top of the table by then and easing towards another title assisted by a prolific goalscoring record at Anfield.

They beat both Notts County and Coventry 5-0 and put six past West Ham and Luton with Rush scoring five against David Pleat's men. Tony Woodcock also scored five in one match when Arsenal beat Aston Villa 6-2. Lawrie McMenemy

Arsenal's new signing from Celtic, 21-year-old Charlie Nicholas, signs autographs at the club's pre-season photocall.

Liverpool players celebrate as Phil Neal (centre, arms raised) gives them the lead in the European Cup Final against Roma. The match ended in a 1-1 draw and the Reds won the trophy after a penalty shoot-out.

was the longest-serving manager in Division One and as part of a superb season Southampton produced the highest scoring performance when they beat Coventry 8-2.

Everton had been having a bad season and Howard Kendall was on the verge of the sack when they recovered from 1-0 down in a League Cup quarter-final match at Oxford United thanks to a late goal by Adrian Heath. It proved to be the turning point they needed and Everton reached Wembley for the first all-Merseyside Final. Liverpool won, for the fourth consecutive season, but Everton were back on track and Kendall made an inspired signing when he bought Andy Gray from Wolverhampton Wanderers.

Having already collected one trophy, Liverpool secured the Championship when they drew 0-0 at Notts County on the last weekend of the season and in doing so became the first team to win three titles in a row since the Arsenal side of the 1930s. Rush finished the season with 48 goals and made it six years of never having been on a losing Liverpool side when he scored.

They rounded off an incredible first year for their new manager, Joe Fagan, by winning their fourth European Cup. AS Roma were beaten on penalties after goalkeeper Bruce Grobbelaar fooled around with wobbly legs on the goal line to try and put them off. It worked. Alan Kennedy hit the winning penalty and Graeme Souness lifted their third trophy of the season.

In the League they finished three points ahead of Southampton with Nottingham Forest third and Manchester United fourth. It was a bad year for the Midlands as Birmingham City, Notts County and Wolves were all relegated and replaced by Chelsea, Sheffield Wednesday and Newcastle United.

With First Division football secured, Kevin Keegan retired from Newcastle aged just 33. His last League game was against Brighton and *Match of the Day*'s cameras followed him onto the pitch at St James' Park as he played for the final time. Having been present at his league debut when he scored for Liverpool, it was fitting that the show should be there to record his farewell. He produced an inevitable goal in their 3-1 win.

Sportscene

Scottish football fans have had their own separate football show broadcast on the BBC on Saturday nights. It began on 20 March 1958 as *Sportsreel* and usually consisted of about 20 minutes of action from Scottish matches. In 1974 the programme changed its title to *Sportscene* and has broadcast continuously, regardless of the contract situation with *Match of the Day*. It has traditionally had more action and less comment and has often also broadcast an edit of one of the main games featured on *Match of the Day*. In 2004 the BBC lost the rights to show league football but, as with *Match of the Day* in the lean years, the title will remain for cup action.

On the same day another English hero, Trevor Brooking, also retired having spent his entire career with West Ham United.

In the UEFA Cup Final Tottenham Hotspur beat Anderlecht on penalties when substitute goalkeeper Tony Parks became an instant hero by saving a crucial spot-kick. Steve Burkinshaw then left the club because of problems he was having with the board, having been their most successful manager since Bill Nicholson.

The FA Cup

The first live FA Cup tie on the BBC as part of the new contract and took place at Anfield on 6 January when Liverpool beat Newcastle United 4-0. Two of the goals came, inevitably, from Ian Rush with the others scored by Michael Robinson and Craig Johnston.

A the same stage in the competition Cup holders Manchester United made a shock exit when they were knocked out by lowly Bournemouth. Harry Rednapp's

Everton celebrate with the FA Cup after beating Watford 2-0 in the Final – it was the first piece of silverware won by the blue side of Liverpool since 1970.

Division Three team beat them 2-0 in one of the biggest ever FA Cup upsets.

Graham Taylor's Watford, who had been in Division Four just six years before, first demonstrated their form in front of the cameras in the sixth round when a brace from John Barnes helped them to a 3-1 away win over Birmingham City. In the semi-final at Villa Park only a goal by George Reilly put them past Plymouth Argyle who were bidding to become the first team ever to reach the Final from Division Three.

In the second semi-final Adrian Heath scored the only goal of the match as Everton beat Southampton 1-0 after extra time at Highbury. This gave manager Howard Kendall the chance to lead out his team at Wembley and take some silverware back to the blue side of Liverpool for the first time since they won the League in 1970.

With Watford's chairman Elton John looking on in the stands, Everton won 2-0 to lift the trophy for the first time since 1966. For the third season in a row the losing League Cup finalists had found consolation by winning the FA Cup.

The BBC were finally allowed to transmit a League match live, a mere 45 years after they had first requested permission from the Football League. Then, they had wanted to broadcast the game between Arsenal and Derby County on 14 September 1938, but the clubs passed a resolution refusing to allow their matches to be televised despite there being fewer than 4,000 television sets able to receive the pictures. The BBC were eventually granted permission to cover a game live and on 16 December 1983 viewers saw Manchester United beat Spurs 4-2 (below). The world did not end.

Goal of the Season
Danny Wallace for Southampton against Liverpool, Division One, March 1984

Footballer of the Year
Ian Rush, Liverpool

European Footballer of the Year
Michel Platini, Juventus

PFA Player of the Year
Ian Rush, Liverpool

PFA Young Player of the Year
Paul Walsh, Luton Town

1984–1985

Presenter
Jimmy Hill

League Champions   Everton

FA Cup winners   Manchester United

League Cup winners   Norwich City

European Cup-Winners' Cup winners   Everton

The show

The show celebrated its 20th anniversary with matches still being broadcast on Fridays as it was felt that the highlights format was beginning to look tired.

Most other sports were now seen live on television so the production team wanted to continue the football experiment as well. Jonathan Martin, the Head of Sport, recalled that the experiment was disappointing.

'We only got six or seven million viewers on Friday nights which was poor for the slot, so we moved to Sundays in the following year.'

This was to be the last time that *Match of the Day* contained weekly League highlights until the beginning of the 1992–93 season.

The season

As the season began, a number of the best-known British players moved abroad. Graeme Souness had left Liverpool for Sampdoria, Liam Brady joined Juventus and Ray Wilkins was in Milan. Although the trend was for our top stars to go to Europe, a few were coming the other way including the Danish pair Jan Molby at Liverpool and Jesper Olsen who moved to Manchester United.

In the first live *Match of the Day* of the season Kevin Richardson's goal for Everton at Chelsea set them off towards the Championship. A few weeks later they

Everton's Graeme Sharp (left) scores with a magnificent volley during the Merseyside derby at Anfield in October. Mark Lawrenson can only admire the technique.

Sunderland's Barry Venison (number 2), David Hodgson (number 9) and Chris Turner (number 1), and Norwich City's John Deehan (on the ground, right), watch as the ball goes wide during a disappointing League Cup Final. A shot by Asa Hartford was deflected into the Sunderland net to win the match for the Canaries.

consolidated their early form when they won the Merseyside derby at Anfield 1-0.

Liverpool had a poor start to the season and won just one of their first five matches, while Everton marched relentlessly toward the title. On the way they beat Manchester United and Nottingham Forest 5-0, Newcastle United 4-0 and defeated Watford 5-4 at Vicarage Road. The highest-scoring match came in September when Newcastle travelled to Queens Park Rangers. At half-time the visitors led 4-0 but an incredible comeback by the home team saw the match finish at 5-5.

Tottenham Hotspur were without Glenn Hoddle and

Osvaldo Ardiles who both had long-term injury problems, but Micky Hazard proved to be a strong replacement in their midfield, and scored when Spurs went to Nottingham Forest in November and won 2-1.

In December two goals by Mark Falco in a televised match helped Spurs win 3-1 at Newcastle, and by Christmas they were level with Everton at the top of the table.

On 16 March Spurs managed to end a 72-year jinx when they beat Liverpool at Anfield for the first time since 1912. Garth Crooks scored the only goal of the match to help finally re-write the record books.

Double impact

Football was hit by two major disasters in 1985. On 11 May, the last day of the season, Bradford City were celebrating their Third Division Championship when fire broke out in a wooden stand during their match against Lincoln City. On that tragic afternoon, 56 people died. In Birmingham on the same day, rioting Leeds supporters injured nearly 100 police officers and caused a wall to collapse, killing a boy.

Just a fortnight later on 29 May, 39 supporters died and more than 400 were injured in a riot at Heysel Stadium in Brussels, just before Liverpool were beaten in the European Cup Final 1-0 by Juventus. Poor policing, a dilapidated stadium, lack of segregation, alcohol-fuelled supporters and trouble between fans produced devastating results. The FA withdrew English teams from European competition and football seemed to some to be on an unstoppable slide. It would get worse before it got better.

The charred remains of the main stand at Valley Parade, home of Bradford City, after a fire swept through it during the last match of the season, leaving 56 people dead and many others injured.

In April Tottenham lost 2-1 at home to Everton, which gave Howard Kendall's team a four-point lead at the top of the table and a month later they clinched the title when they beat QPR 2-0. Everton ended the season with 90 points, 13 ahead of Liverpool and Spurs, with Manchester United in fourth place.

Everton's next stop in a remarkable season was the European Cup-Winners' Cup Final in Rotterdam. Having seen off Bayern Munich in a tough semi-final they beat Rapid Vienna 3-1 to clinch their first ever European trophy.

In a clean sweep of awards, Peter Reid was named PFA Player of the Year, Neville Southall won the Football Writers' award and Howard Kendall was voted Manager of the Year.

Jimmy Hill had been at Wembley to present *Match of the Day* live from the League Cup Final earlier in the season as Norwich City beat Sunderland 1-0. Despite their cup form both teams were relegated at the end of the season along with Stoke City who had managed only three wins and conceded 91 goals to finish bottom.

Oxford United, Birmingham City and Manchester City all won promotion from Division Two. Oxford appeared twice on *Match of the Day* and, thanks to their young striker John Aldridge, provided viewers with great entertainment. In November he scored three as Oxford demolished Leeds 5-2, and in April he hit another hat-trick as part of their 5-2 win over Oldham Athletic.

The FA Cup

In the quarter-finals Norman Whiteside's hat-trick helped Manchester United to a 4-2 win against West Ham United and in the semi-final they beat Liverpool 2-1 in a replay after the original match had finished 2-2.

Everton were still chasing a treble but found themselves 1-0 down against Luton in the other semi-final when Ricky Hill got the opening goal. Kevin Sheedy's famous left foot and an extra-time strike by defender Derek Mountfield saw them through to the Final. It was one of 14 goals that he scored that season.

When Howard Kendall led Everton out at Wembley on 18 May to try and retain the FA Cup, his team were already League Champions and winners of the European Cup-Winners' Cup; but they were unable to complete their treble.

Not even the sending off of Manchester United's Kevin Moran in the 78th minute could help a tired Everton. It was the first dismissal in the history of the Cup Final and came when Peter Reid was denied a goalscoring opportunity. Moran was still able to collect a winner's medal, though, after Norman Whiteside scored the only goal of the match. It was a curling shot that went beyond the reach of Neville Southall's dive with just ten minutes of extra time remaining.

1984 European Championship

Although England lost just one of their eight qualifying games they failed to progress to the finals in France. Their highest score came in December at Wembley when Luther Blissett scored a hat-trick as part of their 9-0 win against Luxembourg. France beat Spain 2-0 in the Final with goals by Michel Platini and Bruno Bellone. In five matches Platini scored nine goals and completed two hat-tricks.

Manchester United's goalscorer Norman Whiteside celebrates their FA Cup victory with team-mate Kevin Moran. Moran had been sent off in the second half for a foul on Peter Reid – he was the first player ever dismissed in an FA Cup Final.

Fact file

On 8 December in the first round of the Scottish Cup, Stirling Albion set a new record for the biggest first-class score of the century in Britain when they beat Selkirk 20-0. The Selkirk goalkeeper, Richard Taylor, was thought to have had a good game and prevented the score from being much higher. Stirling Albion lost 2-1 to Cowdenbeath in the next round.

Goal of the Season
Graeme Sharp for Everton against Liverpool, Division One, October 1984

Footballer of the Year
Neville Southall, Everton

European Footballer of the Year
Michel Platini, Juventus

PFA Player of the Year
Peter Reid, Everton

PFA Young Player of the Year
Mark Hughes, Manchester United

Gerald Sinstadt

Gerald Sinstadt was born in Kent in February 1930, completed his National Service in the Intelligence Corps. and was seconded to forces broadcasting in Europe. He first joined the BBC in 1959 when he succeeded David Coleman in Birmingham as a producer, reporter and manager before moving to London. He later worked for Anglia and Granada as a commentator and presenter. In the early 1980s Gerald decided on a complete change of direction and spent three years working on Ballet and Opera with the National Video Corporation.

'I was invited by Alec Weeks to go to the 1982 World Cup as a commentator, and followed that with the 1984 Olympics, where I described Steve Redrave's first gold medal. At about the same time I asked the BBC if I could have some more regular work and within a week was seconded on to 'Focus' to do a feature on the state of the game. I followed this with a match report on *Grandstand*, live from Liverpool, before being asked to dub the goals round-up that evening. I was then invited into the 'Focus' meeting on the following Tuesday and didn't look back for the next 20 years!

I did a lot of third matches on *Match of the Day* as I had joined behind Barry, John and Tony, but I also covered many games for *Sportsnight* and did a lot of the round-ups. Initially we always had to name every player who touched the ball, but I thought this overcomplicated matters, so I set out to simplify the information for the viewer. I found that the key was to allow room for the pictures to breathe by adding a bit of colour and general background. The secret was to hit the important name at the right moment.

As well as studio-based round-ups I always loved to be out at the games and get as close to the action as possible. I must have worked on hundreds of matches at a huge variety of grounds and venues. My favourite commentary positions were at Highbury and Goodison Park before it was redeveloped. The right location tends to be high enough to see the pattern of play develop but low enough to see the

The ladder was then taken away until the end of the game, so if we needed the loo it was tough.

When I first joined the BBC we had the budget and facilities that were so much greater than those at ITV, where a lot of very good producers did their best within great constraints. Suddenly I found that the speed and standards that people worked to were immense, but the guys who deserve so much of the credit are the assistant producers, then and now. They and their VT editors have the skills to make us commentators look good even when we are off form.

I remember leaving one match feeling I'd had a very bad day. I'd been off the pace, said things I shouldn't have, not said things that I should have and drove home feeling very miserable. One of the young assistant producers, Ken Burton, had been logging the match back at Television Centre and did a great job of rescuing my efforts.

When I sat down to watch the show that night it was with some trepidation, but I was relieved and amazed to see that it looked and sounded fine. That was down to Ken and I have always had tremendous respect for the producers and editors in the football unit at the BBC. They are the real unsung talent who have helped create the show that we all love and are now celebrating as it reaches its 40th anniversary.'

expression on people's faces. After Goodison was rebuilt, it became one of the worst to reach and I had to go right up the top through the main stand, up a ladder, across the roof, lift up a trapdoor and then go down another ladder into the gantry. I can assure you that it is not much fun on a rainy night.

The worst commentary position I ever encountered was the old one at Maine Road. They used to put a ladder in the paddock that was so high it used to bounce like a trampoline. I would climb up, briefcase in one hand, to a crow's-nest halfway up a pillar. Then it was a second ladder to the top and a walk across a catwalk to the commentary position.

1985–1986

Presenter
Jimmy Hill

League Champions Liverpool

FA Cup winners Liverpool

League Cup winners Oxford United

The show

In 1985 the television rights came up for renegotiation and the BBC and ITV offered £16 million for four years. This was in return for 19 live games plus weekend highlights. The Football League met on Valentine's Day and rejected it.

Robert Maxwell, the Oxford chairman, described it as 'mad, bad and sad' as the clubs felt their product was worth far more. Saatchi and Saatchi were appointed to carry out an in-depth analysis of the game and its worth, and valued the contract at many times greater than had been offered.

Football was, however, in a weak negotiating position as the game was rife with hooliganism, and the two sides became deadlocked. The result was a total black-out for the first part of the season which annoyed fans and concerned the sponsors.

The Football League finally backed down and agreed a deal that gave them less money per game than before on a short-term, two-and-a-half-year contract. The remaining six months were worth £1.3 million with a two-year £6.2 million extension confirmed in June. The supporters were delighted and *Match of the Day* resumed in January. It concentrated mainly on FA Cup highlights and the occasional live League match on a Sunday.

The season

The contractual stalemate in the first part of the season meant that very few people witnessed Manchester United's amazing start as they won their first ten matches to secure a nine-point lead over Liverpool by the end of September.

Live football returned in January and Jimmy Hill opened the first *Match of the Day* of the year by saying: 'Football is back on television at the start of a year of renewed hope and determination on all sides to restore the game to health and strength.'

Editor Bob Abrahams selected Watford against Liverpool as the first league game of the season and the future Champions won 3-2. Six days later came the first Saturday night highlights show for many months. In an unusual pro-

Never mind a captain's role, in his first season as player-manager Kenny Dalglish registers his delight as he scores the only goal of the game at Chelsea to secure Liverpool's eighth title in 11 seasons.

With English clubs banned from European competition, domestic trophies came under the spotlight. In a surprising League Cup Final Oxford United beat QPR 3-0 to win the club's first ever major prize. Here (from left) David Langan, Jeremy Charles (with trophy) and John Trewick take part in the lap of honour.

grammc, all three featured matches resulted in away wins. Gary Lineker scored both Everton's goals as they won at Birmingham City; Chelsea put three past West Bromwich Albion and Nottingham Forest beat Manchester United 3-2.

When United went to Anfield in February they drew 1-1 with Liverpool but it was nearly a month before the next *Match of the Day*. Liverpool featured again, this time beating Spurs 2-1 at White Hart Lane thanks to goals by Ian Rush and Jan Molby.

Away from the cameras they were scoring heavily and beat Birmingham City, Coventry City and Ipswich Town 5-0, and also put six past Oxford United. The two highest scores of the year came when Luton Town beat Southampton 7-0 and West Ham United won 8-1 against Newcastle United. Frank McAvennie and Tony Cottee were on prolific form for West Ham that season and scored 53 goals.

On the last weekend of the season Jimmy had the Canon League Championship trophy in the studio as the three teams in with a chance of the title all won their final matches. A Lineker hat-trick helped Everton to a 6-1 win over Southampton at Goodison Park; West Bromwich Albion went down 2-3 at home to West Ham but Kenny Dalglish's volleyed goal in the Chelsea box saw Liverpool win 1-0 to clinch their 16th League Championship. It was his first year as player-manager and their eighth title in 11 seasons. Everton were runners-up, two points behind, with West Ham third.

Ipswich Town, Birmingham City and West Bromwich Albion were relegated, Albion having won just four matches. Norwich City and Charlton Athletic were promoted and Wimbledon completed their astonishing journey from non-League to Division One in nine years.

Jock Stein

Scotland's manager, Jock Stein, collapsed and died from a heart attack towards the end of their World Cup qualifier against Wales at Ninian Park on 10 September. He was 62. They drew the match 1-1 and Alex Ferguson temporarily took charge to see Scotland beat Australia in the play-offs and reach the Mexico finals.

Stein began his managerial career in 1960 with Dunfermline, winning the Scottish Cup with them before joining Hibernian and moving on to Celtic in 1965. Together they won an unprecedented ten Championships, eight Scottish Cups and six League Cups during a 13-year spell. Stein's greatest season was 1967 when Celtic became the first British side to win the European Cup as well as collecting all three domestic trophies. He moved to Leeds United in 1978 but, just 44 days, later was appointed manager of Scotland.

Swansea had performed a similar feat when they went from Division Four to the top of the League, but that journey had now reversed. They were relegated out of Division Three having finished sixth in the top flight just four seasons before.

The season began with all English clubs banned from taking part in the three European competitions as a direct result of the Heysel tragedy, so the only other major competitions were the FA Cup and the League Cup. In a surprising League Cup Final, Oxford United beat Queens Park Rangers 3-0 to lift their first major trophy.

The FA Cup

The BBC's semi-final saw Everton beat Sheffield Wednesday 2-1 after extra time at Villa Park. It meant that Howard Kendall could lead his team out at Wembley for a third successive year. His opposite number was Kenny Dalglish who had just clinched the League title. Two goals from Ian Rush had enabled Liverpool to defeat Southampton in their semi-final at White Hart Lane.

The all-Merseyside Final was a sell-out and the cameras spotted dozens of frustrated fans scaling the Wembley walls, desperate to get into the ground as hundreds waited outside. Those inside saw Gary Lineker open the scoring for Everton in the 28th minute with his 40th goal of the season.

Ian Rush equalized in the 57th minute, Craig Johnston put Liverpool ahead six minutes later and Rush scored a third just before the final whistle. They were only the third team of the century to complete the Double following Tottenham Hotspur in 1961 and Arsenal in 1971.

Liverpool's Ian Rush scores his team's third goal minutes from time to make it 3-1 in the all-Merseyside FA Cup Final. Their FA Cup triumph was the second part of a double this season as Liverpool became only the third team to achieve this feat during the 20th century.

Fact file

When West Ham United beat Newcastle United 8-1 in April, Alvin Martin achieved the unique distinction of scoring a hat-trick against three different goalkeepers. His first goal came against Martin Thomas, who was then injured and replaced by Chris Hedworth. He let in Martin's second before being replaced by Peter Beardsley who conceded the third.

Goal of the Season
Bryan Robson for England against Israel, friendly international, February 1986

Footballer of the Year
Gary Lineker, Everton

European Footballer of the Year
Igor Belanov, Dynamo Kiev

PFA Player of the Year
Gary Lineker, Everton

PFA Young Player of the Year
Tony Cottee, West Ham United

1986–1987

Presenter
Jimmy Hill

League Champions   Everton

FA Cup winners   Coventry City

League Cup winners   Arsenal

The show

With highlights out of fashion there were only 14 editions of *Match of the Day* all season for Bob Abrahams and his team and the only League action came in the seven live games on Sunday afternoons. BBC viewers did get to see the FA Cup and League Cup Finals, but no League action was seen after March and very few clubs were featured in the coverage.

Clive Allen of Tottenham Hotspur scored 49 goals this season including this one against Chelsea at Stamford Bridge. Allen's total was a new club record.

The season

It was a year of change as second substitutes and play-offs were introduced. These were to help reduce Division One from 22 to 20 and meant the team that finished just above the relegation zone in the top three divisions would have to compete against the third, fourth and fifth-placed sides in the division below to determine the final promotion or relegation spot.

Wimbledon, who had been promoted to the top flight at the end of the previous year, found themselves top of the League at the beginning of September, just nine seasons after they were playing non-League football.

The first *Match of the Day* came on 21 September when Everton beat Manchester United 3-1. A week before, Brian Clough's Nottingham Forest had made their ambitions clear when they beat Aston Villa 6-0. They also scored heavily against Chelsea when they won 6-2 at Stamford Bridge.

The second programme wasn't until 2 November when West Ham United beat Everton 1-0, but the big story of the month came at Old Trafford when Ron Atkinson was sacked as manager after five and a half years in charge. He was replaced by Aberdeen's Alex Ferguson, and in the same month Arsenal moved to the top of the table after their 4-0 win at Southampton.

The best televised League match was on 7 December when eight million viewers saw Tottenham Hotspur travel to Manchester United. Norman Whiteside and Peter Davenport put the home team two-up at half-time, but a reply from Gary Mabbutt started the Spurs fightback. An own-goal by Kevin Moran and a third from Clive Allen put the visitors ahead before Davenport's penalty made it 3-3. Allen had an incredibly prolific year and ended the season with 49 goals, seven more than Jimmy Greaves' old club record.

In the penultimate televised League match of the season,

Arsenal's two-goal hero Charlie Nicholas holds up the League Cup after the Gunners' 2-1 victory over Liverpool at Wembley.

Paul Davis and Tony Adams scored when Arsenal won 2-1 at Tottenham Hotspur in January.

Everton were steady rather than spectacular and took the lead in the title race on 4 April when they beat Chelsea 2-1. They eventually finished nine points clear of Liverpool to lift their second Championship trophy in three years, but their neighbours did gain some satisfaction when they beat them 3-1 at the end of April. Spurs were third and Arsenal, who had enjoyed a 22-match unbeaten run, were fourth. Forest finished in eighth place.

Liverpool were also runners-up in the League Cup, this time to Arsenal, who won the Final 2-1. Ian Rush put Liverpool ahead in the 24th minute, but two goals from Charlie Nicholas gave Arsenal the victory. It ended Liverpool's amazing 144-match and seven-year record of never losing a game when Ian Rush scored. Earlier in the competition they had set a new goalscoring record by beating Fulham 10-0.

Having secured the Championship, Howard Kendall resigned as Everton manager and took over at Athletic Bilbao. His assistant, Colin Harvey, replaced him at Goodison Park. Dave Bassett left Wimbledon after taking them to sixth in Division One in their first season. He moved to Watford to succeed Graham Taylor who had surprisingly taken over at relegated Aston Villa. They had gone down with Leicester City and Manchester City. Derby County and Portsmouth were promoted.

Keith Houchen dives to head Coventry's equalizer and *Match of the Day*'s Goal of the Season against Spurs in an exciting FA Cup Final. An own goal by Gary Mabbutt during extra time ensured that the Sky Blues won their first major trophy eventually winning the match 3-2.

Albert Sewell

Albert Sewell, the legendary football statistician, is the longest serving member of the regular *Match of the Day* team having been recruited in 1968 when the show first became a studio-based programme.

Born in 1927 Albert left school at Christmas 1943 and started his first job as a messenger in the sports room of the *Daily Sketch*. He regularly finished his shifts at 2 a.m. before taking the night bus back to Walthamstow in the East End of London as the bombs and V2s were dropping.

'I joined the Press Association as a trainee journalist after the war and then spent two years in the RAF on national service. I then joined a company called Programme Publication who launched the first football match programmes. Previously fans had only been able to purchase small pamphlets, but Chelsea sold the new versions and despite their 6d price, they were a great success. In 1949, a year after it was launched, I became editor of Chelsea's programme and continued writing it until 1978.

Reg Hayter had left the Press Association to set up his own agency and he asked me to become his Saturday afternoon stringer at Chelsea as I was always there. In 1956 he offered me a job as a regular staff football reporter.

In 1968 Sam Leitch asked me to join the 'Football Preview' and *Match of the Day* teams as part of a revamp to compete with ITV. Sam and I had known each other around Fleet Street for many years and with David Coleman moving into the studio as the new presenter, Sam wanted someone on-hand to chase the late football stories.

I would come in on a Saturday morning to work on *Grandstand*, then, after Sam had presented 'Football Preview', the forerunner to 'Football Focus', we would get in a car and go to one of the London matches. At the end of the first half Sam would leave to get back in time to do his one-minute report live on *Grandstand* alongside Frank Bough and I would stay and phone through the details of the rest of the game just before he went on air. Once, when Chelsea won 6-0 he missed all the goals, so I rapidly had to send him the scorers and times.

I have been incredibly lucky to have worked with so many great presenters, commentators and pundits but only became better known when Des devised the tag 'Our Man Albert' during his time in the presenter's chair. I suddenly found I had kids knocking on my door on Sunday mornings asking for autographs.

My main role is to provide notes, facts and statistics to the production and presentation teams ahead of each match, and even though I've been doing it now for 36 years I still enjoy it. I have a lot of letters to reply to, answer questions on the 'Ask Albert' section of the BBC Sport website and I love working with each new generation of young people on the show. It is inspiring to work with them, especially now that I am the oldest on the programme. My wife Betty has been very patient because with all my football jobs she's been a Saturday night widow for over 50 years.'

The FA Cup

ITV had both semi-finals this season as Coventry City reached Wembley for the first time by beating Leeds United at Hillsborough. Tottenham Hotspur reached their third Final in seven seasons when they inflicted a 4-1 defeat on Watford.

At Wembley, Clive Allen headed Spurs into the lead after just two minutes but Coventry quickly equalized through Dave Bennett. A shot by Gary Mabbutt was then deflected in by Brian Kilcline just before half-time to take David Pleat's team into the break with a 2-1 advantage.

After 63 minutes a diving header by Keith Houchen forced the match into extra time, then it was Mabbutt's turn to be on the wrong end of a cruel deflection when the ball struck his knee and looped over Ray Clemence.

It was Coventry's first major trophy, but for Spurs it was to be a frustratingly empty season after they finished third in Division One and were semi-finalists in the League Cup.

1986 World Cup

The finals were staged in Mexico and resulted in mixed fortunes for the British teams. Scotland and Northern Ireland both failed to win a group match and England scraped into the second round thanks to a hat-trick against Poland by Gary Lineker. Having overcome Paraguay 3-0 they were beaten in the quarter-final 2-1 by Argentina after Diego Maradona scored two of the most memorable goals in World Cup history. The first came in the 51st minute when he palmed the ball past Peter Shilton with what he later claimed was the 'hand of God'. Then just four minutes later he completed an outstanding solo run by scoring one of the best goals of all time. In the final Argentina met West Germany and, having squandered a two-goal lead, they won 3-2 when Jorge Burruchaga scored with six minutes remaining.

Maradona's 'hand of God' pushes the ball over Peter Shilton's head and into the England net to give Argentina the lead in their World Cup quarter-final clash.

The pundits

Sir Trevor Brooking

Trevor Brooking was born in Barking in October 1948, joined West Ham United in 1965 and stayed for his entire career. By the time he retired from their midfield in 1984 he had played more than 600 matches; won the FA Cup in 1975 and 1980 and been capped 47 times by England. In 1984 he joined the BBC's television and radio teams and stayed for 20 years until taking up a new post at the FA as Director of Football Development. In June 2004 he received a knighthood in the Queen's Birthday Honours list.

'In 1964 I was still going to watch West Ham with my dad and brother and had just started to talk to the club about playing for them. To be able to see football on *Match of the Day* in the evening after going to a match was great. Before that I had only seen the occasional European match on television.

Once the programme became established on BBC1 everyone involved in football watched it, and it became a ritual. It was also the only chance that we had to take a look at the opposition and work out the strengths and weaknesses of their individual players. At that time we didn't have videos of them all to watch before a game, so *Match of the Day* was valuable as well as exciting.

As a player you have to do interviews and post-match features and that was my first involvement away from the pitch in the 1970s. Our then captain, Billy Bonds, was reluctant to appear in front of the media so he'd ask me to do it for him, and I guess that led to me becoming the public face of West Ham.

As I enjoyed the media work, I started appearing as a studio pundit for England games after I had retired from the international scene in 1982. When I stopped playing in 1984 my main stepping stone was working for Radio Sport, which was then on Radio 2. I was incredibly lucky to learn the craft by working as a summarizer alongside the legendary commentators Peter Jones and Bryon Butler.

I next began doing the same on television and that included the occasional studio spot as well. I worked on the 1986 World Cup coverage and everything developed from there.

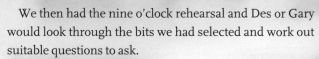

We then had the nine o'clock rehearsal and Des or Gary would look through the bits we had selected and work out suitable questions to ask.

It's difficult sometimes because the edited game might only be ten minutes long. Then there are just three or four minutes of comment to get our points across, and that time might be reduced if something else runs long. The irony was that everyone thought the show was recorded, and even today 90 per cent of the people I speak to don't believe it's live!

Nothing can ever match the adrenalin of playing in a big game, or the satisfaction of getting a result, but a live *Match of the Day* can come pretty close sometimes – especially on a big FA Cup or England match.

The best game I have worked on was the win in Germany in 2001 – a massive game for John Motson and me. It was a momentous performance that no-one had anticipated, especially after we conceded that early goal. To end up 5-1 was unbelievable and Mots was flying. When we got back we were told that the commentary had really added to the occasion, which was a great feeling.'

I know I became known for sitting on the fence, but when I started I knew all the players and didn't want to embarrass them. Over time, as I no longer had the close involvement with them, I adapted my style, but have never wanted to be overly critical. I think you lose the respect of players if you just go for point-scoring rather than being constructive.

On Saturdays the production team would always gather in a special room at Television Centre to watch all the matches on a bank of monitors. Each of the pundits would be assigned a main game to look at and maybe then a player or pattern would develop as we all sat and watched. I would look for a theme, such as striker who was pushing for a place in the England team. I'd listen to fans as I travelled to get feedback on what they'd like to see, and try to include questions such as why a particular team was leaking goals.

I always knew what I wanted to say by the end of the match. I'd make notes and would go up to VT and spool the tapes up and down myself and double-check my notes.

1987–1988

Presenter
Jimmy Hill

League Champions   Liverpool

FA Cup winners   Wimbledon

League Cup winners   Luton Town

The show

The focus was still on the big clubs and the shows were very irregular. They followed the same format as the previous year with a mixture of live League games on Sunday afternoons and highlights shows for the FA Cup.

Everything changed with the launch of satellite TV. British Sky Broadcasting wanted to buy football rights and in May they bid £9 million per season over ten years. The BBC and ITV bid together, offering less, but just when the Football League looked as though they were going to agree the BSkyB deal, the chairman of ITV Sport Greg Dyke negotiated directly behind the backs of the BBC.

In June he invited representatives from Arsenal, Tottenham Hotspur, Manchester United, Liverpool and Everton to a secret lunch in Knightsbridge. ITV wanted live Sunday afternoon football and offered to buy each club individually for £1 million.

Dyke then courted other clubs to try and form a super league, and in the following week it became public knowledge that ITV had bid for the original five plus Nottingham Forest, Newcastle United, Sheffield Wednesday, West Ham United and Aston Villa.

BSkyB and the BBC put in a counter-offer, forcing ITV to switch tactics and bid for all the clubs in the League, offering £11 million a season. On 8 August the League chairmen voted to sell all their matches exclusively to ITV from 1988, leaving the BBC and BSkyB with the FA Cup and England Internationals. This was Jimmy Hill's final season as presenter after a record 15 years in charge of the show.

A season without silverware meant that new faces arrived at Liverpool. Manager Kenny Dalglish signed (left to right) Peter Beardsley from Newcastle, John Barnes from Watford and John Aldridge from Oxford. It worked immediately as they scored 28 goals between them in nine games.

The season

Liverpool's failure to win any trophies in the previous season led to Kenny Dalglish opening his chequebook. Having sold Ian Rush to Juventus, he signed John Barnes from Watford, Peter Beardsley from Newcastle United and Oxford United's prolific goal machine and Ian Rush lookalike, John Aldridge. It seemed to work, as they scored 28 goals in their first nine games and matched Leeds United's record of going 29 Division One matches without defeat.

Two goals from Mark Stein (right) helped Luton Town beat holders Arsenal in the League Cup Final.

They beat Watford 4-0 in November, moved to the top of the table and remained there for the rest of the season. Oxford were involved in many of the season's highest scoring games. They lost 7-4 and 5-2 against Luton Town, drew 4-4 with Chelsea and went down 5-3 to Nottingham Forest and 5-2 against Wimbledon. It was no great surprise that they finished bottom.

In the Football League's centenary season, Third Division Gillingham produced the highest League score since 1964 when they beat Chesterfield 10-0 on 5 September.

In December Nigel Clough delivered one of the best individual performances of the season when he completed a hat-trick inside four minutes at the end of Nottingham Forest's 4-0 win against Queens Park Rangers. It had been a strong title challenge by Forest but their season fell away in April when they lost 5-0 to Liverpool at Anfield.

Liverpool finally lost their unbeaten record when Everton beat them 1-0. It was their first loss in 30 games but made no difference to the outcome of the Championship – they secured their 17th title when Beardsley scored the only goal of the match against Spurs on 23 April.

Manchester United came second, nine points behind, with Nottingham Forest third and Everton in fourth. Watford and Portsmouth were automatically relegated with Oxford, and fourth from bottom Chelsea joined them when they lost the play-off final to Middlesbrough. Also promoted were Millwall and Aston Villa, who returned at the first attempt under Graham Taylor.

In the League Cup Final Luton Town beat the holders Arsenal 3-2. Brian Stein had put Luton ahead after 14 minutes, and the score remained 1-0 until late into the second half when four goals were scored in 15 minutes. Martin Hayes and Alan Smith gave Arsenal the lead; Danny Wilson pulled it back to 2-2 and Stein scored his second in the final moments to give Luton their first major trophy.

Brian Moore

Although this book is about *Match of the Day* it would not be complete without paying tribute to the other great voice of football, Brian Moore. While the BBC had an array of outstanding football commentators, his name was synonymous with the sport on ITV for 30 years.

Brian also presented 'On the Ball' and *Midweek Sports Special* from 1978 to 1986 and covered League matches, Cup finals, European competitions and nine World Cups .He retired after the 1998 World Cup Final between France and Brazil but sadly died in September 2001 aged 69.

Brian was born in Kent in February 1932 and attended the same school as Peter West and Barry Davies. After completing his national service he got a job driving the writer and commentator Jim Swanton around the UK to cricket matches before becoming a journalist and then a radio reporter. He graduated to football commentaries and was part of the BBC's radio team at the 1966 World Cup Final.

In 1968 Jimmy Hill lured him to the new LWT where he hosted *The Big Match* as well as always doing the main commentary. For more than a decade, it completed the second half of the weekend's football axis. For football fans growing up in the 1970s there was a constant battle to stay up late and watch *Match of the Day* on Saturday nights, before bolting down Sunday lunch in time to see *The Big Match*.

The FA Cup

Match of the Day reverted back to a Saturday night highlights show for the FA Cup. Nottingham Forest were one of the early favourites and after they had beaten Arsenal in the quarter-finals it looked as though Brian Clough might at last have a chance to win the trophy that had eluded him. All went wrong at the semi-final, however, when they met Liverpool at Hillsborough and lost 2-1.

The cameras were also following Wimbledon as they progressed against a succession of supposedly unfashionable clubs. Having beaten West Bromwich Albion, Mansfield Town, Newcastle United and Watford, they faced Luton in the semi-final at White Hart Lane. Goals from John Fashanu and Dennis Wise meant that just five seasons after leaving Division Four, the Crazy Gang were in the FA Cup Final.

By the time Kenny Dalglish and Bobby Gould led their teams out at Wembley, Liverpool were already League Champions. The Cup Final was tough and scrappy and is remembered mainly for two crucial moments. In the 37th minute, Lawrie Sanchez headed Wimbledon into the lead; and a third of the way into the second half their skipper, Dave Beasant, made a superb diving save from John Aldridge's penalty kick. Liverpool had missed out on the double and Wimbledon, the unlikely heroes from South London, were the winners of the FA Cup.

Another iconic moment for *Match of the Day* came in the FA Cup Final when Wimbledon keeper Dave Beasant saved John Aldridge's second-half penalty. This save and Lawrie Sanchez's first-half goal proved enough for the Crazy Gang make off with the trophy.

The courts began to intervene in football's disciplinary process by punishing players for misconduct on the field. In Scotland, Rangers' Chris Woods and Terry Butcher were fined and convicted of disorderly conduct and breach of the peace following a goalmouth incident in the Old Firm match. In England, Chris Kamara of Swindon was fined for causing grievous bodily harm to Jim Melrose of Shrewsbury. It was the first time that a player in England had been convicted in a civil court for an on-field incident.

Goal of the Season
John Aldridge for Liverpool against Nottingham Forest, FA Cup, April 1988

Footballer of the Year
John Barnes, Liverpool

European Footballer of the Year
Marco van Basten, AC Milan

PFA Player of the Year
John Barnes, Liverpool

PFA Young Player of the Year
Paul Gascoigne, Newcastle United

1988–1989

Presenter
Desmond Lynam

League Champions Arsenal

FA Cup winners Liverpool

League Cup winners Nottingham Forest

The show

The show celebrated its 25th anniversary, but for the first time since its inception in 1964, couldn't broadcast any League football. It was very difficult for those working on the programme, but they settled into the four-year contract with the intention of breathing new life into the FA Cup.

With the new contract came a totally revamped show. It was now officially titled *Match of the Day – the Road to Wembley*, and was presented by Desmond Lynam.

'Come on, it hasn't been that long... you know it, course you do... one, two, three...' and the opening titles ran.

The season

Before the season began there were two major transfer deals. Paul Gascoigne moved from Newcastle United to Tottenham Hotspur for £2 million and Everton paid West Ham United £2.2 million to buy Tony Cottee. Liverpool also re-signed Ian Rush from Juventus after he had spent just one season in Italy. The fee of £2.8 million was a record sum paid by an English club.

The opening weekend of the League season produced goals for all the main contenders. Cottee opened his new career with a hat-trick in Everton's 4-0 win against Newcastle; John Aldridge matched him as Liverpool won 3-0 at Charlton Athletic, and Arsenal beat Wimbledon 5-1.

Newly-promoted Millwall were the surprise leaders of Division One at the beginning of October while their London neighbours, Spurs, were in bottom place by the end of the same month. At the turn of the year Arsenal were on top having won 3-0 at Aston Villa and on 14 January they beat Everton 3-1 at Goodison Park to open up a five-point lead. Their main challengers, Liverpool, had

suffered a setback when Jan Molby was jailed for three months for reckless driving.

Nigel Clough scored twice in the League Cup Final when Nottingham Forest beat the holders Luton Town 3-1 to win their first major trophy in nine seasons. They returned to Wembley a few weeks later and defeated Everton 4-3 to win the less prestigious Simod Cup.

Just 18 days after the Hillsborough disaster, Liverpool resumed their title challenge with a 0-0 draw at Everton, and beat West Ham 5-1 to send them into the Second Division. The season reached an astonishing climax on 26 May when Arsenal and Liverpool met at Anfield in the final game of the campaign, with the Championship still undecided.

It was complicated: Liverpool led but Arsenal knew they needed to beat them by two clear goals. This would mean

Tony Cascarino (left) and Teddy Sheringham both starred for newly-promoted Millwall as they went top of Division One at the beginning of October.

they'd draw level on goal difference, but win by having scored more goals.

Alan Smith put the Gunners ahead in the 53rd minute, but that didn't look like it would be enough. Then, with the final kick in the final minute of the last game of the season, Michael Thomas added a second to snatch the Championship away from a traumatised Anfield.

Arsenal were Champions for the first time since 1971. Liverpool were second, with Nottingham Forest 12 points behind in third place, and Norwich City fourth. Newcastle United and Middlesbrough joined West Ham in the drop to Division Two. They were replaced by Crystal Palace, Manchester City and Chelsea, who returned at the first attempt having accumulated 99 points.

The FA Cup

As the BBC's only regular football was the FA Cup, the coverage began at the stage when the smaller clubs were all still in the competition. This meant that Motty and Barry found themselves and their microphones at some unlikely venues.

November's first round saw the cameras visit Enfield, where the home team drew 1-1 with Leyton Orient; and Southport for their 2-0 home defeat to Port Vale. It was a long way from the glamour of Division One.

In round three there were major shocks as both teams that had taken part in the Final just two years before were knocked out. Tottenham Hotspur went down 1-0 at Bradford City, while in Surrey it was a battle between the GM Vauxhall Conference and Division One as Sutton United met Coventry City at their tiny Gander Green Lane ground in south London.

Tony Rains and Matt Hanlan were the stars of the day as Barrie Williams managed his side to an astonishing 2-1 victory and into FA Cup folklore. On the Sunday, Norwich City were seen beating Port Vale 3-1 at Vale Park and from there they met the giant-killers in the next round.

That was where the dream ended as Sutton lost 8-0. Malcolm Allen scored four, Robert Fleck three and Trevor Putney one as the Canaries flew into the fifth round draw.

Norwich's great run continued as they beat Sheffield United 3-2 and West Ham 3-1 in a sixth-round replay, before eventually losing to Everton in the semi-final at Villa Park.

Amid extraordinary excitement Michael Thomas (right) scores Arsenal's Championship-winning goal at Anfield in the last few moments of the final game of the season.

Hillsborough

English football suffered its worst tragedy on 15 April when 95 Liverpool supporters died during their FA Cup semi-final against Nottingham Forest at Hillsborough in Sheffield. The BBC cameras were there to cover the game for *Match of the Day* and the producer, John Shrewsbury, and his team had to switch into news mode to stay on air until midnight. John had also been at Heysel, and he explained the horror of the situation they found themselves in once again.

'It was a terrible nightmare. We had to cover the story but ensure at the same time that we didn't show anyone dying, as their loved ones might be watching. It was absolute chaos, a frightening scenario and without any doubt the worst day of my career, and it was a week before I could talk about it. It never goes away.'

The people of Sheffield turned up in numbers to pay their respects to the dead at the gates of Hillsborough.

Sutton United's Matt Hanlan (number 11) beats Coventry keeper Steve Ogrizovic put his side 2-1 up. The GM Vauxhall Conference team went on to win the match – one of the biggest giant-killing acts in FA Cup history.

Liverpool coasted through and in the semi-final they eventually beat Nottingham Forest 3-1 in the re-staged game following the Hillsborough disaster.

The all-Merseyside Final became an emotional tribute to the many people who had so tragically died or been injured in Sheffield. Gerry Marsden sang the Kop anthem 'You'll Never Walk Alone', and both teams stood with their heads bowed before the game began.

John Aldridge put Liverpool ahead after just four minutes and the score remained 1-0 until just before the final whistle when Everton's substitute, Stuart McCall, equalized. In extra-time Ian Rush restored Liverpool's lead, McCall's volley made it 2-2 and then Ian Rush headed the winner past Neville Southall from a John Barnes cross. The result was 3-2 and Ronnie Whelan lifted the trophy, but their win was inevitably overshadowed by the terrible memories of Hillsborough.

1988 European Championship

The finals were held in West Germany and England's journey there included an 8-0 win against Turkey. Unfortunately that was six goals more than they managed in group two of the final stages, and they lost all three matches. Holland won the competition, beating the USSR 2-0 in the Final.

Fact file

On 22 October three brothers, Danny, Ray and Rod Wallace all appeared for Southampton against Sheffield Wednesday. It was the first time in 68 years that three brothers had played together in the same First Division team.

Goal of the Season
John Aldridge for Liverpool against Everton, FA Cup Final, May 1989

Footballer of the Year
Steve Nicol, Liverpool

European Footballer of the Year
Marco van Basten, AC Milan

PFA Player of the Year
Mark Hughes, Manchester United

PFA Young Player of the Year
Paul Merson, Arsenal

Desmond Lynam

Desmond Lynam was born in Ennis, County Clare but moved to Brighton where he launched his broadcasting career as a sports reporter for Radio Brighton in 1968. A few months later he joined BBC Radio 2 where he presented *Sports Report* before moving to BBC Television in 1978. Des was the BBC's main sports anchorman for more than 20 years, presenting *Grandstand*, Wimbledon, the Grand National and many major sporting events including the World Cup and the Olympic Games. He presented *Match of the Day* from 1988 to 1999 when he moved to ITV. Following the demise of *The Premiership* Des returned to the BBC to host a show on Radio Five Live.

'Back in the seventies I watched the show along with everyone else and in those days it got ten or eleven million viewers, which Jimmy Hill never stops reminding me. For a spell it was almost compulsory not to go out on Saturday nights as *Match of the Day* was very big news. It was part of the national fabric at the time.

I loved the show and I liked the way Jimmy presented it. He is the only one who has been both presenter and pundit, performing both roles commendably, and he obviously enjoyed himself.

My first involvement came when I presented a few of the round-ups when Bob Wilson was away – the round-ups being a long, rambling read backed up by still pictures and captions. I think that part of the show probably bored everybody silly, but the producers felt it was their duty to give all the other results and stories back then.

Strangely enough I was also asked to do some football commentary. At the time I was doing presentation mostly for *Grandstand* and I was asked to get involved in commentary for the 1980 European Championship held in Italy. I did a few League matches as a warm-up in 1979 and went out to Italy where I remember doing a couple of games and thoroughly enjoying it.

I was first asked to present *Match of the Day* when I was in Thailand in 1988 doing a film for the *Holiday* programme. The phone rang, at some extraordinary time of the day, and it was Jonathan Martin, the BBC's Head of Sport, who said "*Match of the Day*'s coming back and I'd like you to be the presenter". I was a bit shocked, and asked what would happen to my role as the main presenter of *Grandstand*.

Jonathan was confident I could do both shows, because at that time we just had the FA Cup. Subsequently, of course, we got the League matches back in the early nineties, and I presented those as well. That was a big change for me because I did *Match of the Day* with *Sportsnight* in a job swap with Steve Rider who moved to *Grandstand*.

I loved working with Jimmy Hill. We always had lots of people on the show to play the "nice guy"; and he would adopt the opposite approach, and play the villain perfectly. Even if he agreed with you he'd give the opposite point of view just to make the programme more interesting.

With due respect to Alan Hansen, Mark Lawrenson and Trevor Brooking, my favourite pundit has to be Jimmy. He's irritated people – he's irritated me sometimes – but we always knew we'd get rock solid opinions. Sometimes

they were right, sometimes they were crazy, but he would always have lots to say.

We were at a football ground once and all 30,000 people started chanting at him, but not quite in his favour. "Jimmy Hill's a w****r! Jimmy Hill's a w****r!" echoed around the ground and I asked him how he put up with it. He simply said: "That's fame for you." Jimmy wasn't going to be beaten by a chanting crowd. He's such a great man.

Alan Hansen is also terrific on the show, although it wasn't always the case. He wouldn't mind me saying this because he admits it himself, but on his first few shows he was terribly nervous, and I wondered if he'd get through it. For all his experience as a footballer, being on live television with a camera up his snout giving opinions to millions of people is a different kettle of fish. A lot of people can't do it. Now, of course, he's fantastic, but in his early days he was nervous and a little bit edgy, and he took a while to get used to it.

One of the best parts of the programme was working with the production teams and sitting down with everyone on a Saturday afternoon to watch the games as they came into Television Centre. I used to get in just after lunch, usually about half past one or two o'clock. We'd settle down in a little room and watch the matches, shouting and yelling like everyone else does when they watch football.

It's just like that: we're fans you see and it's great fun. Those Saturday afternoons were a joy. The pundits would each be given a match to concentrate on and they'd make notes for their videotape extracts later. We would suggest interviews to the commentators down the line and then we would put the programme together. I would write the script, and the pundits would go off and select clips from their videotape to illustrate their views later on. It was always a nice day, I promise you.

We were so lucky, just about every great player or manager appeared on the programme at some point and they used to love it as well. I remember Ian Wright coming on to the show as a guest. "Des, this is my Graceland," he said. "Just to be invited on to *Match of the Day*." I thought it was terrific for a famous player to come on to the show and consider it such a privilege.

It's wonderful that *Match of the Day* is celebrating its 40th anniversary, especially as it's been such a large part of my life. I think television is about continuity to a large extent, which is part of the programme's attraction. It's still a very strong product and I think it'll continue for a long time.'

1989–1990

Presenter
Desmond Lynam

League Champions Liverpool

FA Cup winners Manchester United

League Cup winners Nottingham Forest

The show

Desmond Lynam continued to present the show with Jimmy Hill and Terry Venables as his two regular pundits. The audience loved it that the pair seemed to argue about almost every footballing issue, but off-screen they were very good friends. One of the regular causes of disagreement came as a result of the offside law being changed for the first time since 1925. FIFA announced that players who were level were no longer offside and that caused a great deal of debate.

Striker Gary Lineker arrived at Spurs from Barcelona at the beginning of the season scored his first goals at White Hart Lane in a hat-trick in a 3-2 win over Queen Park Rangers.

The season

Newly-promoted Crystal Palace had a harsh lesson in life at the top when they were beaten 9-0 by Liverpool in September. It was the biggest Division One victory since Fulham had beaten Ipswich Town in December 1963.

Perry Suckling was the hapless goalkeeper while Geoff Thomas missed a penalty when they were 6-0 down – he blasted it over the top. Palace got their revenge when they beat Liverpool 4-3 in the FA Cup semi-final.

Before the season began a new British transfer record was set when Chris Waddle moved from Tottenham Hotspur to Olympique Marseille for £4.5 million. Gary Lineker had joined the north London team from Barcelona and he ended the campaign just behind John Barnes, who was top goalscorer this season. Lineker opened his account at White Hart Lane with a hat-trick as Spurs beat Queens Park Rangers 3-2.

Liverpool traveled to Chelsea and won 5-2 to go top of the League on Boxing Day when they beat Charlton Athletic. They displaced Arsenal who had lost to Southampton.

The main football story at the beginning of the new decade came with the publication of Lord Justice Taylor's report into the Hillsborough disaster. As well as calling for better policing, medical facilities and emergency exits, he recommended that all standing should be phased out at football grounds by August 1999. This had major social and financial implications and led to a great deal of debate during the rest of the year.

Liverpool recovered from the shock of the tragic events in Sheffield the previous season and clinched the Championship when they beat QPR. The winning goal was a penalty from John Barnes.

Kenny Dalglish came on for his final Liverpool appearance in their last home game of the season against Derby

Mark Robins salutes his goal at the City Ground that secured a 1-0 win for Manchester United, a place in the FA Cup fourth round and Alex Ferguson's job.

County, the match where Alan Hansen lifted the trophy. It had been an easy win in the end and they finished nine points clear of Aston Villa. Tottenham Hotspur, Arsenal and Chelsea filled the next three places.

Despite Ron Atkinson's best efforts Sheffield Wednesday were relegated along with Charlton Athletic and Millwall. Howard Wilkinson took Leeds United back into the top league as Champions and they were joined automatically by Sheffield United. Sunderland were also promoted after the play-offs.

Brian Clough celebrated his thousandth match as a manager; Nottingham Forest beat Oldham Athletic 1-0 to retain the League Cup; and England's manager Bobby Robson announced he was resigning after the World Cup to return to club management with Dutch side PSV Eindhoven.

The FA Cup

The game that arguably had the biggest impact on British football for the next decade came on 7 January when Manchester United were drawn away in the third round against Nottingham Forest. Having had a poor League season they were just above the relegation zone and the pressure was on manager Alex Ferguson, with many of the papers predicting he would be sacked.

Barry Davies described the action at the City Ground and saw United pull off a surprise 1-0 win when Mark Robins nodded home from a cross by Mark Hughes. The manager was safe, their Cup run secured and captain Bryan Robson later said he thought that match was the turning point for the club and their crop of young players.

For the first time both semi-finals were live on the BBC, and at midday Liverpool took on Crystal Palace at Villa Park

FA Cup semi-finals day this season was truly memorable. Both games were shown live and back-to-back and both were magnificent. The first was won in extra time when Alan Pardew (right) scored to make it 4-3 to Crystal Palace against Liverpool. The second match between Manchester United and Oldham ended in a 3-3 draw.

Sir Bobby Robson

Sir Bobby Robson is the longest serving manager to have been featured on *Match of the Day* having begun his League career with Fulham in 1968. He moved to Ipswich Town in the following year, winning the FA Cup and UEFA Cup, before succeeding Ron Greenwood as the England coach in 1982. He left in 1990 and had great success with PSV Eindhoven, Sporting Lisbon, FC Porto and Barcelona before returning to his native North East in 1999 to take charge of Newcastle United.

'When *Match of the Day* began I was in my second spell as a player with Fulham and the show totally changed our Saturday nights. I stopped going to the cinema, pubs or parties as I used to love watching it and it consumed me. It was a great opportunity to see other teams and great footballers playing.

It was the first time I had seen myself or my team-mates on film, and the way it illustrated our mistakes was very beneficial. It became a great teaching and coaching aid.

If I missed the show because we were playing away and couldn't get home in time it was a terrible wrench. I think it also caught on because it provoked discussion and people could talk about the behaviour of players, the decisions of the referee and all the action. One of the joys of *Match of the Day* has always been the replays and that has also been a marvellous help with training.

I still make sure I am in to see the show whenever it's on, even after all these years. It is wonderful that you can sit at home and see all the top players and teams from your living room, and for virtually no cost.'

after both teams had made steady progress to this stage. Ian Rush put Liverpool ahead and at the start of the second half Mark Bright equalized with a left-footed volley.

As the goals flew in, first Palace and then Liverpool took the lead until, at 3-3 in extra time, Alan Pardew scored to clinch a place in the Final for the Londoners. It was sweet revenge against the side that had beaten them 9-0 in the League earlier in the season.

As the viewers began to recover, the second semi-final kicked off and proved to be just as pulsating. Oldham Athletic took an early lead against Manchester United at Maine Road, but the goals kept coming and the match finished 3-3. United won the replay 2-1 with Robins once again scoring the crucial goal.

The Final proved to be just as exciting and stood at 3-3 after extra time. Both sides had taken the lead, Ian Wright scored twice when he came on as a substitute and Mark Hughes tucked away the crucial goal for United just seven minutes from the end of extra time to secure a replay.

Jim Leighton, the Manchester United goalkeeper, was sensationally dropped and never played for the club again. His replacement, Les Sealey, was on loan from Luton Town and managed to keep a clean sheet on his debut. Lee Martin scored the only goal in the 59th minute and Bryan Robson lifted the trophy for a third time. Before the match Alex Ferguson described it as the most important event in his life and it proved to be the stepping stone to more than a decade of unrivalled success.

Substitute Ian Wright scores to give Crystal Palace a 3-2 lead in the FA Cup Final against Manchester United. The match ended 3-3 and United went on to win the replay 1-0 with a goal from Bryan Robson.

Fact file

Osvaldo Ardiles led Swindon Town into Division One for the first time in their history, but three weeks later fans were stunned when the club found themselves relegated to Division Three instead. It was punishment for irregular payments made to their players by the previous regime.

Swindon's chairman, Brian Hillier, and former manager, Lou Macari, had also contravened rules by placing a bet two years previously that the club would lose an FA Cup match to Newcastle in 1988. They lost 5-0. The club and Macari were fined and Hillier was suspended for three years. On appeal Swindon were reinstated to the Second Division but Sunderland took their place in the top League despite having lost the play-off Final 1-0.

Goal of the Season
Ian Wright for Crystal Palace against Manchester United, FA Cup Final, May 1990

Footballer of the Year
John Barnes, Liverpool

European Footballer of the Year
Lothar Matthaus, Inter Milan

PFA Player of the Year
David Platt, Aston Villa

PFA Young Player of the Year
Matthew Le Tissier, Southampton

1990–1991

Presenter
Desmond Lynam

League Champions Arsenal
FA Cup winners Tottenham Hotspur
League Cup winners Sheffield Wednesday

European Cup-Winners' Cup winners
Manchester United

The show

In the third season of the new contract there were 20 editions of *Match of the Day* covering FA Cup matches. League action was still only to be found on ITV.

FA Cup replays and highlights were seen on Wednesday evenings on BBC1 in *Sportsnight*. It was also hosted by Des who was only the seventh regular presenter after Peter Dimmock, Frank Bough, David Coleman, Tony Gubba, Harry Carpenter and Steve Rider. The midweek show began life in 1954 as *Sportsview* and ran until 1997.

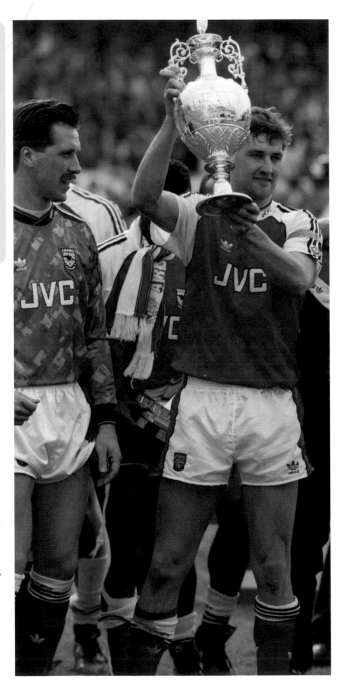

The season

The opening weekend saw contrasting fortunes for the UK's two most famous goalkeepers. At Derby County Peter Shilton played his 900th League game but Neville Southall was fined a week's wages when he walked out of the dressing room at half-time to go and sit in his goalmouth after Everton went 2-0 down against newly-promoted Leeds United. They lost 3-2.

In early September, Liverpool beat Manchester United and Everton on their way to recording 12 consecutive victories, equalling Everton's 96-year-old record. Graham Taylor began his spell as England manager by appointing Gary Lineker as captain for the friendly against Hungary at Wembley in September. Lineker scored the only goal of the match in the 44th minute and a new partnership seemed set to blossom. Just a month before that game one of

Arsenal keeper David Seaman (left) conceded only 18 goals during the season enabling captain Tony Adams to lift the League Championship. The Gunners finished seven points ahead of rivals Liverpool.

Despite good form during the competition, Manchester United were surprisingly beaten by Sheffield Wednesday in the League Cup Final. Here Wednesday's Roland Nilsson (left) beats United's Lee Sharpe.

Taylor's predecessors, Joe Mercer, had died aged 76. He had managed England seven times in 1974 inbetween Sir Alf Ramsey and Don Revie.

In October Arsenal were involved in yet another brawl, this time with Manchester United, and David Seaman was the only player not involved. Both clubs were fined £50,000 and the FA deducted two points from Arsenal and one from Manchester United.

Liverpool's winning run ended on 20 October with a 1-1 draw at Norwich City. Their first loss came in December when Arsenal beat them 3-0 although at the end of the year Liverpool were top, with Arsenal a point behind and Crystal Palace in third place.

In February, Arsenal suffered their only League defeat of the season when they lost 2-1 at Chelsea. It was their 24th match. A few weeks later Liverpool beat Derby 7-1 to keep their Championship hopes alive, but March ended with Arsenal two points ahead and they soon increased

that to five when they beat Aston Villa 5-0.

It was all over by the first weekend in May when Liverpool lost against Nottingham Forest and handed the title to Arsenal. The north London club celebrated by winning 3-1 against Manchester United after Alex Ferguson's players lined up to applaud them on to the pitch.

George Graham's team finished seven points ahead of Liverpool, having lost just one League match and only three of the 50 games they played in all competitions. David Seaman conceded just 18 goals in the entire campaign and Alan Smith was the top scorer in Division One with 22 goals. Crystal Palace came third and Leeds United fourth. One of Liverpool's many injured players was their captain, Alan Hansen, who was forced to retire from the game in February, aged 35.

Sunderland and Derby County were relegated and, in order to increase the size of the division, Oldham Athletic, West Ham United and Sheffield United were promoted.

Wembley played host to the FA Cup semi-final between Spurs and Arsenal – the only venue deemed suitable for such a match. After five minutes Paul Gascoigne scored a magnificent free-kick for 30 yards to put Spurs into the lead. Two goals from Gary Lineker saw Spurs earn a place in the Final with a 3-1 victory.

They were joined by Notts County who beat Brighton & Hove Albion in the play-off final.

It was a year of mixed fortunes for Brian Clough and Nottingham Forest. They finished eighth in the League, racked up the biggest win of the season when they beat Chelsea 7-0, won the PFA's Fair Play trophy and were runners-up in the FA Cup, but also mourned the loss of Peter Taylor who had been Clough's Assistant Manager throughout their great triumphs at Derby County and Forest. He was 62.

John Sheridan scored the only goal of the League Cup Final as Sheffield Wednesday surprisingly beat Manchester United. United had been on good form in the competition earlier in the season when they demolished Arsenal 6-2, but the biggest win came from Crystal Palace when they put eight past Southend United with hat-tricks for both Ian Wright and Mark Bright.

Manchester United's compensation came in the European Cup-Winners' Cup. Following the ban after the Heysel tragedy, this was the first season British clubs were readmitted into the competition, and United reached the Final to beat Johan Cruyff's Barcelona 2-1 in Rotterdam. Mark Hughes scored both goals in the second half to make Alex Ferguson the first British manager to win European trophies with different clubs. He had previously steered Aberdeen to the same title in 1983.

The FA Cup

For the editor of *Match of the Day* the most difficult part of the job is choosing the matches – several weeks in advance – that will produce the most exciting football or best story for the show. With 32 matches to choose from in the third round of 1991, Brian Barwick got it absolutely right when he sent cameras to cover Tottenham Hotspur and Nottingham Forest. Both clubs were subsequently featured in every round as they made it to the Final. In the third round a goal from Paul Stewart was enough for Spurs to win at Blackpool while Brian Clough's Forest took two replays to beat Crystal Palace.

Non-League Woking were the season's main giant-killers when they went to West Bromwich Albion and won 4-2, thanks to a Tim Buzaglo hat-trick. In the fourth round they switched their home advantage to Goodison Park where they lost 1-0 to Everton in front of the cameras.

Everton's next opponents were Liverpool but the match ended in a 0-0 draw. The replay was one of the best games of the season and one which also resulted in the season's greatest surprise. The 4-4 scoreline was overshadowed by Kenny Dalglish's shock resignation as Liverpool manager immediately after the game, having guided Liverpool to three championships and two FA Cups. He was replaced by Ronnie Moran. Everton won the second replay 1-0 but lost in the sixth round to West Ham.

In the semi-finals Forest beat West Ham 4-0 at Villa Park and Spurs beat Arsenal 3-1 in the first semi-final ever to be staged at Wembley.

It proved to be yet another outstanding game for Paul Gascoigne and included an amazing long-range free-kick that flew past David Seaman into the top corner. It was followed by a famously manic interview with Ray Stubbs in the tunnel after the game.

Spurs released their fourth FA Cup Final song since 1981, once again with Chas and Dave, but 'When the Year Ends in One' stalled at number 44 in the charts. Nottingham Forest didn't need a gimmick. They had Brian Clough. Many thought that he would finally win the FA Cup this season, the only honour to have escaped him as both player and manager. He led out a team at the Cup Final for the first time having defined his style of play earlier in the season when he said: 'We don't play football in the clouds. If God had wanted us to play football in the clouds he'd have put grass there.'

Unfortunately Paul Gascoigne took a different view and in an infamous moment of recklessness put himself out of football for a year when he tackled Gary Charles with his feet way above the grass early in the Final.

Both were carried off and Stuart Pearce scored from the resulting free-kick. A few minutes later Mark Crossley

The Final was a different story for Gascoigne as after 15 minutes he lunged wildly at Forest defender Gary Charles and was taken to hospital with a serious cruciate ligament injury – it marked the end of his career at White Hart Lane.

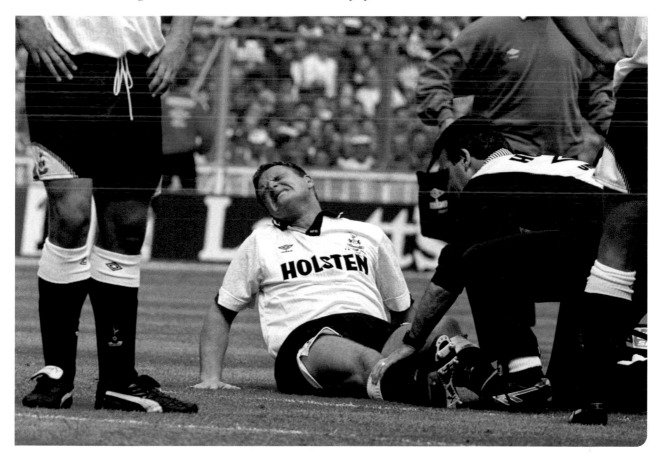

George Best

George Best is still regarded by many as the greatest footballer that the British Isles has ever produced. He played for Manchester United from 1963 to 1973 winning the European Cup and two League Championships as well as being named European Footballer of the Year.

'1964 was my first full season, and we won the title so it was incredible to be a 17-year-old lad coming over from Belfast. It was a very special period and *Match of the Day* was part of it. In those days Saturdays for me were pure heaven. We'd play the game in the afternoon and then I'd go out with my pals to the bowling alley or snooker hall, have a game and chat up a few ladies. When it came to kick-off time for *Match of the Day* the ladies went out of the window, we'd knock back the lagers and get back in time to see the start at 10 p.m. All the men would rush off and leave the women in the pub. That's how big it was.

My favourite goal probably wasn't my greatest but it was quite pleasing as I scored it against Pat Jennings. There were three or four Spurs defenders in front of me and the only way to get out of it was to put it over all their heads, so I lobbed him. The fact that Big Pat was a great friend of mine made it special and it's always nice to score against one of the greatest ever goalkeepers.

I loved it when the *Match of the Day* cameras were there and would try to do things to make people laugh. They call it showboating now but I always used to play up to them. To me it was all just theatre, it always has been and I wanted to play to the crowds. It was all part of the act.

It had a big impact on my life as well because I went from being an unknown kid to having millions watching me on Saturday nights and that led to the commercialism. I wasn't just a footballer but was modelling and advertising Spanish oranges, chewing gum and Playtex bras. It just became massive, and television was mostly the reason for it. I was probably doing more work outside of football than I was in football, a little bit like David Beckham is today.

A lot of it was down to *Match of the Day* and it has lasted because it was the first of its kind. The programme has had some great presenters with Kenneth Wolstenholme, David Coleman, Jimmy Hill, Des Lynam and lastly Gary Lineker. He was useless when he started but now he's brilliant, and the thing they all have in common is that they love football. *Match of the Day* was in there at ground level, and if you survive for 40 years you must be doing something right.'

saved a penalty from Gary Lineker to leave Terry Venables a lot of work to do during the interval to lift his side.

Whatever he said clearly worked and just nine minutes into the second half Paul Stewart equalized. With six minutes left and extra time looming the Forest defender, Des Walker, deflected the ball into his own net to make the final score 2-1 and send the trophy back to north London. It was the fifth successive decade that Spurs had won a major trophy when the year ended in one.

1990 World Cup

England reached the semi-finals in Italy by topping their qualifying group and then beating Belgium and Cameroon but were eliminated by West Germany after a penalty shoot-out in Turin. The match finished 1-1 after extra time and then Chris Waddle and Stuart Pearce both missed their penalties as England lost 4-3. West Germany beat Argentina 1-0 in the Final when Andreas Brehme scored from a penalty a few minutes from the end. It was the third time that the trophy had gone to Germany.

Paul Gascoigne's tears during England's semi-final defeat prompted an outbreak of Gazzamania and helped him to become only the second footballer to win the BBC's Sports Personality of the Year Award. Scottish snooker star Stephen Hendry was second with England's cricket captain, Graham Gooch, in third place following his epic 333 and 123 against India at Lord's. The only other footballers to have won the trophy are Bobby Moore in 1966, Michael Owen in 1998 and David Beckham in 1999. Football teams have, however, collected the Team Award on 12 occasions, beginning with Tottenham Hotspur's double-winning side in 1961. It helps to only be known by one name in order to win the Overseas's Personality of the Year as the only footballers to be presented with it are Eusebio, Pele and Ronaldo.

Top Man at Elland Road this season was Gordon Strachan. His performances in a blossoming midfield saw Leeds finish fourth and earned him the accolade of Footballer of the Year.

Fact file

Arsenal's captain, Tony Adams, was jailed on 19 December for a drink-driving offence and spent two months inside Chelmsford Prison. The jail's previous footballing connection had been in 1979 when it was used to stage the football match in the film version of the BBC sitcom *Porridge*.

Goal of the Season
Paul Gascoigne for Tottenham against Arsenal, FA Cup, April 1991

Footballer of the Year
Gordon Strachan, Leeds United

European Footballer of the Year
Jean-Pierre Papin, Marseille

PFA Player of the Year
Mark Hughes, Manchester United

PFA Young Player of the Year
Lee Sharpe, Manchester United

1991–1992

Presenter
Desmond Lynam

League Champions   Leeds United

FA Cup winners   Liverpool

League Cup winners   Manchester United

The show

After several years of speculation it was announced in February that a new, breakaway FA Premier League was going to be formed. ITV were expected to win the TV rights but the BBC and BSkyB placed a joint counter-bid and had strong influence within the new organization.

The chairman of Tottenham Hotspur, Alan Sugar, was one of Rupert Murdoch's key business partners. Sugar's company supplied the Amstrad satellite dishes for BSkyB who in turn knew they needed sport to increase their subscriber base.

There was also bitterness felt by many club chairmen at the way ITV had favoured big clubs during the previous contract. In May 1992 the rights were decided and each club had one vote. BSkyB were awarded live matches on Sundays and Mondays and the BBC got the Saturday night highlights as part of a five-year, £304 million deal. The two companies also joined forces to sign a new £72 million, five-year deal to cover FA Cup and international matches. ITV would be covering the Football League and the League Cup.

Alan Sugar (left) and Rupert Murdoch were key business partners in the establishment of the new breakaway FA Premier League.

Manager Howard Wilkinson led Leeds United to the Championship for the first time since Don Revie 18 years earlier.

The season

The contrary nature of football was demonstrated on the very first day of the season when Division Four newcomers Barnet lost 4-7 at home to Crewe Alexandra. To their credit they only conceded 16 more goals at home and recovered to finish seventh in the League.

Two former Liverpool heroes had very different experiences of life in Division Two this season. Kevin Keegan took over from Osvaldo Ardiles as manager of Newcastle United and managed to save them from relegation to Division Three. Just eight months after his surprise resignation from Liverpool, Kenny Dalglish joined Blackburn Rovers and took them back into Division One.

George Graham signed Ian Wright from Crystal Palace for £2.5 million and he immediately had a great impact on the Arsenal side. Alex Ferguson was relying on Manchester United's youth policy and it began to pay off with the break-

through of 17-year-old Ryan Giggs. He became the new pin-up and heart throb and was inevitably described as the next George Best.

He helped Manchester United make all the early running and for a while it looked as though they would finally win the elusive title. When they went to Oldham Athletic on Boxing Day and won 6-3 they were League leaders, but needed to see off the challenges of Leeds United and Arsenal. The Gunners were on great form and beat Sheffield United 5-2, Sheffield Wednesday 7-1 and Southampton 5-1, but their away results let them down and they slipped out of contention.

In Yorkshire, Howard Wilkinson felt he might not have had the best players, but was convinced he had the best team. That was strengthened when he persuaded the Frenchman Eric Cantona to choose Leeds over Sheffield Wednesday. He was a gifted player with a reputation for being difficult, but made the difference as Leeds finally went top of the table.

In the run-in to the Championship Manchester United were ahead of Leeds, but had to play four games in a week. They lost twice in three days and it all came down to the final matches. Leeds beat Sheffield United, Liverpool beat Manchester United and Wilkinson's men were Division One Champions for the first time since 1974. They finished four points ahead of Manchester United with Sheffield Wednesday, Arsenal, Manchester City and Liverpool close behind.

Alex Ferguson's team did, however, manage to win the League Cup for the first time when Brian McClair's fourteenth-minute goal was the only score in the Final against Nottingham Forest.

At the other end of the table Luton Town, Notts County and West Ham United missed out on the chance of Premier League football and were replaced by Ipswich Town, Middlesbrough and Blackburn Rovers.

The FA Cup

The biggest FA Cup upset for many seasons came on 4 January when Wrexham beat Arsenal 2-1 at the Racecourse Ground in front of the *Match of the Day* cameras. The Welsh side had been the bottom club in the League in the previous season but managed to knock out the reigning First Division Champions. To complete a humiliating day, Arsenal's coach broke down on the way back.

Football funnies

During the 1970s, football regularly cropped up in mainstream light entertainment shows as the game crossed over on to the front pages, and the *Match of the Day* viewing figures reached twelve million. Although Tony Hancock had once delivered a classic description of his own footballing prowess to Sid James in his eponymous sitcom, and Alf Garnett had become established as the nation's most famous West Ham supporter, it wasn't until *Match of the Day's* second decade that the crossover began.

Mike Yarwood's regular impersonation of Brian Clough and Eric Morecambe's dedicated support for Luton Town led the way, but Eric Sykes, *The Two Ronnies* and many others followed. The approaches varied. *Whatever Happened to the Likely Lads* took a conventional one in the famous episode where Bob and Terry spend an entire day trying to avoid hearing the score of an England game before watching it on

Eric Morecambe and Ernie Wise got lots of laughs out of the fact that Eric was a keen Luton supporter. Here Glenda Jackson gets in on the act during *The Morecambe and Wise Show*.

BBC 1 that evening. The Monty Python team often had a slightly different take on the sport as was evident in their portrayal of the Bournemouth Gynaecologists against The Watford Long John Silver impersonators!

Michael Palin later created one of the greatest ever footballing comedies in a 1979 episode of *Ripping Yarns*. He perfectly captured the frustrations of all supporters who love and loathe their clubs, and caricatured their addiction to following them.

In the 1980s and 1990s Rory Bremner and then Alistair McGowan continued the trend, with Rory taking off Des and Alistair doubling-up as Gary Lineker and Mark Lawrenson.

In the next round Wrexham lost to West Ham United who had almost suffered a third-round humiliation of their own – needing a replay to get past non-League Farnborough Town.

In the semi-final Liverpool drew 1-1 with Portsmouth at Highbury and it took a replay, extra time and – for the first time in the competition's history – penalties before they scraped into the final.

On the way back from the game their manager, Graeme Souness, told the players he needed a triple heart-bypass operation. After the surgery, and with his doctor sitting behind him, Souness made it to the Final where Liverpool met Sunderland – making their first appearance since their famous victory over Leeds United in 1973.

Malcolm Crosby's side had struggled in Division Two and finished 18th, but they arrived with hopes of pulling off another shock. It wasn't to be, however, as Michael Thomas and Ian Rush scored the goals that gave Liverpool a 2-0 victory, and the FA Cup for the third time in seven seasons. It was a new trophy that Mark Wright held aloft as the old one had been retired after 81 years of service.

There was another sensational FA Cup result during the third round when Wrexham, who had finished 92nd in the Football League, met Champions Arsenal at the Racecourse Ground. A goal down with 8 minutes to go, Wrexham did not give up. First, 37-year-old Mickey Thomas (right) crashed a free-kick past David Seaman then, two minutes later 20-year-old Steve Watkin forced the ball home to seal a famous victory.

The financial crisis that had long threatened clubs began to take a grip as Aldershot had to leave the League when they were unable to guarantee their fixtures. The club had been in the Football League since 1932, but collapsed with a £1.2 million debt in March 1992 and were closed down. All games involving them were declared invalid and it was decided that the bottom side, Carlisle United, would not be relegated. Aldershot were the first League club to fold since Accrington Stanley in 1962.

Goal of the Season
Mickey Thomas for Wrexham against Arsenal, FA Cup, January 1992
Michael Thomas for Liverpool against Sunderland, FA Cup Final, May 1992

Footballer of the Year
Gary Lineker, Tottenham Hotspur

European Footballer of the Year
Marco van Basten, AC Milan

PFA Player of the Year
Gary Pallister, Manchester United

PFA Young Player of the Year
Ryan Giggs, Manchester United

1992–1993

Presenter
Desmond Lynam

League Champions Manchester United
FA Cup winners Arsenal
League Cup winners Arsenal

The show

A new season, a new Premier League, a new football contract and a new show, fronted by Desmond Lynam.

'Good evening, I suppose its back to the future tonight with *Match of the Day* returning on a Saturday night after a gap of four years.'

The new deal meant that BSkyB was about to revolutionise football coverage. Pubs were transformed as screens went up around the UK to enable fans to enjoy a new pastime – live Monday night football. Their team of Richard Keys, Andy Gray and Martin Tyler settled into a long residency at the heart of the new football coverage.

Back at the BBC, Des was joined by his new regular pundits Alan Hansen and Trevor Brooking (below), and the show reverted to the classic format of extended highlights from three main games. Now, however, as well as all the extra analysis, viewers were also able to see the goals from all the other matches as well.

As the BBC had both the Premier League and the FA Cup it was free to concentrate on the top clubs without any of the contractual restrictions that it had faced in the 1960s and 1970s. As a consequence Manchester United were featured in a main game on 18 programmes, while Oldham made just two appearances.

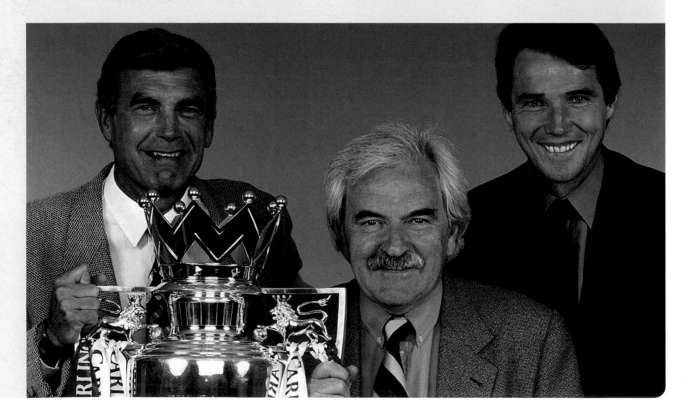

The season

The season started with a goal rush at the Charity Shield when Eric Cantona scored a hat-trick as Leeds United beat Liverpool 4-3. The following weekend saw the launch of the new Premier League and Brian Deane entered the history books as the scorer of the first Premiership goal. He put Sheffield United 1-0 up against Manchester United after just five minutes.

In September, Norwich City, the surprise team of the year, took ten points out of a possible twelve. In early October, however, they had a serious wobble when Blackburn Rovers, led by their new £3.3 million striker Alan Shearer, beat them 7-1. They recovered to lead the table by eight points in December.

Alex Ferguson felt he was a striker short and bought Eric Cantona for £1.2 million. This proved to be the final part of the United jigsaw as the team came together and beat Coventry City 5-0, ending the year at the top of the table tied on 41 points with Aston Villa and Norwich City.

They were regularly featured as the main game on *Match of the Day* and were seen beating Spurs 4-1 in January; defeating Middlesbrough 3-0; winning at Anfield 2-1; drawing 1-1 at Maine Road with Manchester City; beating Sheffield Wednesday 2-1; Chelsea 3-0 and Blackburn Rovers 3-1.

The match against Sheffield Wednesday had been crucial as they went 1-0 down but became a turning point for the club's whole season. Steve Bruce scored twice, leading to the famous images of Alex Ferguson and Brian Kidd as they leapt on to the pitch and took over from Aston Villa at the top of the League.

United were crowned Champions on 2 May when results went their way while they had a day off. Aston Villa needed three points from their home game against Oldham Athletic to stay in the title race, but lost 1-0. At 6 p.m. on that Sunday, Manchester United knew they had won and the whole team went to Steve Bruce's house for a party. Several stayed the night, Bryan Robson cleared the dishes and they then beat Blackburn Rovers 3-1 the following afternoon before Bruce was able to lift the trophy.

Aston Villa finished in second place, ten points behind Manchester United. Norwich were third and Blackburn Rovers fourth. Arsenal could only manage tenth position in the League but won both cups. They beat Sheffield

The sight of Eric Cantona trying something spectacular became a regular one when he signed for Manchester United in November 1992. It was the start of something special as the Red Devils went on to dominate English football for the first decade of the newly-formed Premiership.

Brian Clough

Brian Clough retired at the age of 58 as football's longest-serving manager. After 18 seasons with Nottingham Forest, he had been one of the most charismatic personalities to feature on *Match of the Day*, and was regularly outspoken and controversial. As a player, Clough had been a phenomenal goalscorer. With a record of 251 in 274 League games for Middlesbrough and Sunderland, he began his managerial career with Hartlepool in 1965. He joined Derby County two years later and, having been promoted as Second Division Champions in 1969, won the League title in 1972. After brief spells with Brighton and Leeds United he joined Nottingham Forest in 1975 and led them out of the Second Division and to the Championship in 1978. They also won the European Cup in 1979 and 1980 and four League Cups.

'*Match of the Day* was exciting for me. I was a reasonably young man in those days and it was something which was new and anything that's new, if it's good, remains good. If it's new and it's bad you soon bomb it out, so to speak, but *Match of the Day* stood the test of time. And the people involved with it were enthusiastic as well. You can't produce a programme whether it be a football match or a cricket match or any sporting event unless the people who are working on the other side of the fence, or pitch, are enthusiastic as well. And that's what you lot captured.

Barry Davies and John Motson were fine, unassuming young men. Both had their opinions but were sufficiently intelligent enough not to force them on people who were in the game for a living. There's nowt worse than that. As a manager it was exciting, it allowed me to digest and to work out the odd thing I missed during the match while I was watching it live. Irrespective of how good you are you can miss certain things, and the replays helped. It was the highlight of the week and was for many, many millions.

I think that because I appeared so often it enhanced my reputation fractionally. I was just lucky. I didn't know it was doing it because people just asked me to come on and talk as I'd been in the game a long time. The screen and monitors and all that just never worried me so whatever I said came natural to me, and there were no airs and graces when I went on telly.

I was thrilled and delighted we're getting *Match of the Day* back because it was good and it stood the test of time. To bring it back is a credit to whoever decided to do it and it's going to give pleasure to millions. It might be nostalgia, it might be longing for our youth but we'll tune in. I was thrilled when I heard the news.'

Brian Clough is happy with his haul of silverware in April 1989 as he shows off the Simod Cup, the League Cup and his Manager of the Month cheque.

Arsenal's Steve Morrow (right) completes the first half of a cup double for the Gunners as he scores the winner against Sheffield Wednesday in their 2-1 victory in the League Cup Final in April. Both teams returned to Wembley in May for the FA Cup Final and drew 1-1. They returned again five days later for the replay, and Arsenal won 2-1... again!

Wednesday 2-1 to take the League Cup, but it was the aftermath of Steve Morrow's lift by Tony Adams that made the headlines. Having scored the winning goal Morrow was hoisted up by his captain who then dropped him and broke his arm.

In Brian Clough's final season as manager of Nottingham Forest he saw them relegated having lost 2-0 at home to Sheffield United on the last weekend of the campaign. They were joined in Division Two by Crystal Palace and Middlesbrough. Newcastle United and West Ham United both returned to the top flight along with Swindon Town who beat Portsmouth in the play-off final, despite having finished 12 points behind them in the League.

The FA Cup

Although the main focus was on the newly-revived Saturday night League highlights, the FA Cup still had a prominent role in the BBC's football portfolio. Arsenal reached their first FA Cup Final since 1980 by defeating Tottenham Hotspur 1-0 at Wembley, a reverse of their famous 1991 semi-final at the same venue.

The second semi-final was also played at Wembley and the city of Sheffield was left deserted as the fans of Wednesday and United took to the M1 to take part in a unique FA Cup derby weekend.

Chris Waddle and Mark Bright both scored for Wednesday as they finished 2-1 winners. They returned to a Wembley Cup Final for the second time that season, having already

Graham Taylor led England to the 1992 European Championships in Sweden. Two 0-0 draws, against Denmark and France, were followed by a 2-1 defeat against the hosts. England's sorry exit followed by failure to qualify for the 1994 World Cup – all captured for a fly-on-the-wall TV documentary – saw Taylor resign.

finished runners-up in the League Cup Final to Arsenal.

The FA Cup Final was a disappointing affair that ran to two games when the first finished 1-1 after extra time. Ian Wright put Arsenal ahead after 21 minutes but David Hirst equalized 40 minutes later and the two sets of supporters had to travel back to Wembley for the fifth time that season.

In the replay Ian Wright once again put Arsenal ahead, but Chris Waddle levelled the scores and the match looked set to go to a first-ever penalty shoot-out. Then, in the last minute of extra time, Andy Linighan, who had been playing with a broken nose and finger for most of the game, headed the winner and Tony Adams was able to lift his second major trophy of the season.

1992 European Championship

Neither England nor Scotland progressed from their groups to the semi-finals in Sweden. Although Scotland won one match against the C.I.S, England only managed a solitary goal in their three games and when Graham Taylor substituted Gary Lineker against Sweden he left him one goal short of Bobby Charlton's English goalscoring record of 49. The tournament was won by Denmark who beat Germany 2-0 in the Final, having only been invited to take part in the finals when Yugoslavia were excluded because of United Nations' sanctions.

Fact file

Bobby Moore, the golden boy of English football in the 1960s, died in February 1993 aged just 51. He had been suffering from cancer. As well as leading England to their 1966 World Cup success he had captained his country in an astonishing 90 of his 108 appearances. Moore played in 642 League and Cup matches for West Ham United, and while with them lifted the FA Cup in 1964 and the European Cup-Winners' Cup in the following season. Both wins were at Wembley enabling him to complete a unique footballing hat-trick when he climbed the steps for a third consecutive year in 1966.

Goal of the Season
Dalian Atkinson for Aston Villa against Wimbledon, Premier League, October 1992

Footballer of the Year
Chris Waddle, Sheffield Wednesday

European Footballer of the Year
Roberto Baggio, Juventus

PFA Player of the Year
Paul McGrath, Aston Villa

PFA Young Player of the Year
Ryan Giggs, Manchester United

Tributes to the late Bobby Moore piled up outside Upton Park – home of West Ham United.

Alan Hansen

Alan Hansen was born in June 1955 and began his career at Partick Thistle where he made 108 appearances before being signed by Liverpool in 1977. He made 621 appearances for them and was captain between 1985 and 1990. In an astonishingly successful career, Alan won eight Championships, three European Cups, two FA Cups, four League Cups and 26 Scottish caps. A knee injury forced his retirement in 1991.

'As a youngster I would occasionally get to see *Match of the Day* in Scotland if there were no Scottish matches for them to show, but it wasn't until I joined Liverpool in 1977 that I saw it regularly.

As a player I would watch every football programme and tape each one to see again later. *Match of the Day* at that time was an institution, with such a strong format that it was a great watch. Because there were no live games then and just the terrestrial channels it was so exciting to see any football. I remember on Boxing Day in 1979 we were top, Manchester United were second, and when we played each other there wasn't a camera in the ground. That would be ludicrous now.

I didn't like any of the pundits, I thought they were all talking nonsense and didn't know what they were on about. I thought there was nothing worse than someone going on TV and talking about football because they were always wrong – especially if they were talking about me, and a mistake they thought I had made. I held that view right up to the day that I became one!

When I retired in February 1991 I decided not to stay in football and told my wife that as the phone was never going to stop ringing I'd take six months off and pick the best of the offers. After there hadn't been a single call in three months I thought I'd better find some work, so I called BSkyB and managed to do a bit on their Italian football. *Radio Sport* was on Radio 2 in those days and they asked me to do a few things until Brian Barwick, the editor of TV football, called to see if I could work on the Liverpool in Europe programmes. It meant I had a variety of experiences to learn from as a freelancer, and it was an invaluable year of gaining experience.

When the BBC got the contract for the Premiership in 1992, I joined as a pundit and have been there ever since. The first few shows were very intimidating and I was a nervous wreck. I always found that the worst part of football was the 45 minutes before kick-off, but I was fine when I had my first touch. Television is the same. A lot of nerves before the show but once I start speaking they vanish. It's amazing.

Desmond was fantastic to start working with as he was such a calming influence and would always feed me questions that he knew I could answer. In those early days I didn't do much ad-libbing simply because I didn't know how to, but I gradually relaxed and it became easier.

We decided from the beginning to take a new approach to the analysis by showing different aspects of the game rather than just concentrating on the goals. I wanted to

When I was in my first season at Liverpool we had a bad run and he made some changes on the basis that experience is everything. That was what I was actually trying to say in my own way, but ten years on people are still reminding me about it.

The best part of the job is being with the production team on *Match of the Day*. I have never missed playing or training but I do miss the dressing room with all its characters and banter. The TV team is a very different entity but with lots of similarities, and they are great to work with.

In the end though, it is all about the game and I still love watching the stars when they are playing well. We have had some fantastic goalscorers in recent years and players with great flair such as Cantona and Henry, and I'm really looking forward to *Match of the Day* coming back on Saturday nights so that we can cover the Premiership again.'

show the viewers things they might not realize were happening such as the movement of players off the ball and ways that new players affected teams.

I suddenly found myself as a pundit renowned for being critical, but I have always tried to say it just how I see it. The viewers are not going to be fooled, so if it is bad we should say that it is bad – but I always try and give a balanced view with plaudits and accolades for good play.

The line that probably made me as a pundit is also the one that is quoted back at me most often, usually with a very bad attempt at a Scottish accent. When I said of Manchester United that they couldn't win anything with kids, what I actually meant was that they couldn't win EVERYTHING with kids. It was an adaptation of an old Bob Paisley line.

1993–1994

Presenter
Desmond Lynam

League Champions   Manchester United
FA Cup winners   Manchester United
League Cup winners   Aston Villa

European Cup-Winners' Cup winners   Arsenal

The show

Despite all the changes in both football and television *Match of the Day* had survived to see its 30th season. It was a relatively low-scoring one as far as the show's main games were concerned as teams scored four or more goals only six times in the 92 featured League and cup matches.

In previous years this might have been a problem but now that the programme was also able to feature every goal from every other game the viewers always had plenty of entertainment.

The season

With Kevin Keegan back in the top flight interest was massive and the first full Premier League weekend saw the cameras at newly promoted Newcastle United. They lost 1-0 to Tottenham Hotspur but the following weekend they were featured again, and this time drew 1-1 with Manchester United.

The biggest tally in a televised game went to Everton when they beat Swindon Town 6-2 in January with Tony Cottee getting a hat-trick. Swindon Town, the team Glenn Hoddle had taken into the Premier League and then abandoned to move to Chelsea, crumbled time and again. They

Alex Ferguson (left) and his assistant Brian Kidd hold up the Premier League trophy after Manchester United's second successive Championship victory.

Andy Cole of Newcastle United (right) sidefoots the ball home against Aston Villa. His tally of 41 goals during the season included 34 in the Premiership.

also lost 5-0 to Liverpool, Leeds United and Aston Villa; 5-1 to Southampton and in the season's highest-scoring match, 7-1 to Newcastle. It was not exactly a huge surprise to their fans when they finished bottom of the table having won only five games and conceded 100 goals.

At the top of the Premier League, Manchester United and Blackburn Rovers were competing for supremacy and that was having an impact elsewhere. When Liverpool met Manchester United at Anfield the visitors went 3-0 up. Two goals by Nigel Clough helped them to recover and eventually draw the game, but it was enough for Graeme Souness who resigned as manager. He was replaced by Roy Evans as the club attempted to restore some of its old glory.

On 16 January Alex Ferguson's team were a record 16 points ahead of Blackburn, although they had played three more games. Kenny Dalglish had taken Blackburn out of Division Two and up to second place in the table, but he had been assisted by the philanthropy of Sir Jack Walker who had transformed their Ewood Park ground as well as

spending £27 million on players. They refused to be daunted by the large points gap and steadily began to reduce it.

In March it looked as though the situation might radically change. Eric Cantona was sent off twice in one week against Swindon and Arsenal, missing the crunch game against Blackburn on 2 April. An unmarked Alan Shearer headed in the first goal, his 31st of the season, and then added a second with a thunderous left foot shot after getting the better of Gary Pallister to win 2-0. They were now just three points behind having both played 35 games.

The following weekend the *Match of the Day* viewers saw them both win. United beat Oldham Athletic 3-2 at Old Trafford while Blackburn travelled to Everton and won 3-0.

With two games left Blackburn were five points behind but ran out of steam and lost 2-1 to Coventry City meaning that Manchester United had retained their crown. Newcastle were third and Andy Cole finished as the League's top scorer with 34 goals.

England managers

Graham Taylor resigned as England manager when the team failed to qualify for the 1994 World Cup. Needing to beat San Marino by seven goals to try and reach the finals they instead conceded one after just eight seconds, eventually winning 7-1. Taylor was replaced by Terry Venables who became the seventh England boss during the lifetime of *Match of the Day*.

Alf Ramsey (1963–74), Joe Mercer (1974), Don Revie (1974–77), Ron Greenwood (1977–82) and Bobby Robson (1982–90) had preceded Taylor (1990–93). Since then Venables (1994–96), Glenn Hoddle (1996–99), Kevin Keegan (1999–2000), Howard Wilkinson (1999 & 2000) and Peter Taylor (2000) have all been in charge of England. Sven Goran Eriksson was appointed in 2001 and is the twelfth man to hold the post in the 40 years the programme has been on the air.

Terry Venables' expansive style of management is evident in his gesture at the photocall at Wembley on his appointment to the England hot seat in 1994.

Glenn Hoddle's reign as England manager was reasonably successful but is remembered primarily for his resignation in 1999 following bizarre remarks about disabled people.

Steve Bruce had already missed out on lifting one trophy when Aston Villa beat United 3-1 in the League Cup Final, but this time was able to raise the Premiership trophy in memory of Sir Matt Busby who had died earlier in the year.

With the Championship settled *Match of the Day* focused on the relegation battle, where any two of five could go down on the last day. Everton knew they had to win against Wimbledon, regardless of other results, but after 20 minutes were 2-0 down and looked doomed. With former Norwich manager Mike Walker now at the helm, having taken over in January, two goals by Graham Stuart and one by Barry Horne pulled them back and kept them up.

When the final whistles blew, Swindon Town, Oldham Athletic and Sheffield United were relegated with Crystal Palace and Nottingham Forest returning to the top flight. Leicester City joined them when they beat Derby County in the play-off Final.

Arsenal beat Parma in Copenhagen to lift the European Cup-Winners' Cup after Alan Smith scored the game's only goal in the 19th minute. However, the other side of north London lost one of its heroes when Spurs' double-winning captain, Danny Blanchflower, died aged 67. He had been one of the first pundits to regularly appear on *Match of the Day*.

The FA Cup

Manchester United encountered Oldham Athletic who held them to a draw at Wembley in the semi-finals. Three days later they succumbed 4-1 to United's greater firepower in the replay held at Maine Road.

Glenn Hoddle was the new player-manager of Chelsea and he led them out alongside Alex Ferguson at Wembley, having taken a relatively straightforward route to the Final.

After an initial scare against Barnet in the third round when they were taken to a replay Chelsea had beaten Sheffield Wednesday, Oxford United, Wolverhampton Wanderers and Luton Town.

Although they had beaten Manchester United in both their League encounters that season Chelsea could find no way through the United defence and lost 4-0. Eric Cantona scored twice from the penalty spot with Mark Hughes and Brian McClair adding one apiece to give United the double and an eighth FA Cup win.

Bryan Robson (far right) scores Manchester United's third goal in their 4-1 win over Oldham Athletic in the FA Cup semi-final replay at Maine Road.

Fact file

Sir Matt Busby died aged 84 in January and missed seeing the current Manchester United side win the double for the first time in their history. Sir Matt had become manager in 1945 and in his 24 years in charge they won five League Championships, two FA Cups and the 1968 European Cup. He had twice reached the European Cup semi-finals with the Busby Babes before the club was decimated by the tragedy of the Munich air crash in 1958 when eight of his players were killed. He rebuilt his team around George Best, Bobby Charlton and Denis Law and continued until 1969, briefly coming out of retirement to manage the club again in the 1970–71 season.

Goal of the Season
Rod Wallace for Leeds against Tottenham, Premier League, April 1994

Footballer of the Year
Alan Shearer, Blackburn Rovers

European Footballer of the Year
Hristo Stoichkov, Barcelona

PFA Player of the Year
Eric Cantona, Manchester United

PFA Young Player of the Year
Andy Cole, Newcastle United

1994–1995

Presenter
Desmond Lynam

League Champions   Blackburn Rovers
FA Cup winners   Everton
League Cup winners   Liverpool

The show

To celebrate *Match of the Day's* 30th anniversary a special section in the first show of the new season looked back at all the great moments and games. It was revealed that Arsenal, Everton and Liverpool had been the only teams to stay in the top flight for the full duration of the series while Manchester United were the most featured club, having appeared as a main game on 247 programmes. After 20 years with the BBC, Bob Wilson moved to ITV as their main football presenter.

The season

The new series of *Match of the Day* got off to a great start with 16 goals in the three featured games. Crystal Palace lost 6-1 at home to Liverpool; Manchester United beat Queens Park Rangers 2-0; and Tottenham Hotspur won 4-3 at Sheffield Wednesday. One of Spurs' goals was scored by Jurgen Klinsmann who had joined the team from Monaco for £2 million in the summer and had become an instant hero at White Hart Lane.

Osvaldo Ardiles began the year as manager at Spurs, playing an adventurous system of five up-front. Unfortunately this also meant they conceded in lots of

Jurgen Klinsmann celebrates his first goal for Tottenham in their 4-3 win at Sheffield Wednesday on the first day of the season.

Three goals in four minutes against Arsenal made Robbie Fowler an instant star on Merseyside as Liverpool crushed the Londoners 3-0.

goals and after Manchester City beat them 5-2 he resigned in November and was replaced by former England captain Gerry Francis.

Mike Walker was another who lost his job, leaving Everton after just one win in 14 games. His replacement, Joe Royle, got off to a good start by beating Liverpool 2-0. The Kop, however, had a new star of their own in Robbie Fowler and against Arsenal he scored three goals in four minutes. Another youngster, Steve McManaman, scored twice in the League Cup Final as Liverpool secured the first trophy of the season by beating Bolton Wanderers 2-1.

Jack Walker and Kenny Dalglish had been on another spending spree at Blackburn Rovers and broke the British transfer record for a second time, buying Chris Sutton for £5 million from Norwich. He formed a prolific partnership with Alan Shearer that proved to be the backbone of their Championship challenge.

Newcastle United were the early-season leaders with Andy Cole scoring regularly, but Kevin Keegan surprised everyone in January when he sold Cole to Manchester United for £7 million. Cole's first game as a United player was a top-of-the-table clash with Blackburn where Eric Cantona scored and United won 1-0. Cole began to repay his fee when he scored five times against Ipswich Town, United eventually winning 9-0 to set a new Premiership record.

At Crystal Palace in January, Cantona was sent off by referee Alan Wilkie. As he left the pitch he was abused by a fan in the crowd prompting Cantona to attack him, feet-first. The incident became a front-page sensation: he was banned for nine months, fined £20,000 and the affair had a major impact on Manchester United's title chances.

Arsenal also had problems. Paul Merson confessed to drug, drink and gambling addictions and spent six weeks in a rehabilitation clinic; and their manager George

Oasis

Oasis had their first number one record in May 1995 with 'Some Might Say', but almost as important to Noel Gallagher was that in the same month, Manchester City just managed to avoid being relegated out of the Premier League.

'For me the main memory of *Match of the Day* has to be the tune. I think it's the same for anyone my age because it just means football. We always used to watch the show as kids because our Dad is a big Man City fan, so it was the done thing for us to sit up and watch the programme. It was always really exciting as well to be at the ground as a kid and see the BBC vans and know that the game was going to be on the show that night.

My worst memory is when City lost to Luton in the last game of the season and got relegated. It was a typical Man City afternoon. We had to win the game to stay up, the team we were playing were useless, and then we conceded a last-minute goal. It was just unbelievable.

My memories are now dominated by David Pleat running across the pitch in his white shoes. White shoes on a football manager! I remember walking through the streets after that, through Moss Side, and it's the first time I'd ever seen people crying after a football match.

I suppose my favourite time was the sixties and early seventies with George Best and Rodney Marsh and all that lot. They really used to play football and there wasn't so much emphasis on fitness. You can imagine them sat in a changing room at half-time having a fag and a cup of tea, which by all accounts they used to do a lot. Everybody had cool haircuts, and great names and it was all about standing on the terraces. The pitches were muddy and all the managers smoked – they were the days. Now everyone is sitting down drinking double-decaff lattes.

As for the show now, I love Gary Lineker and Alan Hansen. They're the men and Hansen is just the best. So is Mark Lawrenson. They are streets better than anyone else. I was in the opening titles once after City lost to Charlton – sat there with my head in my hands. They cut to me in the crowd and John Motson said "and he certainly doesn't look very pleased". I was on the phone to everyone afterwards saying "did you see that?!" '

Graham was sacked and banned for 12 months by the FA. This followed an investigation that resulted in Graham returning £425,000 plus interest on money he had been paid by a Norwegian agent Rune Hauge. At the end of the season they met Real Zaragoza in the Final of the European Cup-Winners' Cup but were beaten in the last minute of extra time when Nayim lobbed David Seaman from some 50 yards to make it 2-1.

With six games remaining Blackburn were eight points clear of the pack, but almost blew the lead, reducing it to just two points ahead of Manchester United with just one match each to play. *Match of the Day* cameras were at the crucial matches with Barry Davies at Upton Park for United's encounter with West Ham and John Motson covering Liverpool against Blackburn.

At half-time Shearer's 34th goal of the season had put Blackburn one-up, while West Ham were also leading 1-0. Then in the second half John Barnes equalized for Liverpool before a late Jamie Redknapp free-kick put them 2-1 up. Just at that moment news filtered through that Manchester United had drawn 1-1 with West Ham, meaning Blackburn were Champions.

Jack Walker's millions had paid off and Blackburn finished on 89 points, one ahead of Manchester United. It was their first title since 1914. Because the Premier League was being reduced in size this season four sides were relegated. Crystal Palace, Norwich City, Leicester City and Ipswich were replaced by Middlesbrough and Bolton Wanderers who had beaten Reading 4-3 in the play-off Final.

With 49 League goals between them Alan Shearer (left) and Chris Sutton had reason to smile as Blackburn Rovers won the Championship for the first time since 1914.

Everton's Paul Rideout rises between Denis Irwin and Gary Pallister to head the only goal of the FA Cup Final against Manchester United.

The FA Cup

Since Everton won the FA Cup in 1984, they had lost five consecutive Wembley Finals and in a season of indifferent League form, the competition had become their main focus. They beat Derby County, Bristol City, Norwich City and Newcastle United to reach the semi-finals where they faced Tottenham Hotspur at Maine Road. Two goals from Nigerian striker Daniel Amokachi helped Everton to a 4-1 win and ensured that Joe Royle would be leading them out at the Final in his first season in charge. At the 50th post-war Cup Final at Wembley they met Manchester United who were aiming to retain the trophy having needed two attempts to get past Crystal Palace in their semi-final at

Villa Park. They had also beaten Sheffield United, Wrexham, Leeds and Queens Park Rangers but were without three key strikers for the Final as Eric Cantona, Andy Cole and Andrei Kanchelskis were unavailable.

The only goal in the match came after half an hour when Paul Rideout headed Everton into the lead. At the end of 90 minutes Dave Watson lifted the Cup, leaving Manchester United without a major trophy for the first time in six years and the double winners of the previous season had the frustrating accolade of being double runners-up.

There was special satisfaction for Joe Royle who had lost the 1968 Final as an Everton player when West Bromwich Albion had won 1-0 and had twice seen his

Oldham Athletic side beaten in the semi-finals by Manchester United.

1994 World Cup

With none of the home nations making it to the finals in the USA many British fans put their support behind Jack Charlton's Republic of Ireland team. They pulled off one of the shocks of the tournament by beating Italy 1-0, coming second in their group and reaching the second round where they lost 2-0 to Holland in Orlando.

Brazil and Italy drew a dull Final 0-0 but the South Americans' lifted the trophy for the fourth time when they won the penalty shoot-out 3-2. It was the first time that a World Cup Final had ended goalless and been won this way. The critical moment came when Roberton Baggio hit the ball over the bar to give South American teams an 8-7 lead over European nations in the list of titles won.

For two men from that continent the competition had appalling postscripts. Diego Maradona failed a drugs test and was sent home in disgrace while Colombian defender Andres Escobar was murdered when he returned home after his side were eliminated.

Although never a prolific scorer, Southampton's Matt Le Tissier scored the BBC's Goal of the Season at Blackburn Rovers in a 3-2 defeat in December.

Blackburn Rovers' Championship win was a record ninth English title for their manager Kenny Dalglish. He won five as a Liverpool player, three as their manager and now one with Blackburn. He became only the third manager to win the League title with two different clubs. The others were Herbert Chapman with Huddersfield Town and Arsenal and Brian Clough who won with both Derby County and Nottingham Forest.

Goal of the Season
Matt Le Tissier for Southampton against Blackburn, Premier League, December 1994

Footballer of the Year
Jurgen Klinsmann, Tottenham Hotspur

European Footballer of the Year
George Weah, AC Milan

PFA Player of the Year
Alan Shearer, Blackburn Rovers

PFA Young Player of the Year
Robbie Fowler, Liverpool

Ray Stubbs

Ray Stubbs was born in May 1956, played football for Tranmere Rovers and says he stumbled into a media career by accident when he read the results of pub matches on BBC Radio Merseyside in the early 1980s. He later joined BBC Manchester and worked as a producer on *A Question of Sport* and *On the Line*, before becoming a reporter and presenter.

Ray joined BBC Sport in 1990 as a *Match of the Day* reporter and first presented the show in the mid-1990s. He has also hosted *Sportsnight*, *Grandstand* and coverage of the Winter Olympic Games. More recently he has become the face of darts and snooker on the BBC, presented 'Football Focus' since 1999 and now presents 'Final Score'.

'I was a professional for five years with Tranmere Rovers although I wasn't touched with success in any shape or form. I had lots of enthusiasm but precious little else and as a player I was absolutely nowhere near *Match of the Day*. As a footballer I loved the life but it was a dream that wasn't going to be fulfilled. I was one of thousands of kids who wanted to make the grade and I was very proud to have represented my home town club.

Match of the Day is part and parcel of footballing society, and one of the things that stands out for me is Jimmy Hill's face in those opening titles. I'm no different to anyone else and the show was my window on the world of football when I was growing up. Suddenly the characters became real in our homes and the players and clubs embraced it.

You say the name, "*Match of the Day*", and the song pops into your head. It is like a trigger. You can go into any bar, with a crowd of 60-year-olds or a bunch of students, say "*Match of the Day*" and someone will start singing the theme tune. I did that myself on the first show I presented and I still do – I can't help it! When the music starts you find yourself humming along.

There have always been three soundtracks to football for me. The roar of the crowd when a goal goes in; the sound of

studio". Broadcasters, production teams and supporters have this huge romance for the show, so it's great when the players have it as well.

I think it is especially true for the smaller clubs in the early rounds of the FA Cup. There is a feeling of the fairground when the vans and cameras roll into town and we always get such a great reaction.

I love the buzz of being part of a team of football fans. As with every show, for every presenter on screen there are dozens of people off camera who make the programme work. It's great to talk football so what we try to do is share the experience with the fans – we do our best and hope that they like it. If they don't they are quick to let us know!

As a reporter I was able to interview some memorable characters but my favourite has to be Paul Gascoigne. I would happily talk to him anywhere, any place, any time. He is such an amazing and unpredictable person. It was always a challenge to interview Sir Alex Ferguson as he often tries to create an intimidating atmosphere. I always enjoy interviewing Alan Shearer because of the slightly different challenge of trying to break through his protective shield, and also because I have such respect for him as a player.

The interview I have never been able to do is to congratulate an England manager or captain on winning an international trophy. I just hope that Garth gets to do it soon.'

the vidi-printer bringing us results on a Saturday afternoon; and the opening music of Match of the Day.

To present Match of the Day, Sportsnight, Grandstand and 'Football Focus' – some of the biggest brands on TV – has been a huge privilege and a great thrill. For a football fan, working with the pundits is as good as it gets. They all have such authority and the reaction of players when they come on to the set is great. John Salako just sat there in awe saying, "I'm sitting in the Match of the Day

1995–1996

Presenter
Desmond Lynam

League Champions Manchester United
FA Cup winners Manchester United
League Cup winners Aston Villa

The show

Manchester United had a major clear-out of their more established names including Mark Hughes and Paul Ince, replacing them with a raft of new younger players. On the opening day of the season they lost 3-1 to Aston Villa, their only goal coming from 21-year-old David Beckham. When Alex Ferguson's side were discussed on *Match of the Day* that night, Des remarked: 'United were scarcely recognizable from the team we've known over the past couple of seasons, what's going on, do you feel?'

Alan Hansen replied: 'You can't win anything with kids... he's got to buy players, it's as simple as that.' He was almost accurate in his analysis – apart from Manchester United winning the double!

David Beckham's performances for Manchester United proved Alan Hansen wrong for once. And how wrong was he? Well, they only went and won the double.

The season

The season began with Stan Collymore moving from Nottingham Forest to Liverpool for a British record fee of £8.5 million. It was his new team-mate Robbie Fowler, however, who made the biggest impact in the early stages when he scored four against Bolton Wanderers as part of a 5-2 win. On the same day Alan Shearer completed a hat-trick for Blackburn Rovers against Coventry City and Tony Yeboah scored three as Leeds United beat Wimbledon.

At Newcastle Kevin Keegan had added Les Ferdinand and David Ginola to his Newcastle squad and they made a great start, winning nine of their first ten games to lead the Premiership from mid-August.

Eric Cantona returned to the Manchester United side when his ban ended in October. In his first home game, against Liverpool, he supplied the cross for Nicky Butt to score, and then at 2-1 down, scored the equalizing penalty.

Also in-form was Shearer who hit another hat-trick, this time against Nottingham Forest as Blackburn won 7-0 to end Forest's 25-game unbeaten run in the League. It was the biggest win of the season and they later added to Forest's woe by beating them 5-1 at the City Ground.

By 20 January the title race looked over as Newcastle had opened up a 12-point lead but the pressure began to show and the gap began to close. Manchester United got it down to four points in March when they notched up a 6-0 away win at Bolton Wanderers before beating Newcastle 1-0 at St James' Park.

At the end of March, Manchester United were in top place and remained there for the rest of the season. They invited ridicule by changing out of their grey shirts at Southampton when 3-0 down at half-time – the new blue and white strip made no difference and they eventually lost 3-1.

In April Liverpool met Newcastle on a Monday night in a match that was one of the most exciting for years. It prompted the editor of *Match of the Day*, Brian Barwick, to broadcast a special programme on the evening after it was played.

Robbie Fowler opened the scoring for the home side; Les Ferdinand equalized then David Ginola put Newcastle ahead. Fowler's second made it 2-2; Faustino Asprilla put the visitors ahead again and then Stan Collymore scored twice to make the final result 4-3.

Kevin Keegan later said it was the best game he had ever been part of, as player or manager.

In a crucial week Leeds United played both title contenders. Their goalkeeper, Mark Beeney, was sent off against Manchester United and after they lost 1-0, Alex Ferguson suggested that the Leeds players were trying harder against his team than they would against Newcastle. The comments provoked a famous outburst on Sky from Keegan, after they had also beaten Leeds 1-0. He lost all composure and ranted: 'I tell you, honestly, I will love it if we beat them, love it'.

It was not to be, and on the following weekend Manchester United beat Middlesbrough 3-0 to clinch their third title in four seasons. They finished on 82 points with Newcastle second on 78 and Liverpool in third with 71.

Queens Park Rangers and Bolton were relegated along with Manchester City, who ended with 38 points, the same number as Southampton and Coventry City. In the last game of the season Manchester City were level at 2-2 with Liverpool when their manager Alan Ball was told a draw was enough. It was the wrong information and bewildered fans watched as Steve Lomas time-wasted with the ball in the corner when they needed a win. They went down for the third time in 13 seasons.

Robbie Fowler opens the scoring for Liverpool in their Monday night thriller against Newcastle in April. The Reds eventually won 4-3 with two goals for Stan Collymore.

They Think It's All Over

In October 1995 a new and irreverent BBC television sports quiz began and quickly established itself as the anarchic younger sibling of *A Question of Sport*. It took its name from the most famous commentary line of all time, *They Think It's All Over*. Originally hosted by Desmond Lynam on Radio 4, the TV show featured regulars Gary Lineker and Rory McGrath against David Gower and Lee Hurst. Comedian, writer, Sport Relief stalwart, prolific angler and Stoke City fanatic Nick Hancock presents the show.

'I always used to go and watch Stoke play so saw plenty of football, but as a youngster in the seventies I was incredibly anal about football knowledge. The great thing about *Match of the Day* was it gave me loads of information about players from all the divisions. I remember being especially taken by the double nickname given to Warboys and Bannister of Bristol Rovers – Smash and Grab. It gave us all a perspective so we could talk about the game with a greater authority.

The greatest *Match of the Day* in my memory came on 26 September 1970. It was to be Arsenal's double-winning season but we beat them 5-0 at home. I must have done something wrong as I hadn't been allowed to go to the match, but my parents relented when the show came on. Terry Conroy's goal in that game won the second ever Goal of the Month award and at that age it was really something to celebrate. Apparently more than 35,000 people entered the competition and I was shocked that such a momentous achievement didn't merit an open-topped bus tour around Stoke.

I loved working with Gary on *They Think It's All Over* and think he has made a terrific presenter. When Stoke beat Wigan in the FA Cup I heard he said "I know someone who will be very happy with that". To be mentioned on the great show in the same breath as Stoke was probably the defining moment of my life!'

Men of the Moment: Eric Cantona (left) challenges Liverpool's Stan Collymore during the FA Cup Final. Cantona started the season in disgrace and ended it as a double winner and Player of the Season. Collymore's career had gone well so far at Liverpool, but his life was soon to take a turn for the worse.

Sunderland, Derby County and Leicester City all returned to the top division, and Aston Villa won the League Cup for the second time in three years when they beat Leeds United 3-0 in the Final.

The FA Cup

Manchester United reached the Final for the third year in a row by beating Chelsea 2-1 in their semi-final at Villa Park. A straightforward qualifying campaign saw them meet Liverpool in the Final, the Reds having put three past Aston Villa at Old Trafford.

Sadly, despite two star-packed sides, the cream Armani suits of the Liverpool team were more memorable than the game. It looked to be heading for extra time when Manchester United's captain, Eric Cantona, drove the ball into the Liverpool net with just a few minutes remaining. It gave them the Cup for a record ninth time.

Cantona had begun the season in disgrace – still banned as a result of the Crystal Palace incident – but ended it as a double winner and Player of the Year. It was a remarkable transformation and led to the unprecedented achievement by his team of a second double in three seasons.

1996–1997

Presenter
Desmond Lynam

League Champions Manchester United
FA Cup winners Chelsea
League Cup winners Leicester City

The show

During recent years the word 'pundit' has become a standard description for any ex-professional player who sits alongside the main presenter on a sports show. It is most closely associated with *Match of the Day*, however, and there has been a long and distinguished line of regular guests who stretch back to the first series in 1964. Walley Barnes and Danny Blanchflower appeared pitch-side to give their views in that initial season; Jimmy Hill became the first to combine opinion and presentation; and from Desmond Lynam onwards the presenters have always had a regular line-up of friendly faces to throw questions to.

Jimmy Hill and Terry Venables made a famous and controversial double act in the 1990s. Alan Hansen, Trevor Brooking and Mark Lawrenson have been the regulars for recent seasons and they have been supplemented by a variety of others including Garth Crooks, Ian Wright, David O'Leary, Peter Reid, Martin O'Neill, and more recently Peter Schmeichel.

The BBC's coverage of Euro '96 won a BAFTA and an RTS award for the editor, Niall Sloane, and the producer, Vivien Kent. Viv made history by becoming the first woman to produce *Match of the Day*.

The season

The new season began as the old had ended, with Manchester United collecting yet another trophy when they beat Newcastle United 4-0 to win the Charity Shield. Charity was apparently lacking at Highbury, however, where Bruce Rioch was sacked as the manager of Arsenal after just 61 days. A few weeks later Arsène Wenger moved from the Japanese club Grampus Eight to take charge.

The first League show featured David Beckham's extraordinary goal against Wimbledon scored from the half-way line. It also included Middlesbrough's new £7 million signing Fabrizio Ravanelli hitting a hat-trick on his debut as they drew 3-3 with Liverpool. The Italian was the first to win the programme's new Man of the Day accolade that was announced at the end of each edition.

A special midweek programme saw Alan Shearer make his home debut for Newcastle following his record-breaking £15 million move from Blackburn Rovers. He scored in their 2-0 win over Wimbledon and by the end of the season

it was clear that the investment had paid off as finished as the Premier League's top marksman, with 25 goals.

The first half of the season saw the lead regularly change hands as Manchester United, Liverpool, Arsenal and Newcastle vied for top spot. This tussle at the top ensured *Match of the Day* featured many exciting games such as Liverpool beating Chelsea 5-1 to regain the lead. At another stage, Newcastle won seven in a row including a 4-3 win against Aston Villa and a 5-0 win against Manchester United. It sent Kevin Keegan's team top and inflicted the biggest defeat for 12 years on the Champions.

It was the start of a wretched run of form for Manchester United who lost their next game 6-3 at Southampton. Their third consecutive defeat came at Old Trafford when they lost 2-1 to Chelsea in front of more than 55,000 people, a record crowd for the Premier League. The run finally ended when they beat Arsenal 1-0 in mid-November at a time when Newcastle were heading the table. At the end of the month the lead changed again when Arsenal got a 2-1 win at Newcastle, but by the end of the year it was Liverpool who were in charge after a run that included a 5-1 win over Middlesbrough, with four goals by Robbie Fowler.

Middlesbrough had splashed out on many big signings including the Brazilians Juninho and Emerson but they struggled all season. On 20 December they took the unprecedented step of cancelling their game against Blackburn as 23 of their players were injured or ill. That decision cost them a three-point fine and meant they were relegated at the end of the season.

At the end of January, Manchester United beat Wimbledon to go top of the League, and they remained there for the rest of the season. March saw the most entertaining match of the campaign when Liverpool beat Newcastle 4-3, and the most entertaining moment on *Match of the Day* when Alan Hansen pressed a button and finally stopped Jimmy Hill from talking. He blew him up in the studio as part of a gag for Comic Relief.

The conclusion of the Championship was an anti-climax. Manchester United were crowned without playing when Liverpool lost to Wimbledon and West Ham held Newcastle to a 0-0 draw on 6 May. They eventually finished on 75 points with Newcastle, Arsenal and Liverpool on 68, separated by goal difference.

The final *Match of the Day* of the year featured the highest-scoring game as Newcastle ended a barren spell with a 7-1 win against Tottenham Hotspur. Less than a fortnight later Kevin Keegan stunned players and fans by resigning after five years in charge, and another former Anfield hero, Kenny Dalglish, was installed as the new manager.

Middlesbrough were joined in the drop to Division One by Sunderland and Nottingham Forest. To compound a frustrating season for Middlesbrough's supporters, they also lost both Cup Finals. In the League Cup they drew 1-1 with Leicester City in the Final at Wembley but lost the replay 1-0 at Hillsborough ten days later.

Fabrizio Ravanelli scores from the spot against Liverpool. It was the 'White Feather's' debut for Middlesbrough and he scored all three goals in a 3-3 draw.

The music

The most instantly recognisable aspect of *Match of the Day* is its iconic theme tune. Thousands of people have had the tune played at their wedding, including one of the programme's producers, Emma Josling and many others have bade their final farewells to it including Cardinal Basil Hume, who had it played at his funeral. The tune was written by Barry Stoller and introduced at the start of the 1970–71 season. It is called 'Offside' and replaced the original tune, 'Drum Majorette', written by Arnold Stock.

Another famous footballing tune grew out of *Fantasy Football League* presented by Frank Skinner and David Baddiel. The show spawned the number one single 'Three Lions' that Baddiel and Skinner performed with The Lightning Seeds and which became the unofficial anthem of Euro 96.

Roberto Di Matteo (left) punches the air after scoring Chelsea's opening goal in the FA Cup Final. The goal, scored 42 seconds from the kick-off, remains the fastest in FA Cup Final history.

Barnsley manager Danny Wilson (left) is congratulated by his assistant Eric Winstanley after leading the club into the top flight for the first time in 110 years.

The FA Cup

Bristol City made the early FA Cup headlines when they beat St Albans 9-2 in the second round, but the tie of the competition came in April when Chelsea met Liverpool, live on *Match of the Day*. Robbie Fowler and Stan Collymore put the visitors 2-0 up at half-time before Chelsea hit back, inspired by Mark Hughes and Gianluca Vialli. They won 4-2 and kept that form all the way to

There was more to look forward to for the clubs who won promotion into the Premier League, especially for the fans of Barnsley who saw them reach the top flight for the first time in their 110-year history. Bolton Wanderers were the Division One Champions and Crystal Palace beat Sheffield United 1-0 to win the play-off Final.

Wembley, having beaten Wimbledon 3-0 in the semi-final at Highbury.

Their opponents were Middlesbrough who had defeated Second Division Chesterfield in a semi-final replay. Boro couldn't have got off to a worse start when Roberto Di Matteo scored the fastest Cup Final goal at Wembley after just 42 seconds. Eight minutes from the end, Eddie Newton added a second and Dennis Wise lifted the cup to celebrate Chelsea's first win in the competition for 27 years.

QPR's Trevor Sinclair scored the Goal of the Season in the R's FA Cup 5th round tie against Barnsley.

1996 European Championship

Britain's biggest sporting event since 1966 saw England record memorable wins: beating Scotland 2-0 and Holland 4-1 before progressing to the quarter-finals by defeating Spain 4-2 on penalties. The tournament, which featured 16 teams, was twice the size of any that had gone before and dominated national life for a month. When England met Germany in the semi-final at Wembley the nation came to a halt, but, agonizingly England lost another penalty shoot-out after the game had finished 1-1. This time Gareth Southgate missed the crucial kick. Germany won the Final by beating the Czech Republic 2-1 following Oliver Bierhoff's golden goal.

Peter Shilton played his 1000th League game when he turned out for Leyton Orient against Brighton in December. He is England's most capped player, with 125 appearances between 1970 and 1990. Shilton began his goalkeeping career as a 16-year-old with Leicester City in 1966 and also had long spells with Stoke City, Nottingham Forest, Southampton and Derby County. While at Forest he won two European Cups, the League Championship and the League Cup. He later played for Plymouth Argyle, Bolton Wanderers and Leyton Orient where he ended his career after 1005 league appearances and 1390 first-class games.

Goal of the Season
Trevor Sinclair for QPR against Barnsley, FA Cup, February 1997

Footballer of the Year
Gianfranco Zola, Chelsea

European Footballer of the Year
Ronaldo, Inter Milan

PFA Player of the Year
Alan Shearer, Newcastle United

PFA Young Player of the Year
David Beckham, Manchester United

1997–1998

Presenter
Desmond Lynam

League Champions Arsenal

FA Cup winners Arsenal

League Cup winners Chelsea

European Cup-Winners' Cup winners Chelsea

The show

Des introduced the start of the new season with the knowledge that football on the BBC was secure for at least another four years. This was the beginning of a record new deal between the FA and Sky/BBC, worth £670 million from Sky and £73 million from the BBC for highlights. Mark Lawrenson joined Alan and Trevor as a regular pundit during the second part of the season.

As part of the new FA Cup TV contract, ITV regained the rights to show live matches, including the Final, while the BBC retained Saturday night highlights.

The season

Dion Dublin was the star of the opening day of the Premiership when he twice equalized for Coventry against Chelsea before completing a hat-trick with the winner after 88 minutes. It was the start of an outstanding season for Dublin who was to end up as the joint leading goal scorer alongside Michael Owen and Chris Sutton.

Manchester United opened their title defence with a 2-0 win against Tottenham Hotspur. The Spurs fans were still upset that Teddy Sherringham had left them in the summer for Old Trafford but they got a small dose of satisfaction when he missed a penalty against his old team.

Having waited a fortnight for their next game, Chelsea travelled to Barnsley where four goals from Gianluca Vialli helped them to a 6-0 win. August ended with Blackburn Rovers and Manchester United as the early joint leaders, three points clear of the rest.

On 13 September Ian Wright's hat-trick against Bolton Wanderers at Highbury took him to 180 goals and past Cliff Bastin's 58-year-old Arsenal record of 178. Wright celebrated wildly but the rest of his season was to be dogged

On a day when the Rest of the World came to Yorkshire, Italian superstar Gianluca Vialli scores the second of his four goals as Chelsea beat Barnsley 6-0 at Oakwell. The other goals came from Romanian Dan Petrescu and Uruguayan Gus Poyet.

by injury and he scored only four more League goals. On the same weekend Manchester United beat West Ham United 2-1 to go top while Blackburn lost 4-3 at home to Leeds United. Incredibly all seven goals came in the first 34 minutes.

By the end of the month Arsenal had captured the lead by scoring four against West Ham and putting five past Barnsley, but Manchester United regained the top spot when an Andy Cole hat-trick helped them to a 7-0 win against the same side. They followed that by beating Sheffield Wednesday 6-1 and stayed at the top of the Premier League for the next six months.

The best recovery of the season came from Leeds who turned a 3-0 deficit into a 4-3 victory against Derby County but Gerry Francis was unable to inspire his Spurs side to do the same when they found themselves 4-0 down at home to Liverpool. A week later he was replaced by the Swiss coach, Christian Gross. The change of manager made little difference and Chelsea moved into second spot after beating Spurs 6-1 at White Hart Lane. It was their worst home defeat for 62 years.

Despite that victory and going into the new year in second place, Chelsea shocked the footballing world in February when they sacked their manager Ruud Gullit and replaced him with their Italian striker Gianluca Vialli.

By late February, Manchester United had moved 11 points clear at the top of the Premier League and a local bookie, Fred Done, was so convinced they wouldn't be caught that he paid up to all those who had bet United would be Champions. It proved a costly mistake.

Their season turned on 7 March when they lost 2-0 to Sheffield Wednesday and a week later Arsenal beat them 1-0 to cut the lead to just six points. On 18 April the Gunners beat Wimbledon to go top and remained there for the rest of the season.

On 3 May their record tenth consecutive win set a new League record and made Arsène Wenger the first foreign manager to win the title. They clinched it by beating Everton 4-0 to secure the Championship for the 11th time.

Arsenal's captain Tony Adams shows off the FA Cup and the Premiership trophy during their victory parade through Islington in north London.

Ian Wright

Ian Wright was a late starter as a professional footballer and didn't join Crystal Palace until he was 21. After six seasons with them he moved to Arsenal in 1991 and went on to become their highest ever scorer with 185 in 288 games. Ian played 33 times for England scoring nine goals. He is an occasional pundit on *Match of the Day*.

'My best early memory is just Jimmy Hill and the original goatee and, of course, the music. I always remember how nice his beard was with that amazingly long chin. It was always so pristine. There was a strange thing that used to happen in school playgrounds as well. When somebody used to say something that wasn't quite right or tell an obvious lie you'd say, "Yeah, yeah, Jimmy Hill, Jimmy Hill" and stroke your chin!

There always seemed to be great goals as well when I was younger, and it was fantastic to first appear on it when I was at Palace. After matches, friends would ask if I was going to go out with them for a drink, and I'd say I just wanted to relax, but really all I was doing was getting home to tape *Match of the Day* so I could see myself on the programme. They may pretend that they haven't seen their goal on the show but all players do it.

When I first appeared on the show I sat and heard the countdown; listened to the music and watched the opening titles. Then when Des asked me something I told him that this was my Graceland. It was so weird because it was so small, but for me, *Match of the Day* is so big. It was quite a surreal moment for me.

Match of the Day is like an institution, it's just like the Queen's speech on Christmas Day; it's always going to be there and always should be there.'

Arsenal finished the season on 78 points, one ahead of Manchester United with Liverpool in third place on 65 points and Chelsea fourth with 63. Crystal Palace, Barnsley and Bolton Wanderers were all relegated.

Charlton Athletic and Sunderland drew the play-off final 4-4, but the Londoners won 7-6 on penalties to join Nottingham Forest and Middlesbrough back in the top flight.

In the League Cup Final Chelsea met Middlesbrough and the winning goals from Frank Sinclair and Roberto Di Matteo both came in extra time. Chelsea completed a 2-0 victory and lifted the trophy for the first time since 1965. In his first season as manager Gianluca Vialli led them to a cup double when they also won the European Cup-Winners' Cup beating VfB Stuttgart 1-0 in the Final with a goal from substitute Gianfranco Zola. Their only previous European success had been in the same competition 27 years before.

The FA Cup

Arsenal's route to the Final had been a tough one after they had scraped past Port Vale on penalties in third round, beaten Middlesbrough in the fourth and needed a replay to defeat Crystal Palace in round five. They were taken to penalties again in the quarter-final by West Ham and came away from Villa Park with just a 1-0 win against Wolverhampton Wanderers in the semi-final. Newcastle United were chasing their first FA Cup victory since 1955 and had overcome Sheffield United at Old Trafford to reach Wembley.

They were, however, to be disappointed once again as Arsenal emulated their 1971 side and completed the double, winning the Final 2-0. Marc Overmars scored the first after 23 minutes and in the second half Nicolas Anelka's shot secured the win. Tony Adams lifted the FA Cup for the second time in six seasons.

Marc Overmars knocks the ball past Newcastle keeper Shay Given to give Arsenal the lead in the FA Cup Final.

Michael Owen (right) had become the youngest England international of the century when he played against Chile at Wembley in February. After his instant impact in France, he went on to become the second youngest winner of the BBC's coveted Sports Personality of the Year award. Scottish swimmer Ian Black, who collected the trophy back in 1958, remains, at 17, the youngest winner.

Goal of the Season
Dennis Bergkamp for Arsenal against Leicester, Premier League, August 1997

Footballer of the Year
Dennis Bergkamp, Arsenal

European Footballer of the Year
Zinedine Zidane, Juventus

PFA Player of the Year
Dennis Bergkamp, Arsenal

PFA Young Player of the Year
Michael Owen, Liverpool

Mark Lawrenson

Mark Lawrenson was born in Preston in 1957 and played for Preston North End and Brighton before Bob Paisley paid £900,000 to take him to Liverpool in 1981. He formed a legendary partnership with Alan Hansen at the heart of their defence, winning five League titles, the European Cup, FA Cup and three League Cups. Capped 39 times by the Republic of Ireland, Mark was forced into retirement by an injury when he was just 30. He has been a regular guest and summarizer on Radio 5 Live and a *Match of the Day* pundit since 1997, although Alistair McGowan's regular impersonations have also introduced him to a wider audience.

'I was brought up in Penworthan near Preston and can clearly remember that my Saturday night treat was to sit up and watch *Match of the Day* with a bowl of sweets. This would be at the end of the 1960s when I got my pocket money on a Saturday, so if I was good I had spearmint chews and the football.

Both parents were big football fans and my Dad had been a very good player with Southport in the old Division Three (North) as well as working as a draughtsman. My Mum later re-married and my stepfather was a director of Preston while I was there as a youngster. At that age I supported them and Manchester United but my overwhelming early memory of *Match of the Day* was of watching Trevor Brooking at West Ham and thinking how much time he always seemed to have to play the ball.

If you played professional football, then *Match of the Day* was like breathing and taxes. Totally essential. Everybody watched it. I still have a few performances recorded from my playing days as well as a couple of post-match interviews. They were complete fashion disasters – long hair, shaggy perm and clothes that a scarecrow would have rejected.

After I signed for Liverpool we played Arsenal and I remember Jimmy doing a nice piece on me about playing out from the back and the techniques that I used. At training on the following Monday Bob Paisley called me over. That was rare occurrence and only usually happened when

there was a problem. "Did you see *Match of the Day*?" he asked. "Just remember that the whole country saw it." In other words, it might have been good for the ego but it also exposed your tricks.

My favourite memory is from the first year that we won the League after I joined Liverpool. On Boxing Day we had lost 3-1 at home to Manchester City and were having a torrid time. We turned it around and after a great run had to win on the last day of the season at home to Spurs. Glenn Hoddle scored one of the best goals I have ever seen when he was 35 yards out. I backed off thinking "go on then, try and score from here", and he did! I equalized with an 18-

some take it personally and I fell out with Kevin Keegan after England lost 3-2 to Portugal in the European Championships having been 2-0 up. I criticized him about tactical naivety and we haven't spoken since, but I was just being honest. I also fell out with Peter Reid a couple of times but he's a big mate now.

The best bit of the job is seeing all the games come in at the same time. We have small bets on the scores with nine or ten of us in a room and it's good fun. Not having that for the past three years has been very strange. It has been difficult to do 'Final Score' without seeing a ball kicked and we relied a lot on Radio 5 Live, which has really come into its own for the BBC.

To have been a viewer, a player and a pundit on the show means a lot to me. Everyone is delighted that we've got the show back on Saturdays, just in time for the 40th anniversary.'

yard header past Ray Clemence and then played Kenny Dalglish in for the second before Ronnie Whelen got the third. It was my first championship medal and the best.

I got involved with television after Niall Sloane rang me in March 1997 and asked if I wanted to do some punditry. I'd already done quite a bit on Radio 5 Live and a few television commentaries, and I leapt at the chance. It came quite naturally as I turned from poacher to gamekeeper but *Match of the Day* was also a bit daunting as it was a show I had always watched. By that time Des, Alan and Trevor were fixtures.

I still watch football primarily as a fan but try to be honest with my opinions. Most people are fine with that but

1998–1999

Presenter
Desmond Lynam

League Champions Manchester United

FA Cup winners Manchester United

League Cup winners Tottenham Hotspur

European Cup winners Manchester United

The show

In the early years of the show the match commentaries were monopolized by the household names. They were supplemented by Tony Gubba, Gerald Sinstadt, Alan Parry and Clive Tyldesley but toward the end of the 1990s the vast increase in the amount of football on TV meant more opportunities were created.

In 1998–99, for example, 11 different commentators were used on the main games during the campaign with John Champion's (right) voice being heard most often. He covered 38 matches and was followed by John Motson (29), Tony Gubba (26) and Barry Davies (25). Simon Brotherton (9) and Gerald Sindstadt (7) were also used as were Ian Brown (6), Mark Pougatch (4), John Murray (3), Steve Wilson (2) and Ian Gwyn Hughes (1).

The season

New boys Charlton Athletic got off to a strong start when Chris Mendonca's hat-trick helped them beat Southampton 5-0 on the second weekend of the season. Across the Thames, however, Tottenham Hotspur were struggling. Just a month into the campaign they sacked manager Christian Gross and replaced him with George Graham. He had resigned from Leeds United in order to take the post and was succeeded there by David O'Leary. Ruud Gullit was the new man in charge at Newcastle United following Kenny Dalglish's departure and he got away to a strong start as they won four in a row including a 5-1 victory at Coventry City.

Paul Merson was another on the move, in his case for £6 million from Middlesbrough, and he scored on his Aston Villa debut as they beat Wimbledon 2-0 in September. Villa were the early leaders and after two months were four points ahead of Manchester United.

Liverpool had been in poor early form but that changed at the end of October when they beat Nottingham Forest 5-1 thanks to four goals by England's 18-year-old hero, Michael Owen. They reverted to type, however, in the following two weekends, losing to Leicester City and Derby County.

Aston Villa were still unbeaten on 7 November when they met Spurs and paraded their latest signing, Dion Dublin, who had joined from Coventry for £5 million. He scored twice and had a third controversially disallowed as they won 3-2.

Liverpool lost 3-1 at home to Leeds and, having dropped to 12th, they decided to split their double-headed managerial partnership. Roy Evans left, leaving Gerard Houllier in sole charge. It seemed to work as they promptly beat the League leaders Aston Villa 4-2 at Villa Park.

In the weekend before Christmas Manchester United lost 3-2 at home to Middlesbrough but it was to be their last defeat of the season as they embarked on an incredible 33-match unbeaten run. Gianluca Vialli was also celebrat-

Middlesbrough's Paul Merson (centre) gets between Aston Villa's Ugo Ehiogu (left) and Lee Hendrie. His performance obviously impressed Villa as they bought him shortly afterwards for £6 million.

ing as Chelsea beat Spurs 2-0 on the same afternoon to go to the top of the League for the first time in nine years, although Villa regained the lead a week later.

Chelsea returned to the top in January when their 1-0 win at Newcastle meant that they had been unbeaten for a club record 20 games. The show on 16 January was one packed with goals as Manchester United won 6-2 at Leicester City, Sheffield Wednesday put four past West Ham at Upton Park and Liverpool thrashed Southampton 7-1.

New signing Dwight Yorke had scored a hat-trick in that victory over Leicester and he added two more in early February when United went to Nottingham Forest four points ahead of the pack and won 8-1. Andy Cole also scored two but the star performance came from Ole Gunnar Solskjaer who scored four after coming on as a substitute.

Aston Villa fell away having led the Premiership regularly during the season, but Leeds United were beginning to make a strong challenge, as were Arsenal. On 24 April they became the eighth different team to head the League since August when they travelled to Middlesbrough and won 6-1, but Manchester United replaced them on the following weekend.

In a surprising break from tradition at Anfield, Gerard Houllier (right) joined former boot-room boy Roy Evans as joint manager of Liverpool. The experiment was not a happy one for Evans and he resigned a few months later.

Reds' treble

Alex Ferguson finally achieved his dream of winning the European Cup when Manchester United met Bayern Munich in the Final in Barcelona. United were 1-0 down at the end of 90 minutes but injury-time goals by substitutes Ole Gunnar Solskjaer and Teddy Sheringham secured them an astonishing 2-1 victory and meant that they had achieved the ultimate football treble. They also became the first British club to win the World Club Championship in its 40-year history when they beat Palmeiras 1-0. At the end of the year Alex Ferguson was knighted by the Queen.

The League's climax came on Sunday 16 May when goals from David Beckham and Andy Cole helped Manchester United beat Spurs 2-1 to ensure they won the Championship by just one point from Arsenal. Chelsea were third and Leeds finished fourth.

Charlton, Blackburn Rovers and Nottingham Forest were relegated and Sunderland, Bradford City and Watford all won promotion.

The one trophy that eluded Manchester United was the League Cup. Now known as the Worthington Cup, it was won by Spurs who beat Leicester City 1-0. It was the first time they had won the trophy since 1973.

The FA Cup

Having secured the League title, the second part of Manchester United's historic treble came six days later when they met Newcastle United in the FA Cup Final. It had been a tough route to Wembley and on the way they had beaten Middlesbrough, Liverpool, Fulham, Chelsea and Arsenal. It took a replay to get past the Gunners in the semi-final at Villa Park but a goal by David Beckham and a magnificent strike by Ryan Giggs in extra time helped them win 2-1.

Their opponents had lost to Arsenal in the 1998 Final and were determined not to suffer the same fate. Alan Shearer had scored twice in their 2-0 semi-final victory over Spurs and Ruud Gullit led them on to the pitch convinced that this would be their day.

It wasn't, however, and Manchester United lifted their fourth FA Cup of the decade. Teddy Sheringham scored in the first half and Paul Scholes in the second as they won 2-0 and completed the double for the third time.

Ole Gunnar Solskjaer (centre) steers the ball into the Bayern Munich net to win the European Cup for Manchester United.

Huge crowds pack Manchester's Deansgate as the triumphant Manchester United team show off the three trophies they captured in the 1998–99 season.

1998 World Cup

Scotland and England both qualified for the finals that were held in France. Scotland failed to win a match but England, managed by Glenn Hoddle, reached the second round where they met Argentina in the most dramatic match of the tournament. Argentina took an early lead, Alan Shearer levelled from the penalty spot and then 18-year-old Michael Owen scored an outstanding solo goal to put England ahead. Javier Zanetti's free-kick made it 2-2 and then, just after half time, David Beckham was fouled by Diego Simeone. A prostrate Beckham kicked out and caught the leg of the Argentinian who threw himself theatrically to the ground. Beckham was sent off, the ten men clung on until the end of extra time but lost the resulting penalty shoot-out 4-3 when Paul Ince and David Batty missed. The host nation won the Final when they beat Brazil 3-0, but the match will be remembered as much for the controversy that surrounded Ronaldo's fitness as the goals from Zinedine Zidane and Emmanuel Petit.

On 1 May the whole footballing world mourned Sir Alf Ramsey who died aged 79 following a long illness. His most recent successor as England manager, Glenn Hoddle had been sacked a few weeks before and after a brief caretaker spell by Howard Wilkinson, was replaced by Kevin Keegan.

Goal of the Season
Ryan Giggs for Manchester United against Arsenal, FA Cup, April 1999

Footballer of the Year
David Ginola, Tottenham Hotspur

European Footballer of the Year
Rivaldo, Barcelona

PFA Player of the Year
David Ginola, Tottenham Hotspur

PFA Young Player of the Year
Nicolas Anelka, Arsenal

1999–2000

Presenter
Gary Lineker

League Champions Manchester United
FA Cup winners Chelsea
League Cup winners Leicester City

The show

Just before the start of the season, on 2 August, Desmond Lynam resigned from the BBC and moved to ITV to become their main football presenter. Niall Sloane was the editor of *Match of the Day* at the time and recalled:

'When I heard that Des had left to go to ITV, I was in genuine shock for 30 seconds. Then I thought that it was a fabulous opportunity to develop Gary Lineker and he is now a fantastic presenter.'

The Head of Sport at the BBC was Bob Shennan and he felt the same way:

'If we hadn't lost Des we'd have lost Gary, but although it seemed like a disaster at first and the press gave us a hard time, it quickly became apparent that Gary was ready to take over.'

The season

Once again the opening weekend was dominated by Manchester United. The *Match of the Day* cameras were at Old Trafford to see them parade all their trophies and beat Sheffield Wednesday 4-0 in their opening home game. From then on they were almost unstoppable.

Ruud Gullit was the first managerial casualty of the new campaign when he resigned from Newcastle in August complaining about bad results and press intrusion. Two days later Andy Cole scored four against them in Manchester United's 5-1 victory and Bobby Robson ended his decade on mainland Europe when he returned as the Magpies' new manager.

United themselves had a major shock at the beginning of October when they lost 5-0 at Chelsea. In the same month they lost 3-1 at Spurs but apart from one more blip in their return against Newcastle in February they had no more defeats.

David O'Leary's young Leeds side led the Championship for much of the early part of the season, winning 14 of their first 19 matches. On 28 December, when still in top position, they lost 2-0 to Arsenal on the final *Match of the Day* of the century. They followed that with three defeats in the next month to Aston Villa, Liverpool and Manchester United as they began to slip away from the leading clubs.

One of the biggest League wins of the season came in March when Glenn Hoddle, who had been resurrected as a club manager with Southampton following his dismissal as England coach, took his new team to play his old. Steffan Iversen scored three as Spurs won 7-2.

The other high score came, inevitably, from Manchester United who beat West Ham United 7-1 and by 22 April they had secured their sixth title in eight seasons when they won

3-1 at Southampton. They finished the season a staggering 18 points ahead of Arsenal who were second. Leeds United came third and Liverpool fourth.

Going into the final games Watford and Sheffield Wednesday knew they were relegated but the third spot was still to be decided. Bradford City, who had been in the bottom three for most of the season, managed to defeat Liverpool 1-0, while Wimbledon lost 2-0 against Southampton and dropped into Division One after 14 years in the top flight.

Charlton Athletic, Manchester City and Ipswich Town were all promoted and there was good news for Leicester City. Having sold Emile Heskey to Liverpool for £10 million they bounced back from defeat in the previous year's League Cup Final to beat Tranmere Rovers 2-1, although they lost their manager, Martin O'Neill, who moved to Celtic.

The FA Cup

There was wide condemnation of Manchester United when, despite being the holders, they withdrew from the FA Cup in order to take part in FIFA's Club World Championship in Brazil. It was a wasted trip as they failed to qualify beyond the group stage but other managers were unhappy that it effectively gave the club's players a winter break.

Above Bradford City's players celebrate retaining their place in the Premiership after their final-day victory over Liverpool.

Previous page Michael Bridges (left) and Lee Bowyer were hugely influential in the success of David O'Leary's young Leeds side.

Below Bobby Robson's appointment as manager of Newcastle was a popular one and the fans turned out in numbers to welcome him to St James' Park.

Mark Bright

Mark Bright was born in Stoke in 1962 and had a successful football career that spanned 574 games with Port Vale, Leicester City, Crystal Palace, Sheffield Wednesday and Charlton Athletic. He scored 209 goals, played in two FA Cup Finals and is remembered for a legendary striking partnership with Ian Wright at Palace. Mark has become an established broadcaster within the BBC's football team where his versatility has seen him regularly appear as a presenter, reporter, pundit or summarizer on a range of television and radio shows.

'As a kid I was devoted to football, but could only watch ITV's *The Big Match* on Sunday afternoons. *Match of the Day* was on too late. From my early teens I can remember being allowed to stay up and see it, and it was always one of my ambitions to become a professional footballer and score goals just so that I could get on the show. It was great to be able to go through the whole experience: watching it as a youngster and dreaming of scoring a goal and then turning pro at Port Vale, transferring to Leicester, scoring a goal and seeing it on the programme.

The first time I scored in a match that was being televised I went back to Stoke to meet with some mates at the Out of Town bar. They had *Match of the Day* on the big screen and when I scored the whole bar cheered – but I just felt embarrassed. All that time waiting and I didn't know how to react other than thinking that my shorts were too small!

It was a real downer for us all at the start of the 1985-86 season when a contractual dispute meant that there was no football on TV. I scored two cracking goals against Everton when Gary Lineker played his first game back at Leicester, but the only images I have of it are from a fuzzy club video camera.

I did my first stint as a pundit on *Match of the Day* one Christmas when Gary was presenting and I really enjoyed it. We ran through the matches in advance, I was given one to watch, made some notes and pulled out the bits for analysis.

Then, just after going into make-up I began to get nervous. I was suddenly worried that I would forget all my analysis as none of it's on autocue. Then the music began and I thought "this is it, I'm going to be on *Match of the Day*". Not many get the opportunity so it was amazing to remember watching it as a kid and as a player and now actually sit in the studio.

Having been a player I know that a lot of them don't like being criticized. When I'm a pundit or a summarizer I try and call it as I see it, but try to be constructive with my comments. It would be easy to just be nice to my old clubs and criticize the ones I disliked but I try to give honest opinions while being positive wherever possible.'

The last Final to be played at Wembley before it was knocked down was between Chelsea and Aston Villa. Both semi-finals had also been played there, Aston Villa needing penalties to overcome Bolton Wanderers while Chelsea beat Newcastle United 2-1. The Final was a fairly dull game with the only goal coming in the 72nd minute from Roberto Di Matteo. Dennis Wise lifted the trophy for the second time in four seasons. Everyone had hoped for a classic match to celebrate the old stadium's farewell, but sadly it wasn't one of the more memorable games to have been played in the 77-year history of the ground.

It was Chelsea's fifth FA Cup Final at Wembley (1967, 1970, 1994, 1997, 2000) and Aston Villa's third (1924, 1957, 2000). Manchester United hold the record with 14 appearances, plus two replays. They can also claim the record for lifting the trophy most times at Wembley as their captains have been presented with it on nine occasions between 1948 and 1999.

Other FA Cup Final record holders for the stadium include Mark Hughes who was on the winning side four times (1985, 1990, 1994, 1997), Stan Mortensen, who hit the only hat-trick (Blackpool v Bolton, 1953), Kevin Moran, the only player to be sent off (Manchester United v Everton, 1985) and Ian Rush, who scored the most goals (5).

West Ham's Paolo Di Canio calls for the ball against Wimbledon... and with reason. Moments later he scored a magnificent volley which was judged Goal of the Season.

Fact file

Rangers collected their 11th title in 12 years in Scotland, finishing an astonishing 21 points ahead of second-placed Celtic. They completed yet another double by beating Aberdeen 4-0 in the Cup Final while Celtic had the consolation of the League Cup.

In the 40 years that *Match of the Day* has been on the air only five teams have won the Scottish title. Celtic top the table with 19 Championship victories, Rangers have 16, Aberdeen have won it three times while Kilmarnock and Dundee United have won it once each.

Goal of the Season
Paolo di Canio for West Ham against Wimbledon, Premier League, March 2000

Footballer of the Year
Roy Keane, Manchester United

European Footballer of the Year
Luis Figo, Real Madrid

PFA Player of the Year
Roy Keane, Manchester United

PFA Young Player of the Year
Harry Kewell, Leeds United

The presenters

Gary Lineker

Born in 1960 Gary Lineker was one of English football's greatest ever goalscorers. He began his career with Leicester City before moving to Everton in 1985 and scoring 38 goals in 52 games. After just one season he moved to Barcelona and collected winners' medals in the Spanish Cup and European Cup-Winners' Cup. That was followed by the FA Cup in his time at Tottenham Hotspur before Gary ended his career in Japan with Grampus Eight. He played 80 times for England and is the second highest scorer of all time with 48 goals. Six of those came in the 1986 World Cup when he won the Golden Boot. After retiring in 1994 Gary joined BBC Sport and in 1999 he became the main presenter of *Match of the Day*.

'*Match of the Day* was something I grew up with because I was obsessed by football, and as a young lad when I wasn't playing it, I was watching it. I went down to Filbert Street with my Dad and Grandad on Saturdays, and then later that night, when I was good, they used to let me stay up. I watched it from quite an early age, probably about eight or nine.

I grew up with David Coleman who I thought was just a fantastic football commentator. I know he drifted away from football and concentrated on athletics, but that old "One nil!" just said it all. It was always brief but somehow added to the occasion and he didn't speak too much – I think over-commentating can occasionally be a fault nowadays.

Now we're dealing with a really well-educated football audience on *Match of the Day*, so it's no good sitting there saying "he goes down the wing and then he crosses it and then he heads it in the back of the net, etc". Everyone can see that for themselves so the really good pundits will make a technical or tactical point and explain it. They will tell you something you can't see for yourself. I think the best is Alan Hansen although there are one or two others who are also exceptional. On *Match of the Day*, however, I think he's been the best.

Looking back at the presenters of both *Match of the Day* and football in general I always thought there was a dearth of people who'd actually played the game. In other sports such as tennis or cricket, all the pundits and even the presenters were former players who really understood the game. In football it wasn't always the case, although there were obvious exceptions such as Jimmy and Bob Wilson. I thought there might be a bit of a niche there when I retired from football.

I was very lucky in the way things fell for me and to get the job in the way that I did, but it was always something I wanted to do. I was ambitious to be the presenter rather than the pundit although I know it means that I can't always get my view in. However, if I feel strongly about something I can still put it in a question.

I joined the BBC and started doing some summarizing, and then I did a bit of presenting on Radio 5 Live, which was a great experience. When Bob Wilson left for ITV, 'Football Focus' became available and I was asked to front it. It was a terrific opportunity and I gradually became the number two presenter behind Des, so when he left as well I was able to inherit his mantle. He was a difficult act to follow of course: he's a master presenter. He is brilliant, and I learnt so much from him. I loved it but, at the same time, it was fairly scary in the early days.

Des was one of the great characters associated with *Match of the Day* and the show has seen many others, both in front of the camera and on the field. I think some people add to the programme, such as the managers who are genuinely funny. Brian Clough would come out with some incredible things, and in the modern generation I would say the most entertaining of them all is Gordon Strachan. We wanted to hear from Gordon in every programme, because he's so funny – let's hope he gets back into football soon because it's not quite the same without him although he is doing a terrific job for us as a pundit on *MOTD2*.

Match of the Day has been an amazing part of my whole life, from watching it as a kid and playing on it to being a pundit and presenting it. Who would have thought when I was growing up that I would become the anchorman on *Match of the Day*? I think people hold a genuine affection for the show and I think that is partly to do with the music.

The theme tune is just synonymous with football. Not just football on the BBC or the fact that it's called *Match of the Day*; it's a tune that is associated with the game of football itself. When the highlights disappeared to ITV for a while, it was still nice to keep hearing that tune, albeit on the odd live game.'

2000–2001

Presenter
Gary Lineker

League Champions   Manchester United

FA Cup winners   Liverpool

League Cup winners   Liverpool

UEFA Cup winners   Liverpool

The show

On 14 June BBC Sport's football unit was thrown into disarray when it heard that ITV had won back the Premier League highlights as part of a three-year £183 million deal starting in August 2001. They also obtained Nationwide League rights while the BBC regained the FA Cup and England games.

It was a major blow to the BBC who had offered double their previous contract of £20 million per season but, as in 1988, it was decided to keep the *Match of the Day* name alive through the FA Cup and European games. After some debate, 'Football Focus' also survived although the show's editor, Andrew Clement, had to restyle the programme to account for the absence of any Premiership material. Ray Stubbs was joined by regular guests every Saturday morning and 'Focus' remained essential viewing for football fans as it concentrated on previews, profiles, interviews and features. For 2000-01 however *Match of the Day* remained in its regular slot although Gary Lineker ended the final show of the season with 'We'll be back after the break.'

Liverpool's Emile Heskey scores his third goal as the Reds win 4-0 at Derby.

The season

Chelsea claimed first blood when they beat Manchester United 2-0 to win the Charity Shield, but a month later their manager Gianluca Vialli was sacked despite having won the European Cup-Winners' Cup, FA Cup and League Cup. He later moved to Watford and was replaced at Stamford Bridge by Claudio Ranieri.

Manchester United made a good start to their title defence with a 2-0 opening victory against Newcastle United, but despite that loss Newcastle were the early leaders with Leicester City in second place. Arsenal's 1-0 win against Manchester United on 1 October was United's first League defeat since February, although they recovered to beat Southampton 5-0 in front of a record Premiership crowd of more than 67,000.

There were several outstanding individual performances in the early part of the season. Emile Heskey's hat-trick helped Liverpool win 4-0 at Derby County; Jimmy Floyd Hasselbaink scored four of Chelsea's six against Coventry City and Mark Viduka also hit four when Leeds United beat Liverpool 4-3.

Kevin Keegan walked out on England after they lost 1-0 to Germany in a World Cup qualifier at Wembley despite there being another vital match against Finland just four days later. Howard Wilkinson took over for that 0-0 draw, Peter Taylor stood in for the rest of the season and Lazio's manager, Sven Goran Eriksson was appointed as the England team's first foreign coach.

A former England manager was also on the move: Terry Venables continued his travel around the UK's clubs, pausing this time at Middlesbrough to give assistance to the beleaguered Bryan Robson. Within days they were bottom but Venables' experience made a big difference to the side and their form steadily improved. West Ham United's defender Rio Ferdinand became the most expensive British player when he moved to Leeds United for £18 million.

Arsenal's form was unpredictable. Ray Parlour and Thierry Henry scored hat-tricks as they beat Newcastle 5-0 and Leicester City 6-1, but in between they lost 4-0 at Liverpool and were then humiliated by Manchester United who won 6-1 in February to open up a 16-point lead at the top of the table.

The Championship, inevitably, went to Manchester United and they clinched it on 14 April by beating Coventry 4-2 with five games remaining. It was their third title in a row. Arsenal finished second, ten points behind, and Liverpool were third. Leeds United came fourth and Ipswich fifth.

The Premiership lost three cities as Manchester, Coventry and Bradford were all relegated. They were replaced

It was a great season for strikers. Mark Viduka (centre, white shirt) joined the list of fine individual performances with four goals for Leeds as they beat Liverpool 4-3 at Elland Road.

by Blackburn Rovers, Bolton Wanderers and Fulham, who had won the Division One title with 101 points.

As well as finishing third in the League, Liverpool collected a unique hat-trick of trophies for manager Gerard Houllier. The first silverware came in February when they beat Birmingham City to lift the League Cup. Played at the Millennium Stadium in Cardiff, the game finished 1-1 but Liverpool won the penalty shoot-out 5-4 to give them the trophy for a record sixth time. Their most outstanding performance in their cup run came in the fourth round when they won 8-0 at Stoke City. It was Stoke's heaviest home defeat in 97 years.

Having added the FA Cup to their trophy cabinet, Liverpool beat Alaves 5-4 to win the UEFA Cup. It was their first European trophy for 17 years and was won by a golden goal after the game stood at 4-4 at the end of extra time. Shown live on *Match of the Day* the climax came when Delfi Geli headed an own goal to end the Final and start Liverpool's celebrations.

The FA Cup

Liverpool's first FA Cup win since 1992 came after they edged past Division Two side Wycombe Wanderers to reach the first FA Cup Final to be held at the Millennium Stadium in Cardiff. Having won that semi-final 2-1 at Villa Park they faced Arsenal in the Final.

Niall Sloane

Niall Sloane is the BBC's Head of Football and in June 2000 he was in Brussels leading the BBC's coverage of the European Championship. There he learned that ITV had won the rights to the Premiership highlights from August 2001 meaning that *Match of the Day* was once again under threat.

'It was 14 June and the news was devastating for us. Having been told just after 5 p.m. I had to drive to the television compound to tell all the staff just before they went on air. I had been away from London for three weeks at the Championship but we were all expecting to get the contract. It was interesting to see that it became a massive story and made just about every front page. It had been a sealed bid and I don't think we were the only ones disappointed when the envelopes were opened. We lost out because ITV bid more money. It was as simple as that.

It is fair to say that we came under immense pressure about talent, but we were very happy with everyone we kept on board both in front of the camera and behind the scenes.

As the *Match of the Day* brand is probably the best in television football it was an easy decision to keep it going because we still had FA Cup and England matches to show. I also insisted 'Football Focus' kept its Saturday lunchtime spot, even though we were unable to show Premier League action.

We beefed up the features, stories and the range of debate and managed to see off the challenge from 'On the Ball'. It was a great reward for Ray Stubbs and the production team to see the viewing figures regularly hit a 24 or 25 per cent share.'

Arsene Wenger's team had beaten Tottenham Hotspur 2-1 at Old Trafford in the other semi-final and were looking for their second win in four seasons.

The first half of the Final was fairly subdued but the game livened up after half-time with several good chances for both sides, although Arsenal always looked stronger. They finally went ahead in the 72nd minute when Freddie Ljungberg, whose chip had just been headed off the line, shot past Sander Westerveld.

Michael Owen equalized 11 minutes later and then, with just two minutes left on the clock he ran on to a long ball from Patrik Berger, evaded the Arsenal defence and put the ball just inside the far post. The Londoners were devastated but part two of Liverpool's treble was complete.

Euro 2000

France added the European Championship to their collection when they beat Italy 2-1 in the Final of Euro 2000 with a golden goal from Trezeguet. England failed to make it past the group stage having lost 3-2 to both Portugal and Romania. The only small satisfaction was beating Germany at Charleroi. More teams than ever before had taken part and 49 different countries competed in the qualifying rounds.

Swede Sven Goran Eriksson was installed as England manager in 2000 – he was England's first foreign coach.

Liverpool's Michael Owen celebrates scoring the equalizer in the FA Cup Final against Arsenal. He scored again five minutes later to secure the second part of the Merseyside club's season treble.

Sheffield Wednesday's goalkeeper Kevin Pressman (right) made headlines on the first day of the season when he was sent off after just 13 seconds of their Division One match against Wolverhampton Wanderers. He was shown the red card by referee Mark Halsey for deliberate handball outside the box. It was the quickest dismissal in League history, although replays suggested that he had been very unlucky as the ball appeared to have hit his chest, not his hands. The match ended 1-1.

Footballer of the Year
Teddy Sheringham, Manchester United

European Footballer of the Year
Michael Owen, Liverpool

PFA Player of the Year
Teddy Sheringham, Manchester United

PFA Young Player of the Year
Steven Gerrard, Liverpool

2001–2002

Presenter
Gary Lineker

League Champions   Arsenal
FA Cup winners   Arsenal
League Cup winners   Blackburn Rovers

The show

With Saturday night highlights now being shown on ITV's *The Premiership*, *Match of the Day* reverted to being an occasional show that concentrated on live FA Cup and England matches as well as some UEFA Cup games. Despite intense press speculation Gary Lineker remained with the BBC football team as did the majority of commentators and pundits.

The Premiership was launched on 8 August but had a difficult start because viewers were not used to seeing so many adverts in a football programme. After just a few weeks it was moved from its much heralded early-evening slot back to the traditional *Match of the Day* start time.

ITV's digital channel also had severe problems and collapsed before the end of the season. This caused financial chaos for the clubs in the Nationwide League who had set their budgets based on the expected income from television.

The season

Leeds United set the early pace in the Championship and led for most of September and October with a steady series of results. The most outstanding domestic scoreline in the early part of the season came when Manchester United recovered from 3-0 down at Tottenham Hotspur to win 5-3, but that was nothing compared to the shock of England's World Cup qualifier against Germany.

The match was live from Munich on *Match of the Day* and produced arguably the greatest result for the national side since 1966. Despite going 1-0 down, England recovered to win an incredible match 5-1 thanks to a hat-trick by Michael Owen. The feelings of all football fans were

A major feature of *Match of the Day* during the Premiership years has been Alan Shearer, one arm raised, celebrating another goal – this one against Middlesbrough. Alan's haul of almost 250 goals makes him the undisputed leading goalscorer in Premier League history.

On a magnificent night for England fans, Germany were beaten 5-1 in Munich in a World Cup qualifier. Michael Owen (left) scored a hat-trick and further goals from Steven Gerrard and Emile Heskey produced the finest victory for the national side since 1966.

summed up by John Motson: 'Oh this is getting better and better and better – one, two, three for Michael Owen'.

Sadly for those same fans, the legendary ITV commentator Brian Moore passed away on the morning of the match, aged 69.

Just a few weeks later, England supporters were celebrating again after a match against Greece, also live on *Match of the Day*. England were trailing 2-1 with just a few seconds left when captain David Beckham curled a free-kick in from 25 yards to ensure they topped their group and qualified automatically for the World Cup finals.

In the Premier League Blackburn Rovers beat West Ham United 7-1, Bolton Wanderers stunned the Old Trafford crowd when they won there 2-1 and Robbie Fowler's hat-trick helped Liverpool to the top of the table by defeating Leicester City 4-1. Fowler also provided one of the biggest shocks of the season when he moved to Leeds United in November for £11 million.

In early December, Manchester United hit poor form and were beaten at home by both Chelsea and West Ham.

That proved to be bad news for Derby County and Southampton as Ferguson's side turned things around with 5-0 and 6-1 victories against them. The end of the year saw Arsenal just ahead of Newcastle in the race for the title, though their lead lasted just a week and they didn't top the table again until April.

Liverpool began the New Year with a 4-0 win against Leeds at Elland Road before putting six past Ipswich to move into second place. Spring saw the game lose two more of its most famous names when Kenneth Wolstenholme, the original presenter and voice of *Match of the Day*, passed away at the age of 81; and the former England manager, Sir Walter Winterbottom, died at the age of 88. One of his successors, Graham Taylor, returned to club management with Aston Villa while at Manchester United, Sir Alex Ferguson announced that he would not, as had been expected, retire.

In February Arsenal beat Everton to start a run of 13 consecutive wins that would sweep them to the title. They clinched it at Old Trafford when Sylvain Wiltord's 57th minute goal gave them a 1-0 win and they finished

Football on film

There is a long history of football being featured in films and one of the most successful of all time was released this year. *Bend it like Beckham* told the story of the daughter of an orthodox Sikh family who rebelled against her parents' traditionalism by playing football. There were similarities to the classic *Gregory's Girl* made in 1980 by Bill Forsyth, but the standard of football was much better than most of the movies that have tried to cover the sport. One of the earliest attempts at a football drama came in 1911 with *Harry the Footballer*, although the best-known of the pre-war films was *The Arsenal Stadium Mystery* that featured both the team and their manager, George Allison.

Possibly the worst ever sequence came in a 1952 Alec Guiness film, *The Card*. In one of the main scenes the camera tracked a star player running the full length of the pitch to score his team's 15th goal of the match. This was especially remarkable as he is seen beating 15 opposition players before putting the ball past the goalkeeper!

The end of the old order? Sylvain Wiltord scores the only goal of the game as Arsenal beat Manchester United at Old Trafford to win the Championship.

seven points ahead of second-placed Liverpool. The three Uniteds, Manchester, Newcastle and Leeds, filled the next three spots.

Ipswich Town, Derby County and Leicester City were all relegated and Manchester City, West Bromwich Albion and Birmingham City replaced them.

Blackburn Rovers had their first major cup success for 74 years when they beat Spurs 2-1 in the Final of the League Cup. Matt Jansen gave Blackburn the lead before Christian Ziege equalised for Spurs. The winning goal came from striker Andy Cole who had joined them from Manchester United for £8 million.

Arsenal's Freddie Ljungberg chips the ball over Chelsea keeper Carlo Cudicini to score Arsenal's second goal in their 2-0 victory in the FA Cup Final.

The FA Cup

The semi-finals saw two recent Cup holders triumph as Arsenal beat Middlesbrough 1-0 to return to the Final. Having been runners-up to Liverpool last year, they had their revenge in the fourth round when they knocked out the holders, beating them 1-0 at Highbury. Chelsea, the winners in 1997 and 2000, beat Fulham 1-0 in the other semi-final to make it an all-London affair in Cardiff.

Ten different nationalities were represented by the 28 players who appeared in the Final. There were nine Englishmen, six from France, four Dutch players, two each from Italy and Nigeria and one apiece from Denmark, Iceland, Sweden, Brazil and Cameroon. Ray Parlour gave Arsenal the lead after 70 minutes and Freddie Ljungberg added a second ten minutes later. Those goals were enough to give Arsenal their second FA Cup triumph in five seasons, and their eighth in all.

Fact file

The biggest story at the end of the season didn't involve any football clubs at all. Attention was focused on David Beckham's left foot. His fractured metatarsal became the most talked-about bone in Britain as he struggled to get fit for the World Cup.

Footballer of the Year
Robert Pires, Arsenal

European Footballer of the Year
Ronaldo, Real Madrid

PFA Player of the Year
Ruud van Nistelrooy, Manchester United

PFA Young Player of the Year
Craig Bellamy, Newcastle United

2002-2003

Presenter
Gary Lineker

League Champions Manchester United
FA Cup winners Arsenal
League Cup winners Liverpool

The show

The BBC began the new season in strong form following the success of their World Cup coverage, hosted by Gary Lineker and a variety of pundits. They had won a 62 per cent share of the available audience for the Final and broadcast eight of the top ten most watched matches.

The coverage had been supplemented by a new service that was offered via Radio 5 Live and the BBC's Interactive platform, when Ray Stubbs and Russell Fuller led the live bi-media 'World Cup Talk Forum'. Fans were able to interact via phone, e-mail and text. For the first time in a major competition the BBC was also able to offer supporters the opportunity to watch highlights and analysis 24 hours a day on their Interactive and on-line sites.

On the domestic front, *Match of the Day* was restricted to showing FA Cup, international and UEFA Cup matches. Behind the scenes, however, Peter Salmon, the BBC's Director of Sport and Niall Sloane, the Head of Football, were preparing a strong bid for the new football contract.

The season

Just before the start of the season Rio Ferdinand moved from Leeds United to Manchester United for a record British transfer fee of £30 million. Terry Venables was the new man in charge at Elland Road and he was confident that he could bring fresh glory to the Leeds fans despite the club's crippling debts. They would, however, struggle all season and the pattern was set at the end of August when they lost at home to Sunderland. That proved to be a rare celebration for Peter Reid's team who failed to win another away match in the Premiership and only won three more in

total. After more than seven years in charge Reid was sacked just a few weeks later and replaced by Howard Wilkinson.

Tottenham Hotspur led the table at the end of August but a month later Arsenal had taken the top spot when they beat Leeds 4-1 to score in a record 47th consecutive league match. They had also gone a record 30 Premiership matches without defeat when they came up against Everton on 19 October and had their run ended by 16-year-old substitute Wayne Rooney. He became the youngest-ever Premiership scorer.

Manchester United were beginning to show some form after a mixed start to the season and although they lost the Manchester derby 3-1, Ruud van Nistelrooy's hat-trick helped them to a 5-3 win against Newcastle United. In early December they halted Arsenal's run of scoring in 55 successive Premiership games by winning 2-0 at Old Trafford. On the same day Chelsea beat Everton 3-1 at Goodison Park to move into second place behind Arsène Wenger's team. Boxing Day proved to be unlucky for Rooney who was sent off against Birmingham City and saw 16-year-old Leeds prodigy James Milner take his record as the Premiership's youngest scorer.

In January Thierry Henry's hat-trick against West Ham United took Arsenal five points clear at the top of the Premiership, and the Hammers finally managed to win at home when Jermain Defoe scored the winning goal against Blackburn Rovers. There was more disappointment for Leeds fans as the selling spree continued with Robbie Fowler moving to Manchester City and Jonathan Woodgate joining Newcastle. A former Geordie hero, Paul Gascoigne, was also trying to resurrect his career, this time with a short-lived move to China where he joined their Division Two side, Gansu Tianma.

English football's newest star, Wayne Rooney, set another record in February when he became the youngest player to win an England cap, although the side lost 3-1 to Australia after fielding different teams in each half. In the same month, David Beckham was cut above the left eye when Sir Alex Ferguson kicked a boot at him following Manchester United's FA Cup loss to Arsenal.

A month later the Old Trafford dressing room was a far happier place after the team moved to the top of the Premiership for the first time that season when van Nistelrooy's hat-trick gave them a 3-0 win against Fulham. The managerial merry-go-round began again when Mick McCarthy replaced Howard Wilkinson at Sunderland and their former boss, Peter Reid, took over Leeds on a temporary basis after Terry Venables was sacked.

Right A legend is born as Wayne Rooney celebrates after scoring in Everton's 2-1 win against Arsenal at Goodison. Everton's victory ended Arsenal's 30-game unbeaten run and Rooney's goal made him the Premiership's youngest ever goalscorer.

Below Ruud van Nistelrooy scores in Manchester United's 2-0 win over Spurs at White Hart Lane. The Dutchman's 25 goals played a major part in United's eighth Championship in 11 years.

As the run-in to the Championship began, Arsenal were once again on top, but on 5 April, Manchester United beat Liverpool 4-0 to draw level on 67 points apiece. From that point they surged ahead with a 6-2 win at Newcastle, a 2-2 draw with Arsenal, a 3-1 win against Blackburn Rovers and a 2-0 victory at Spurs. On 3 May, van Nistelrooy's third triple strike of the season helped them to a 4-1 score against Charlton Athletic. When Arsenal lost 3-2 at home to Leeds on the following day it meant the trophy returned to Old Trafford for the eighth time in 11 seasons. They ended the campaign on 83 points, five ahead of Arsenal. Newcastle were third and Chelsea in fourth so they both qualified for the Champions League. On the last day of the season Liverpool lost 2-1 to Chelsea and so finished three points behind in fifth. Their one consolation came in the League Cup when they beat Manchester United 2-0 in the Final.

Despite rallying under the caretaker management of Trevor Brooking following Glenn Roeder's illness, West Ham were still relegated. West Bromwich Albion and Sunderland joined them in the drop to Division One while former West Ham manager, Harry Redknapp, returned to the top flight with Portsmouth. Leicester City finished in second place and Wolverhampton Wanderers finally returned to the top division after a 19-year gap when they beat Sheffield United in the play-off final.

The FA Cup

The FA Cup Final between Arsenal and Southampton made history when it became the first to be played indoors. Bad weather meant the roof over the Millennium Stadium in Cardiff was closed, creating a unique atmosphere for almost 74,000 fans inside.

Gordon Strachan's south-coast team had already achieved their highest-ever Premiership position of eighth and beaten Watford 2-1 in the semi-final. This was their first FA Cup Final since their victorious 1976 campaign. Arsenal made it three consecutive Finals by defeating Sheffield United 1-0 in the other semi, having also beaten Chelsea, Manchester United, Farnborough Town and Oxford United.

The match was settled by a 38th-minute goal by Robert Pires, as Arsenal became the first side to retain the trophy since Spurs in 1981 and 1982. The commentator was John Motson, describing his 24th FA Cup Final – one more than the previous record holder Kenneth Wolstenholme.

Arsenal's David Seaman(left) and Patrick Vieira hold the FA Cup after the Gunners' 1-0 victory over Southampton at the Millennium Stadium in Cardiff.

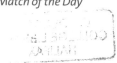

Laying the ghost to rest. As every English fan holds his or her breath, David Beckham scores England's winner from the penalty spot in their World Cup group game against Argentina.

2002 World Cup

Brazil had become World Champions for a record fifth time when they beat Germany 2-0 in the Final in Yokohama. Ronaldo scored both goals in the second half to take his tally to eight in the competition and restore his reputation following the controversy that surrounded his appearance in the 1998 Final in Paris.

Japan and South Korea jointly staged a memorable tournament that saw the Koreans exceed all expectations by reaching the semi-finals. There were 32 teams taking part in the final stages and the shocks began on the opening day when the defending champions, France, lost to Senegal. France went home without winning a match but England made it to the quarter-finals before losing 2-1 to ten-man Brazil. David Seaman had allowed himself to be lobbed by Ronaldinho's speculative long range free-kick. England's most memorable game came against Argentina when David Beckham's 44th-minute penalty was enough to avenge their 1986 and 1998 World Cup defeats.

The most astonishing result of the season came on 29 October when Grimsby Town beat Burnley 6-5 in their Division One encounter. Burnley's manager, Stan Ternent, was staggered that his side had scored five goals in an away game and still lost. Unfortunately, it was to be a rare success for Grimsby who only managed 20 goals in their other 22 home games and they were relegated in bottom place.

Footballer of the Year
Thierry Henry, Arsenal

European Footballer of the Year
Pavel Nedved, Juventus

PFA Player of the Year
Thierry Henry, Arsenal

PFA Young Player of the Year
Jermaine Jenas, Newcastle United

2003–2004

Presenter
Gary Lineker

League Champions Arsenal
FA Cup winners Manchester United
League Cup winners Middlesbrough

The show

In August 2003 came the news that all fans of *Match of the Day* had been hoping for. The BBC had regained the rights to Premiership highlights which meant that from the start of the 2004–05 season the show would return to its natural home in the Saturday night schedules. It also vindicated the decisions to keep the brand alive and maintain 'Football Focus' rather than throw in the towel and take the show off the air. Sky retained the rights to live matches in a three-year deal that cost more than a billion pounds. The BBC's share was just over £100 million. In October, the BBC and Sky also signed a four-year contract to continue showing the FA Cup and England games.

Teenage sensation Wayne Rooney registers his first goal for England against Macedonia in a European Championship qualifier.

The season

It was the season of the Russian, the Italian, the Frenchman and the Swede as well, of course, of David Beckham. Despite denials he finally left Manchester United for Real Madrid but allegations concerning his private life ensured that he was rarely out of the papers. The same was true of Chelsea. From the moment that Russian oil billionaire, Roman Abramovich, bought out the long-time chairman, Ken Bates, the club was centre stage. By the end of his first year, Abramovich had spent an astonishing £190 million on additions to the squad with, as yet, no silverware to show for it.

Frenchman Arsène Wenger coached Arsenal to their third title in seven seasons as they set an incredible record of going the entire league season unbeaten. They won 26 and drew 12 matches to become the first side to achieve the feat since Preston North End in 1888–89. With 90 points they finished 11 ahead of second-placed Chelsea, but even achieving the south-west London club's highest position for almost 50 years was not enough to save Claudio Ranieri from

the sack. There had been press speculation all season about the Italian's fate and the smart money was on Sven Goran Eriksson taking over. In the end Sven signed an extension to his England contract and Ranieri was replaced by José Mourinho who had just won the Champions League with Porto.

Wolverhampton Wanderers and Leicester City were relegated as, after one of the most spectacular footballing decline and falls of recent times, were Leeds United. Peter Reid was sacked in November after a string of poor results. Former player Eddie Gray became the fourth manager in less than two seasons but with the club's crippling debts and a Board that was constantly in crisis, he was unable to prevent relegation.

Manchester United, who finished third in the Premiership, were also rarely out of the news. In August they spent more than £12 million on 18-year-old Cristiano Ronaldo. In September the fans were shocked when Chief Executive Peter Kenyon left to join Chelsea and in October the whole club was left reeling when it was announced that Rio Ferdinand had

'You win some, you draw some' said the Arsenal T-shirts as they completed an incredible unbeaten season winning 2-1 at home to Leicester on the last day of the campaign. It was fitting that captain Patrick Vieira scored the final goal.

missed a routine drugs test. After several weeks of wrangling he was banned for eight months by the FA.

Another teenager in the headlines was Everton's Wayne Rooney. On 6 September, aged just 17 years and 317 days, he became the youngest player to score a goal for England when he helped the team to a 2-1 win in Macedonia.

The main British focus in Europe came in the quarter-finals when Arsenal, who were chasing the treble, met Chelsea. Chelsea were the surprise victors but lost in the semi-finals to Monaco, the eventual runners-up.

Liverpool just managed to clinch fourth spot in the league, but even qualification for the Champions League couldn't convince the board at Anfield to retain the services of Gerard Houllier, and after six years in charge he was sacked.

The substitutes

Despite being on-air for four decades there have only been a handful of presenters who have stood in when the main line-up of Wolstenholme, Coleman, Hill, Lynam or Lineker have been absent. Bob Wilson and Ray Stubbs have each clocked up many appearances, whilst in the first decade Frank Bough, Walley Barnes, Maurice Edelston and Barry Davies all had brief spells at the helm. Others to have had the experience of hearing the famous music precede their voices include David Davies, who is now the FA's Executive Director, and Harry Gration, longtime presenter of BBC's *Look North*.

Harry remembers it as a great experience. 'I was already a regular part of the production team, voicing the round-ups for several years in the 1980s, when I got a call from the editor, Niall Sloane, asking if I could present a hastily arranged *Match of the Day* from Leeds. It was an FA Cup replay against Barnsley and I duly turned up at the ground, did the link into Motty's commentary, linked into the interviews and closed the programme. It was probably one of

the easiest things that I have ever done on TV but it was one of the highlights of my career. Nothing can ever take away the fact that on one special night the famous music played, the titles rolled and I popped up in vision.'

The most recent new presenter is Mark Pougatch who has been presenting *Sport on Five* on Radio Five Live since August 2000. Like Harry, his was a memorable experience. 'It was FA Cup third round day in 2004 and I came straight from a six-hour stint on *Sport on Five* to front the show. Mark Lawrenson and Garth Crooks were very supportive and generous and made it very easy even though Garth managed to give away the result of one of the games before we had seen it!

It was unbelievably exciting, especially the music. I just remember telling myself not to make too many cock-ups and thinking that my Dad, Michael, who died in 1991 and loved sport, would have found the whole thing very amusing. I'd love to do more shows as it was a great experience, whatever else I do I can say I've presented *Match of the Day*.'

Joseph-Desire Job (red shirt) scores for Middlesbrough in the League Cup Final against Bolton. Boro's 2-1 victory earned the first piece of silverware in the club's 128-year history.

Norwich City and West Bromwich Albion won automatic promotion from Division One and were joined by Crystal Palace who beat West Ham United 1-0 in the play-off Final in Cardiff. The League Cup, went to Middlesbrough who beat Bolton Wanderers 2-1 to finally break their silverware duck. Steve McLaren became the first manager in their 128-year history be labelled a winner.

The FA Cup

Manchester United won the FA Cup for a record 11th time when they beat Millwall 3-0 at the Millennium Stadium in Cardiff. The south Londoners first appearance in the Final had been secured when Tim Cahill scored the only goal of their semi-final against fellow Division One side Sunderland. Arsenal were the other losing semi-finalists.

The Portuguese teenager, Ronaldo, opened the scoring in the 44th minute. Two more goals from Dutch striker Ruud van Nistelrooy earned him the Man of the Match award and ensured that yet another piece of silverware went back to Old Trafford. For Wise and his men there was the consolation of an open-top bus tour around South East London.

Goalscorers Cristiano Ronaldo (left) and Ruud van Nistelrooy celebrate with the spoils after winning the FA Cup Final.

Fact file

Millwall's Dennis Wise was appearing in his fifth FA Cup Final this year. He had won the trophy with Wimbledon in 1988, lost with Chelsea against Manchester United in 1994, won it again with Chelsea in 1997 and 2000 against Middlesbrough and Aston Villa respectively. In only his second season as player/manager he led Millwall to the FA Cup Final for the first time in their history.

Footballer of the Year
Thierry Henry, Arsenal

PFA Player of the Year
Thierry Henry, Arsenal

PFA Young Player of the Year
Scott Parker, Chelsea

2004–2005

Presenter
Gary Lineker

The show

On Saturday 14 August the famous music began, Gary Lineker opened the new season with a cheery 'Good evening, welcome back. Now where were we before we were so rudely interrupted'. *Match of the Day* had resumed as normal. Alongside him were Alan Hansen and Mark Lawrenson as the show celebrated its 40th anniversary with more football on the BBC than at any time in its history. The first programme of the new series was edited by Andrew Clement who had previously steered 'Football Focus' through the difficult period when no footage of Premiership football was available. The contrast could not have been greater as he had commentators at all eight matches and a wealth of action to choose from.

The increased programming has meant a new look for the BBC's coverage. It starts on a Saturday lunchtime with Manish Bhasin presenting a revamped 'Football Focus' and continues throughout the afternoon with 'Final Score Interactive' hosted by Ray Stubbs. It includes Tim Gudgin reading the football scores, as he has for the past decade since Len Martin passed away after almost 40 years with BBC Sport. Tim is still a relative newcomer having only joined *Grandstand* to read the racing and rugby results in the mid-1960s! Gary presents *Match of the Day* on Saturday evenings; there is a Sunday morning repeat for younger viewers and a new Sunday night edition, fronted by Adrian Chiles, on BBC2, shows highlights of the day's games plus features and follow-ups.

FA Cup action begins with live action and highlights from all rounds as well as midweek replays, one of the semi-finals and the Final. On top of all that the BBC will show live coverage of every England home game, both competitive and friendly and are planning ahead for the next World Cup, the African Cup of Nations, the European Championship, and the Women's FA Cup.

The season

The season began with transfer activity, renewed speculation about the ability of Sven Goran Eriksson to remain as England manager and a total rebranding of the Football League. Division One became The Championship; while Divisions Two and Three are now know as League One and League Two.

A trio of big name overseas managers had taken up residence in the Premiership as Rafael Benitez, José Mourinho and Jacques Santini all began their spells in charge at Liverpool, Chelsea and Tottenham Hotspur respectively.

Several members of England's Euro 2004 squad changed colours before the start of the new season. Michael Owen left Liverpool to join David Beckham at Real Madrid, Emile Heskey moved to Birmingham City, while Nicky Butt switched Uniteds, joining Newcastle from Manchester. Alan Smith, who had narrowly missed out on selection, switched from Elland Road to Old Trafford. A few weeks

Gary Lineker, Peter Schmeichel and Mark Lawrenson watch all the matches alongside members of the production team.

later Smith was joined by Wayne Rooney who ended months of speculation by requesting a transfer from Everton. Sir Alex Ferguson signed him for a deal that was reputedly worth up to £27 million.

All clubs made several changes but, once again, Chelsea played the most expensive game of footballing musical chairs. Nearly 20 players left Stamford Bridge for varying reasons but their Chairman, Roman Abramovich, was still able to find almost £100 million for new talent including Didier Drogba who moved from Marseille for £24 million.

The opening month also saw two managerial changes in the Premiership when Paul Sturrock left Southampton after just 13 matches in charge and Sir Bobby Robson was sacked by Newcastle.

Sven clung onto his job after yet another media frenzy that saw Mark Palios resign as Chief Executive of the FA but one manager likely to be safe for a very long time is Arsène Wenger. On 25 August Arsenal broke Nottingham Forest's 26-year-old record of 42 consecutive league games without defeat. Their 43rd unbeaten match came when they beat Blackburn Rovers 3-0 at Highbury to establish a record that looks likely to last many more years.

Match of the Day 2

The return of Premiership football to the BBC has seen the introduction of a second *Match of the Day* show. *Match of*

the Day 2 is on Sunday nights on BBC2 and has a more relaxed feel with the guests on a sofa rather than behind a desk. The first edition was on Sunday 15 August and was presented by Adrian Chiles. Adrian has previously fronted BBC2's *Working Lunch* and several shows on Radio Five Live including *Chiles on Saturday* and *606* and is joined by his regular guests Gordon Strachan and Kevin Day. The show features extensive highlights of the Sunday matches plus a full round-up of the Saturday games as well as features and profiles.

Producer Phil Wye and VT Editor Chris Kaye editing a match.

Paul Armstrong

The current Editor of *Match of the Day* is Paul Armstrong and, like the show, he turns 40 this autumn. Having joined BBC Sport 15 years ago he took on the role in 2001.

'I sometimes have to pinch myself to realize that I'm doing this job as I have strong memories of the early 1970s when our babysitter let me stay up to watch the show. After that I was hooked.

My role includes allocating the commentators to each game and, along with Niall Sloane, choosing the main matches that we will cover. The biggest change for us with the new contract is that whereas in the past we had just two or three main games, any match can now lead the show as, for the first time; there will be full coverage and a commentator at every single game.

During a match day I'm constantly in communication with everyone around the grounds and also watching the games with Gary and the pundits as they spot things that we never would. At 5 p.m. on a Saturday afternoon we'll determine the running order and durations of the show and select the interviews. I'll talk to all the main match producers and the production team who have been logging the matches at Television Centre. They are the eyes and ears of the show and will tell me about the main incidents and quotes.

The first series I did was with Des which was a great privilege as I was something of a novice and he taught me a huge amount about the discipline of a live show.

However, I really enjoy working with Gary as he is that rare person, a great footballer who then served a media apprenticeship to get to the top of the tree as a presenter. I liaise with him during the evening but the script is mainly his words. He is totally adaptable and very calm, as you'd expect from someone who has taken penalties in the World Cup finals

It is a very exciting job but we are always conscious of what has gone before and that we're custodians of something that is massive in television history.'

Gordon Strachan, Adrian Chiles and Kevin Day.

Tim Gudgin reading the football results on 'Final Score'.

Euro 2004 – Portugal

Greece produced the greatest shock in the history of the European Championship when they beat the host nation, Portugal, 1-0 in the Final of Euro 2004. England had begun with great hopes of success, especially when Wayne Rooney emerged as an early candidate for player of the tournament. Having lost their opening game 2-1 to France, they recovered to beat Switzerland 3-0 and Croatia 4-2 to finish second in Group B. Sven's team faced Portugal in the quarter-final but lost after the inevitable penalty shootout. David Beckham and Darius Vassell were added to the lengthening list of those who have missed from the spot at the crucial moment.

Phil Bigwood

Phil Bigwood became the Series Producer of *Match of the Day* in December 2000 having joined the programme as a trainee Assistant Producer in 1992.

'For me it is the best job in the world. I grew up watching it as a kid in Essex and would regularly see Gary, Alan and Mark as players when I used to travel the country to watch Southend and Liverpool. It seems strange that I have gone from yelling at them on the pitch to shouting in their ears.

The role is immensely varied and includes directing the studios, overseeing the set design, the graphics and the look of the show, planning OBs and consulting with the match directors. The best aspect is that it is a team effort and we are all totally reliant on everyone else in the chain. BBC Resources and our Engineering Managers are crucial to making it all work and everyone has an important role,

especially the riggers who are the first on site and the last to leave and they deserve just as much credit as the talent.

Although the viewers might only see the presenter and pundits on screen, there are lot of people working hard behind the scenes including the Producers and VT Editors and our Production Manager, Assistants and Secretaries. They are the people who put the show together every week and it is a privilege to work alongside them.'

Schmeichel and Lawrenson work on their analysis.

Gary Lineker prepares to open the show.

Match of the Day's 40th anniversary was marked by BBC1 with a special documentary that celebrated the programme and its stars. The Producer, Paul Wright, found that many of his earliest memories of the programme were matched by those of the guests.

'Martin Johnson recalled running downstairs in his pyjamas as the music began and the memory that being allowed to watch the show as a kid made you feel like an adult for the first time. It was a real privilege to be able to talk to Brian Clough, George Best and David Beckham and hear that they have a real and genuine passion for the show. They all wanted to be part of the programme and the toughest part was simply working out how to fit four decades of great characters, players and action into 60 minutes.'

index